CHILDREN AND
YOUTH IN
LIMBO

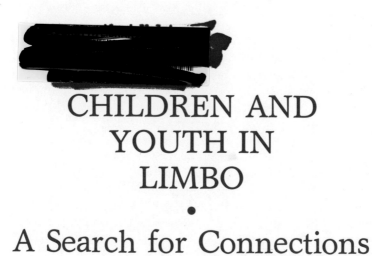

CHILDREN AND YOUTH IN LIMBO

•

A Search for Connections

Nadia Ehrlich Finkelstein

PRAEGER

New York
Westport, Connecticut
London

Library of Congress Cataloging-in-Publication Data

Finkelstein, Nadia Ehrlich.
    Children and youth in limbo : a search for connections / Nadia
Ehrlich Finkelstein.
        p.   cm.
    Includes bibliographical references and index.
    ISBN 0–275–93992–8 (alk. paper)
    1. Social work with children—United States.   2. Social work with
youth—United States.   3. Family services—United States.
I. Title.
    HV741.F56   1991
    362.7′0973—dc20   91–21703

British Library Cataloguing in Publication Data is available.

Library of Congress Catalog Card Number: 91–21703
ISBN: 0–275–93992–8

First published in 1991

Praeger Publishers, One Madison Avenue, New York, NY 10010
An imprint of Greenwood Publishing Group, Inc.

Printed in the United States of America

∞™

The paper used in this book complies with the
Permanent Paper Standard issued by the National
Information Standards Organization (Z39.48–1984).

10 9 8 7 6 5 4 3 2 1

For Joseph,
and our children,
Sharon, Jonathan, and Neal

Contents

Preface

"Nothing comes from nowhere." Everything has a history and a beginning. The ideas for this book were first conceived in the early 1970s when, as director of Parsons Child and Family Center's Residential Program, I was still chairing intake conferences to evaluate children for admission to the then predominant program of that agency, historically rooted in the American orphanage. It was astounding to me then that 97 percent of the children in the Residential Program did not have two biological parents living together; I needed to understand who these children and families were and find out about them as meaningful groups. These early ideas were published in *Social Work* [Finkelstein 1980].

As we got to know the families of the children in need of residential placement, my colleagues and I began to understand that our efforts must focus on the whole family, if the child's life situation is to have a constructive, meaningful outcome. This thinking stimulated some of my earlier work on family participation in residential treatment [1981, 1988]. While working on these ideas professionally, I was also deeply involved in parenting my own children, and naturally empathized with the many painful problems parents of children in placement had to confront and deal with.

As the years passed, I assumed a larger administrative role at Parsons; I became responsible for the agency's community-based programs in 1978, and all agency professional programs by 1983. This involved nineteen separate components of an agency whose largest caseloads today are out-patient and preventive, although it still provides family foster care and an array of residential services for youth who cannot live with their families either temporarily or permanently. Every program at Parsons functions within the same basic philosophy of care, validating roots and connections regardless of where the young person lives.

The book further grows out of my many years of experience in voluntary not-for-profit child care, mental health, and family services, as a direct service-providing practitioner, social work supervisor, and child-care manager. Many of the perceptions and concerns in this book are taken from practical experience in New York State. Through participation at national conferences, as trainer and consultant at agencies across the country, working on national committees, and reviewing the literature, I find the New York experience does not stand in isolation. It reflects the major national concerns in the delivery of services to children and families.

A major reason for this book is the day-to-day challenges and frustrations in trying to understand and administer a service delivery system for children and their families, while struggling with the reality that many clients continue to fall through the cracks. The current national fiscal crisis makes it more imperative than ever to allocate dollars to provide optimum client services in the most cost-effective way. For years I have felt that "more" is not necessarily "better"; at times "more" may even be "worse." And all too frequently we are able to intervene only when it is too late.

In 1986 the Board of Directors of Parsons Child and Family Center allowed me to take a three-months' leave, which was spent with my husband as a guest at Kansai University of Foreign Studies in Hirakata Shi, Osaka, Japan. The first draft of this volume in its entirety was written there while looking out over a Japanese park and watching groups of little nursery children come and go with their soft-spoken, nurturing caretakers. I was able to distance myself from my own professional environment and to evaluate more dispassionately my perceptions of the American system and how we care for our children. I am grateful to the University's President, Sadato Tanimoto, LL.D., for his generous hospitality and for that of his very thoughtful staff.

I am most indebted to the Parsons Board of Directors, its Executive Director, John Carswell, and his predecessor, Edwin Millard, for creating a stimulating work environment that rewards innovation and self-direction. It is this orientation that has allowed me to train and consult nationally and become acquainted with similar issues in other parts of the country. I had the privilege of participating as workshop leader and speaker under the auspices of the University of North Carolina, Group Child Care Consultant Services in 1982–1983. Later in 1984–1985 I served as consultant to a joint effort of five North Carolina child-caring agencies that chose to move from a child-centered to a family-centered practice approach under the creative, energetic leadership of Rochelle Haimes [Coyle et al. 1986]. These opportunities allowed me to crystallize my own thinking. I am grateful to the many participants in these projects who challenged my assumptions until they were articulated clearly enough to become useful and usable in practice.

My colleagues Mary Louise Baum, Dr. Wander deC. Braga, Dr. Richard Kagan, Larry Krohmal, Thomas Luzzi, Lynn Pauquette, Raymond Schimmer, Shirley Schlosberg, Debbie Singer, Dr. Lenore Sportsman, and their staffs have made daily contributions to my ongoing refinement of issues and challenges. Dr. Margaret Griffel and Dr. Alan Klein were my earliest mentors in refining systemic thinking. Dr. Alan Keith-Lucas offered new stimulating perspectives in both the literature and through dialogue. Shirley Cohen, William Martone, Adele Pickar, and Tom Walsh participated in thinking through and first implementing some of the ideas articulated in family rather than child-focused residential care. I am grateful to Bill Brunt, manager of system development for Parsystems, for all diagram production. My secretary Elizabeth Roemer has helped in so many ways. Cathie Wells, my friend, colleague, and assistant, has been tireless in her support and contribution of superb editorial and technical skills. Malcolm Willison has had major editorial input into the final drafts. His competence and enthusiastic encouragement are deeply appreciated. Nan S. Robinson, a friend of many years, commented on the draft and shared her remarkable editorial and language skills most generously. I am indeed indebted to Deborah Klaum of Praeger Publishers for her careful, professional, attention to the production of this volume. Professor Joseph Finkelstein, my husband, has read every part of the manuscript and provided invaluable assistance in helping me articulate ideas in understandable language. Without his belief that "there is a book there," I would have given up many times. I, of course, remain responsible for all views expressed in this volume.

In developing the thesis of this book, I am further influenced by the values and beliefs generated in my own earlier life experience. Dispersed over Europe, East Asia, and the Western Hemisphere during my growing-up years, my family kept its ties intact and closely connected despite war and distance. The opportunity to live and grow in many parts of the world as both child and adult has helped sensitize me to the universality of basic human needs, regardless of race, gender, creed, and culture, yet with an awareness that these very basic needs are expressed in different ways by different ethnic and cultural groups. How people express their needs, feelings, and desires can easily lead to miscommunication and misunderstanding. As the world shrinks with newly developed communications and with more awareness of global interdependence, we are learning more about and from each other, while facing increased chances for misunderstanding and conflict.

To my parents and their parents I am indebted for a belief system that acknowledges concern for others to be of primary importance. Most important is what I have learned from my most valued life experience as a wife and the mother of three now adult children. This book is, therefore, dedicated to Joseph, Sharon, Jonathan, and Neal with love and admiration.

CHILDREN AND
YOUTH IN
LIMBO

Introduction:
Why This Volume?

THE PROBLEM

The American family and child care system is in trouble. This volume was conceived and written some time before the International Children's Summit of 1990. Seventy heads of state then gathered at the United Nations in New York City to address the well-being of children all over the world. They were confronted "just a few blocks from the shining glass tower of the United Nations ... [by] a lengthy and chilling sequence on what is happening to children in this the wealthiest nation of the world" [Hartman 1990:483]. Yet there should be no surprise at recent horrifying developments. According to Sen. Daniel Patrick Moynihan, we are revealed to be "the first society in history in which the poorest group ... is children" [Phillips 1990, as cited in Hartman 1990:483].

The number of traditional families with a clearly defined child-bearing and child-caring role is declining. In 1987, of the 62,932,000 children under the age of eighteen in the United States, approximately 24 percent lived in a single-parent household, and that number continues to increase. The increasing need for foster care beds is symptomatic of the breakdown in family competence and commitment to nurturing its young. In New York State alone, "From 1986 to 1988, the foster care caseload increased by 58 percent.... The number of children in care [was] projected to increase an additional 36 percent in 1989 to a year-end total of 59,300, and to grow to 72,300 by the end of 1990" [New York State 1990:7]. The American child-care and child welfare system lacks the necessary philosophic, functional, and comprehensive thrust to deal with the tens of thousands of children floating in limbo, many in abject poverty. These children do not know who will care for them until they can care for themselves.

Furthermore, the problem does not end when these youngsters attain their majority. In a poignant article, "When Foster Care Ends, Home Is Often the Street," J.C. Barden writes:

A large and disproportionate number of the nation's homeless are young people who have come out of foster care programs without the money, skills or family support to make it on their own. . . . The lack of skills that are necessary in a more technical marketplace and the absence of family members to lean on in hard times were mentioned repeatedly by the experts as major factors in the homelessness of former foster care youths. [*New York Times* 1991:1, 15]

These increasing problems point to a lack of community effort to prevent family breakdown that leaves children without homes. We lack a potent and comprehensive national child and family policy that articulates a value system accompanied not only by rhetoric but by allocation of resources. What programs there are often operate under funding, monitoring, licensing, and accrediting bodies that set up conflicting standards for the provision of services. Too often programs designed to meet the needs of children and families must meet expensive, artificial, inappropriate contracting, reporting, and monitoring requirements to qualify for funding.

The number of children, youth, and their families in need of service is increasing, while the number of dollars allocated to human services has been constantly decreasing. Young people are avoiding careers in the human services professions. The demands, prestige, and salaries of these professions are often not compatible with the aspirations of many talented people entering educational institutions and the job market. During times of economic recession, however, these frequently undervalued and underpaid professions are more successful in their recruitment efforts.

THESIS AND FOCUS

"No one comes from nowhere": Each human being was created through the reproductive capabilities of a man and a woman. Each woman and man was in turn created by another woman and man. Yet children and adults flounder for survival without any meaningful, functional human connections. How has this come about?

This volume attributes the complexity of the American family structure and the value confusions and inconsistencies of our society to the migrant, multicultural, and multiethnic origins of this country. Each wave of voluntary or involuntary arrivals has left behind part of their meaningful past. We are a nation of uprooted people—individuals and families who have all experienced some historical and geographical dislocation and loss of connections. Yet the proverbial "melting pot" has not really melted us into one culture. As people of different cultures and backgrounds intermarry, the complexities surrounding communication and expectations are at risk of increasing geometrically with each generation. With the pressures of a rapidly changing world, these challenges place the American family, and therefore American children, in serious jeopardy.

In attending to our value systems, we will have to take a very close look at the impact these values have on the preservation of the human species. Survival is a natural function. In a broader context, this means not only survival of self but survival of all whom we are creating for future generations. No value system, therefore, should be articulated that does not place a high priority on creating, nurturing, and educating the next generation.

The historical origins of the American child welfare system are rooted in Elizabethan poor law, and the nineteenth-century rescue of children from "bad" and "immoral" adults by breaking their ties. But now, rather than permitting dysfunctional separations, critical and needless losses, and the maintenance of "family secrets," our work with people, big and little, must focus on strengthening and enhancing connections to the past, through the present, and into the future. Although current child welfare practice validates the need for "work with families," absence of ties and communication haunts the lives of too many children who too soon become dysfunctional adults. We need inclusive programs validating the roots and origins of every human being regardless of age.

The literature abounds with innovative, creative practices that work. This volume draws on many of these examples, identifies some of the underlying issues affecting American families, and moves on to suggest the design for an array of family-focused programs that emphasize wellness, strengths, and assets, regardless of the family and individual's level of disability or dysfunction. A unifying philosophical focus is presented with program options on the need for family connections and how to make them work.

PART I

Problems and Responses

This volume begins by identifying the multiple challenges affecting services to children and families in the changing and complex social environment of the United States today. The critical state of the American family is examined in the context of its voluntary and often involuntary migrant, immigrant, and multiethnic origins. The failure to give priority to nurturing our young leaves thousands of children in limbo, not knowing who will care for them until they can care for themselves.

These children and their problems can be clearly identified and a variety of social support systems and program responses developed to prevent family dissolution and assure lifelong connections. When family dissolution cannot be averted, an alternative set of program options can be offered, based on the philosophic premise that "nobody comes from no place" and that children's permanent roots must be identified and strengthened to help them grow into effective, productive adults.

1

Children's Services: Issues and Challenges

Families engaged in childrearing in the United States today face serious difficulties. The challenge is to understand the nature of these difficulties, to articulate a clear, manageable philosophy of care, and to identify a variety of ways to strengthen families in accomplishing their childrearing tasks.

SOCIAL CHANGE

These are complex, challenging, historically significant times. In order to gain maximum benefit from ongoing changes, we must first comprehend their origin and impact.

We have entered into a Third Industrial Revolution that is reshaping our industrial processes and dramatically changing the basis of industrial and technological growth. It will affect all aspects of our society over the next fifty years. The shift in products and markets is already in evidence. . . . All of these are information driven. Their interaction and synergies open a new age of opportunity and challenge, but also one of uncertainty and unpredictability. The impacts of the Third Industrial Revolution are overwhelming. The pace of changes threatens our individual and institutional capacities to cope with change. [Finkelstein 1986]

The previously economically secure and even affluent position of the United States relative to other nations is challenged. Other countries are actively and successfully competing with us for leadership in industrial production and international markets. These pressures and changes challenge our country's capacity in trying to meet highly specialized, continuously changing demands, and they require a highly motivated work force. Jobs go unfilled, or their turnover rate is often too high for adequate performance, and it is difficult to maintain an ethic of work quality essential to assure our competitive edge.

The quality of the work force of tomorrow is directly related to the models our children follow today. Do the significant adults in their lives believe that work is important and that completion and accomplishment is gratifying—whether the task is weeding a garden, designing a fixture, milling a part, filling a rut in a road, or writing a book?

Furthermore, parents' sense of work-related accomplishment is only possible if their life is sufficiently manageable and supported so that family tensions do not creep into the workplace and work experience. The parent concerned about sick or unsupervised children at home finds it difficult, if not impossible, to get any work-related gratification. Quality child care for working families is essential, regardless of income. Moreover, respite services also are needed in a world in which people live longer, both parents are in the work force, and many single people are parents. Families now find themselves responsible for caring for disabled members, especially the elderly, who previously would not have survived at all or would have been cared for in institutions. These caregiving tasks must now be incorporated into people's family living. Families, particularly those who must work and also care for young children, the ill, the dependent, and the elderly, need occasional relief from their tasks. These respite breaks occur naturally with stable family structures. Grandparents, uncles, aunts, cousins step in. Socially competent people have friendship groups or can purchase services to help. Community planning and organizations, however, must step in where gaps exist, to strengthen such services as day care for nonseriously ill children, homemaker services, and respite care. The number and proportion of Americans in these situations will increase. Recognition of this need should facilitate a variety of community initiatives.

There are many work-related issues that impact on family life and human wellness. Should we work a four-day workweek? Should we work a six-hour workday? Should work hours and times be flexible? Should all family members work? Should spouses share jobs? How young do people need to begin work, and how old should they be when they cease to work? What tasks are there for the population with average or even below-average performance? Will most work be so automated that there will be little need for jobs that make people feel useful and productive? Are a shorter workweek and more unstructured time really an improvement in the quality of life for most people? These and many other questions will have to be addressed while rationally defining a human services delivery system for the next century.

As human life designed and affected by the economy of modern science, technology, and organization becomes more complex and demanding, so life tasks for the majority of our population may become too complicated to be managed successfully by the average individual, including the ordinary parent. Inevitably we in America and in human services find ourselves pursuing narrow reactive policies to what are in fact symptoms of much larger issues. Society must be so organized that necessary structural supports can be built in to accommodate these pressures on families.

For example, the increase in child abuse reports,[1] rather than simply being due to better reporting mechanisms and protective services, in fact can be considered symptomatic of tensions beyond people's coping abilities. The heavy tasks of daily life in a rapidly changing world, accompanied by constantly changing expectations, require the emotional and psychological fiber provided through nurturance and role-modeling in a person's formative years. Given the complex nature of the world we live in, more and more children are at risk. These children in turn will be the parents of tomorrow's endangered children unless comprehensive, well-thought-through intervention can cut this destructive cycle.

CONSENSUS AND SOCIAL POLICY

Democratic society is exciting and invigorating because of its recurrent shifts in national, state, and local political leadership and government policies. But with each change in political leadership comes a philosophic shift in the application of social values. This impermanence and unpredictability filter down to family services and their impact on individual families and children. We in family and children services are faced with a dilemma: how in a democracy to find a national and local consensus for family social policy that meets the needs of its most vulnerable populations—children and others in need of special care and support.

The questions raised and principles proposed in this chapter are devised to move the United States toward consensus on family and children services policy. All of us, as Americans, must first look at our values and beliefs. Do we all value every citizen equally? Do we really care about children? Do we count on the family? Because we live in a multicultural society, individual human behavior, values, and types of activities vary widely. Yet a broad national consensus is needed on fundamental values, or we will continue to flounder. In other words, if we in child and family services cannot articulate appropriate and acceptable belief systems and attitudes on which to base a predictable, comprehensive service philosophy, we cannot persuade the electorate and policy-makers to adopt appropriate service delivery and fiscal policy proposals.

Broadly held American political and social attitudes toward family and children would assist the building of a consensus on social policy. For this consensus to produce effective policies, however, there must be close scrutiny of where and how such attitudes would be consistent or in conflict with basic human needs. From this analysis a philosophy and a structural design for needed services to American families and children can be developed.]We shall touch on existing and potential public child and family services policies in the United States, and on their assumptions and consequences, as we lay out the philosophy of care presented in this volume.

CONSENSUS AND DIVERSE ROOTS

There are, of course, difficulties in reaching a consensus on values. We in the United States think of ourselves as a single nation. Yet we are a very special nation: Inhabiting almost a whole subcontinent, many left their homelands in search of freedom and economic opportunity; others were uprooted and brought into slavery by force. Native Americans have been displaced from indigenous environments and cultures. As a nation of voluntary and involuntary migrants, our families of origin brought the values, beliefs, lifestyles, and communication modes of their original cultures. These have been at least partially transmitted since then down succeeding generations of Americans, although some groups were so completely cut off from their past that any cultural continuity was very difficult.

The timetables of arrival, acculturation, and—most difficult of all—intermarriage, have varied from one migrant wave to another, from one ethnic group to another, and from family to family. As soon as each set of new arrivals with their family subcultures has settled in, a new ethnic group has arrived or moved, settling in various parts of the country and creating further regional differences.

Bowenian theory defines the family system as "an interlocking series of relationships bound together by blood and marriage extending over three to four generations" [Guerin 1984b:10]. But these family scripts and messages, expressed through their members' beliefs, feelings, and behaviors, are often in conflict. These conflicts are expressed by us as individuals in our nuclear and extended families, our organizations and communities, and through our elected officials.

PUBLIC AGENCY OVERLAP AND SERVICE-PROVIDER DILEMMAS

An Example

Providing mandated state services for various aspects of children's problems often creates inconsistencies and disagreements (see Figure 1.1).

Figure 1.1
To Whom Does Johnny Really Belong?

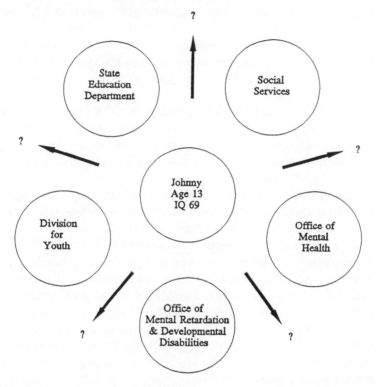

Although these services vary from state to state, let us take the hypothetical but very possible case of Johnny, a thirteen-year-old resident of New York State, which has an elaborate service system for children.

Johnny's mother and father have been separated for a long time. Johnny's mother is receiving assistance from the county department of social services to maintain herself, Johnny, and his four other siblings, some with other fathers. Since the child's mother has limited intelligence, sporadic drinking problems, and no supportive kin nor apparent community support network, her management of Johnny has been inconsistent at best, and occasionally abusive. Johnny is a dependent and neglected child, and as such his service planning is the responsibility of the New York State Department of Social Services.

Johnny has a measured I.Q. of only 69; he had a traumatic birth and shows some developmental lag. Because of his developmental deficits, he is also the responsibility of the State Office of Mental Retardation and Developmental Disabilities.

The youth also has an intense—at times self-destructive—fantasy life. Although it is difficult to determine which of these symptoms is primary and which secondary, he could come to the attention of the State Office of Mental Health.

In his day-to-day functioning, Johnny is impulse-ridden, with little regard for law and order; he has had several brushes with the law, and has been adjudged a delinquent child. He thus comes under the jurisdiction of the State Division for Youth.

Given Johnny's complex learning difficulties and his tendency to act out and thereby jeopardize himself and his schoolmates, there is no question that the local public school cannot set up adequate programs for him. Therefore, the State Department of Education is mandated to place him in either a day or a residential away-from-home educational program.

Once services are provided, case coordination becomes very complicated, not only for the child but the whole family, since inevitably other members of the same family are also in need of services. The problem of multiple jurisdictions and services is compounded when each agency looks to another for help in providing services but none accepts full responsibility for the individuals served. And sooner or later, interagency rifts turn up over philosophy of care. Johnny's mother undertakes one program's parent educa tion to help her deal with sister Susie's difficulties, but another agency, working with Johnny, does not believe that program is useful or effective. On the other hand, the child in need may be dropped from some or all services because of reaching a particular age, a change in family income, or some other arbitrary cutoff point.

Service models are forced to adapt to the requirements of their funders, not those they are supposed to serve. State-mandated programs, design of funding, and monitoring mechanisms can often be seen to have little to do with the needs of the service recipient and much more to do with how to fit the unique individual into preconceived categories and demands when viewed within a systems context. Systems analysis is an engineering concept that ties the parts of a system into a whole to understand not only their relationship but also how the interacting components work together to support or hinder appropriate functioning [Fogarty 1984a:18]. Licensing and monitoring requirements grow more extensive each year. In fact a great deal of agency and government energy is wasted on monitoring programs and methods that do not work. How services are articulated and delivered—sometimes duplicated or not delivered at all—is a serious problem.

Multiple and overlapping state agencies and bureaucracies for family and child services cost a great deal. The larger the administrative budgets of public agencies, the less money is available to filter down to the services for recipients. Thus, more money does not necessarily mean better services, especially when funding for effective programs is cut off in favor of new, experimental, not-yet-tested programs.

Furthermore, budgeted service positions often go unfilled because of low salaries and poor working conditions. Family and child services are not portrayed attractively in the media. The helping professions remain on the lower economic and prestige rungs of the occupational ladder. There is a shortage of social workers, nurses, home health aides, day care and child-care workers. Even medicine in general, and psychiatry in particular, are experiencing a significant decline in young people entering what used to be highly esteemed professions. Law, finance, and technical occupations in the last decade at least temporarily displaced such service positions, which are often omitted from job fairs and career selection programs.

These problems in federal, state, and local programs and private not-for-profit agencies for child and family services exist in all parts of the country. When provider problems become severe enough, an effective society must take a close look at whether shifts in the human services system are needed to enhance the quality of life and even the survival of the many who depend on it.

In response to these critical issues, Governor Mario Cuomo appointed a task force to study the service delivery system to children and their families in the state of New York. The task force was comprised of the commissioners of all government agencies providing services to children and families and members of the legislature dealing with these issues. An impressive report, "There ARE Better Ways to Serve Children," was submitted to the governor on 1 August 1989. This could become a national model for the implementation of child and family services based upon a carefully thought-through child and family policy driven by a belief system which in turn would drive responsible government agency organization to optimally provide for the needs of children and families. Early on it became quite clear that "the multiple service needs of families are not neatly divided along government agency organizational lines. In order to meet the needs of New York's children and families in the 1990's, government systems serving families will have to operate in a much closer alignment with each other" [Dullea 1989:i].

Further complicating these overlapping bureaucracies, systems flaws, and often conflicting funding structures are inconsistencies, discrepancies, and confusions on the practice level. The service providers scapegoat the funding agencies, which in turn return the criticism to the service providers for ineffective and costly services. The professional literature and professional conferences add more jarring voices: We hear much about different schools of family therapy, individual versus systemic approaches, and much worship of this guru or that. Disciples of a viewpoint are sometimes more rigid than its creator. There seems to be no inclusive and comprehensive philosophy of care around which the needs of children and their families can be organized and integrated. While practitioners get mired in philosophic controversies, children and their families desperately in need of service fall between the cracks. Yet those of us in practice and program design know a wide range of programs and methods that work. Some integrating principles need to be proposed that could be accepted by most family and child service providers.

A PHILOSOPHIC BASE FOR CHILD AND FAMILY SERVICES

This book suggests a practical framework for an integrated philosophy of care based on human needs rather than on any single theoretical school. The underlying commonalities of many philosophic systems provide enough basis for latitude in the application of different styles and methods to reveal these alternatives as opportunities for an array of services, rather than as obstacles to the creative provision of appropriate care.

Human problems should be perceived, defined, and experienced as interactions within a social and economic milieu. "All people exist in a relationship, an internal and an external relationship. . . . Thoughts, feelings, memories, etc.—exist in relationship to each other. A thought may give rise to a memory which activates a feeling. . . . No portion of self lives in isolation. At the same time, every person lives in relation to other people" [Fogarty 1984a:21]. Especially today, however, this environment very often does not have the built-in organizational capability to support individuals trying to cope with the usual human problems. Therefore, comprehensive services to benefit children must be only a part of overall family services, and cannot be designed apart from their wider social context.

Besides carrying the genetic contribution of our biological parents, as well as a constitutional predisposition for certain kinds of behaviors [Guerin 1984a:3], it must be recognized that most children are the product of a necessarily mixed culture consisting of the often conflicting values, rules, messages, and communication styles of two often very different families, the mother's and the father's. When these messages are compatible, the integration and functioning of the child's personality are easier. But when inherited messages conflict, it is harder for the family to work out acceptable resolutions that the children can ultimately take on as their own.

Working out the problems of "Who am I?" "What do I believe in?" "What is right?" "What is wrong?" "What do I stand for?" "What do I want my life to be?" is crucial to the development of the young human being. Where adult commitment is ambivalent or lacking, young people attempting to sort out their individual identity are constantly threatened by the fear of ultimate abandonment. In view of their long period of dependence, they experience this as fear of death itself. All sorts of personality mechanisms are adopted to ward off such a terrifying thought. Therefore, the less predictable and secure, the less caring and nurturing the childrearing environment, the more complex the child's maturation tasks.

Children need to know who will care for them during their years of dependence, if they are to grow optimally. Only in a social network of mutual commitment, where, no matter how severe the stress, the unspoken rule is that the players are so bonded that they will get through any task without questioning their commitment, may adults take many risks in their lives without necessarily jeopardizing their children's optimal growth. At best, every human being should be able to develop within a caring, connected system where there is no question about the child's belonging and about the other participants' commitment to work through the stresses we all experience in the course of our lives.

The child's sense of belonging must transcend the nuclear family, since no two adults alone, no matter how committed, can create a full sense of safety for a growing child. The safety net is widened through the commitment of grandparents, uncles, aunts, and cousins, whether or not they are biologically related or "adopted" by the family. Children who grow up in an extended family have a wealth of linkages and options that children who live in an isolated nuclear family never have. The extended family provides validation to the childrearing couple, as well as back-up support in case of stress or hardship.

We are all outcomes of the genetic, social, psychological, and cultural heritage of our families, yet we so often are told that particular children or youth are in need of care because they are "without families." We know that every human being is the product of two families, whether present or absent, alive or dead. Our task is to identify who these families are and what has prevented some of them from adequately nurturing their young, not to deny their very existence.

For family service practitioners, developing genuine empathy toward these families is a major challenge. The children in need may not know their families well, or even who they are, but these families are there in the children's minds. Since these children know only too well that they do have families, as long as we claim that Johnny and Susie have no family, we prevent our own trusting and trustworthy relationship not only with the children but with their families.

Of course, the children's view of their families may be a fantasy; these fantasies create the most difficulties. They may be based on faint memories, hearsay, or an unspoken message that their biological family must be neither asked nor spoken about. But these families must be recognized and sought, discovered and helped if possible to join in assisting the child.

Philosophically, therefore, children's services must be family services. We cannot justify placing children and youth in state institutions for months or years on end, while insisting that they have no family. We cannot seek adoption for children, even infants, while claiming that the child's need to search for an understanding of its family of origin can be disregarded. The real or imaginary connections of people with each other are always going to be more powerful than the interventions of the most self-confident therapist or the most legally sanctioned agency.

CHILDREN AND YOUTH IN LIMBO—THE NEED FOR PERMANENCY PLANNING

The Child Welfare League of America uses the following definition of permanency planning: "Permanency planning is the systematic process of case planning, service delivery and monitoring necessary to assure a lifelong, legally recognized nurturant family for every child who is in foster care or at risk of removal from his or her biological family" [Cole 1984:2]. But it is very hard for practitioners and supervisors with heavy caseloads and insufficient consultation and training to apply this principle.

At times, the ties with the biological family are legally severed and separations enforced without a clear understanding as to what this means for the child. In fact, legal termination of parental rights is hardly psychologically binding if the child is still bonded with its family, even if the placement worker perceives that family to be detrimental to the child's growth.

Any permanency planning effort, therefore, requires a clear assessment of the quality and extent of bonding with the original and subsequent primary care systems. Only then can a plan be developed with any reasonable possibility of success. The ideal permanency plan is that which assures the child a sense of identity, of belonging, of being cared for, regardless of the crises a family may encounter. The social system with which a young person is bonded must also be one to which the young person in turn will contribute as he or she grows and matures.

Practitioners often confuse permanence, which is essentially a feeling, with the physical place in which a child may need to grow up. In our zealousness to assure their permanent bonding with a family, we lose those youngsters who cannot be separated from their biological kin emotionally but whose families, whether nuclear or extended, will never be able to raise them to adulthood. Permanency planning too often has become an either/or proposition, with insufficient attention to the many in-between options in the child's and families' evolving situations.

⌊When validating and strengthening the original family system is not possible, a coordinated approach to services needs to be set in motion so that children do not remain in limbo for months and years. We know too well that with each new move or rejection the child's ability to adjust is further jeopardized.⌉

⌊The professional's casework, based on theoretical and practical understanding, is made operational through those who legislate, mandate, oversee, and fund client services. Within this context, the complicated but often oversimplified concept of "permanence" and "permanency planning" has been federally mandated by Public Law 96–272 (the Adoption Assistance and Child Welfare Act of 1980). This law gives "widespread ideological approval and philosophic support for the effort to keep families whole if possible, to reestablish them if they are broken up, or to make other 'permanent' plans for children" [Kamerman and Kahn 1989:16]. Even prior to the federal mandate, the principles had been effectively articulated and operationalized in Oregon [Regional Research Institute 1976] and legislatively mandated by the Child Welfare Reform Act of 1979 in the state of New York [Seaberg 1986:469]. Yet as we gain experience with permanency planning, it raises many unresolv d problems that go beyond the obvious issues created by underfunded mandates, such as an enormous increase in bureaucratic monitoring and voluminous paperwork, which divert limited resources from direct service provision to clients.⌉

SOCIAL NETWORKS AND SOCIAL SERVICES

Human individuals are social beings. We all need social networks to assure our ongoing social support and connections. This has always been expected of family, kin, and the wider community. Isolation and loneliness lead to depression. Depressed people are not productive people; they do not enhance their own well-being or that of others.

Above all, the philosophic thrust of service organization should emphasize people's ongoing wellness and health. Many people in our society have the know-how and skill to organize themselves, their environment, and their lifestyle to meet their basic health and survival needs. But even the most self-contained and seemingly competent remain healthy only until their threshold of overload is reached. A developmentally disabled child, the life-threatening illness of a loved one, long periods of unemployment, can create stress that makes coping marginal for anyone.

Social networks provide surcease, respite, and support in times of stress. Of course, help is more easily acceptable and accepted from people with whom one has an ongoing relationship; a time of stress is not the best time to develop new relationships. Groups of people so organized that they know and care about each other in a natural way are in the best position to provide these extra supports.

To what extent can support networks, later-life friendships, and special-interest groups substitute for family, kin, and early, long-established friendships? In fact, adult support and friendship groups can easily relate to and help meet the special needs of a family in crisis. Ordinarily they are nearby; in our very mobile society that is important. Under stress, family and friendship groups often pull together. Linkages and connections perceived as lost or nonfunctioning are reestablished. Recognizing these linkages provides an unspoken sense of loyalty and safety.

A philosophy committed to wellness must therefore take into account the intense needs human beings have for acknowledgment of their cultural roots, biological connections, and early ties. Because each human being has a unique configuration of connections, every person is thereby special. But this recognition needs validation of and by these other people. Taking this as a philosophic premise, we can design programs to enhance well-being by legitimizing and reinforcing the individual's social roots and connections. Even though there may be a qualitative difference between old and new ties established in specific life situations, such as the neighborhood, work, or religious affiliation, all potentially constructive friendships should be reinforced.

FAMILY SERVICES AND EDUCATION

Child care must be organized to provide supports for wellness that aim at teaching life skills to children and parents for coping with constantly changing social demands. When we speak of human services organized with a wellness and health approach, we are really seeking education to reward and reinforce all human assets.

Our educational systems have lost touch with these realities. Academic secondary and postsecondary education is a worthy investment in our youth. But we have the illusion that everyone should go to college, that higher education is the only entree to a better life, and that cap-and-gown graduations should begin in kindergarten. When inappropriately used, higher education and even secondary education as we often know it have created prolonged dependency and a sense of failure in many young people forced to remain in what to them is an unhealthy, counterproductive environment.

Once a failure script is inscribed, the opportunity for a personally and socially productive future is jeopardized. Youth in inappropriate educational systems become dropouts.

We squander incredible resources on the chronic school truancy of youngsters who have never learned to read, programmed for failure by educational systems neither designed nor intended to meet their needs. These failures, in turn, label these youths as "different," leading many a family to lose hope for a productive future for their child.

We often speak of "remedial" training, "special" education, and other educational "assistance." Our present assessment systems seem to focus on identifying people's deficits; we pay only lip service to emphasizing and capitalizing on identifying and enhancing people's assets. Many individuals need hands-on education in an apprentice relationship rather than a classroom setting. The years of apprenticeship may be very different from high school or college, but the benefits to both employer and apprentice may be equally substantial. Furthermore, tasks are mastered at different speeds by different people, and some need to be retaught again and again. For example, a skill at which we fail at one time in our lives may be learned successfully when retaught later. This learning pattern is true in some degree for everyone.

Teachers constantly ask, "What's wrong with Johnny and what can be done to correct his failures?" They also ask, "What is wrong with Johnny's parents and how can these parents be improved?" But the better questions to ask are: "What is right with Johnny and what can we do to reinforce those strengths? What is right with Johnny's parents and how can we strengthen them?"

FAMILY SERVICES AND VALUES

Enough agreement probably exists in American values [Williams 1970] to develop some clear, bold guidelines in harmony with our Constitution and history. First of all, as a society we can reinforce the concept that family life, broadly defined, is important for raising children. Although it can be defined and experienced in many different ways, our government needs to commit itself to family life as a social institution we believe in and will support.

We should acknowledge as a second American value that work is important and constructive for human beings to accomplish their own and society's goals of self-preservation and self-enhancement. This commitment would lead to clearly articulated educational institutions for all, and to enough employment opportunities that most people can participate, contribute, and benefit from their own efforts.

Above all else, do we believe that children are important? Are children truly valued in our society? Are they equally valued by all ethnic and cultural groups? Are all children equally valued by society regardless of their ethnic and cultural origin? Children do not vote and have no political power. Children no longer provide labor on the farm, necessarily continue the family business, or are seen as a future resource to care for aging parents (although children do care for their parents more frequently than is recognized). Yet children are the vehicle through which a society perpetuates itself. The absence of children creates an empty space for many who have not experienced parenting.

Furthermore, how childhood is experienced by children today will determine the type of society we will experience tomorrow. Simply stated, if children are nurtured, cared for, and able to grow in a caring, predictable environment that allows them to optimize their human potential, we can hope for a more reasonable, productive, and empathic nation and world. If, on the other hand, we in the United States tolerate child neglect, abuse, and unbroken cycles of poverty, we can look forward to a further deterioration of our society. Violence and substance abuse will increase as Americans search for relief from inner tensions and harsh disappointments.

If, indeed, we do believe that the children of today are our most important national asset, we will design programs and allocate both material and human resources according to such beliefs. Given the uncertainties that inevitably accompany massive technological changes, we will have to put greater energy into making childhood more predictable in an increasingly complicated, unpredictable world. A safe childhood is only possible if the primary institution entrusted with childrearing—the family—is understood, valued, and supported.

CONCLUSION

Child welfare services as a component of the human services delivery system in the United States are in trouble, and the challenges are enormous. Our society's democratic process produces periodic change in leadership and frequent shifts in human service priorities, compounded by the multiethnic background of Americans, with their roots in many parts of the world. We are, furthermore, living in an era of economic turmoil and a rapidly shrinking globe, multiplying the impact of other nations on our well-being.

New technologies rapidly change the demands made in the workplace and the lifestyle expectations in home and community. Scientific and medical advances leave us caring for partially disabled children and adults who previously would not have survived. The quite appropriate rejection of institutional care as a universal solution has left families and communities burdened with the task of adapting their own structures. We must focus on all these issues as we search for an appropriate service philosophy out of which service policy, models, and funding mechanisms need to flow, not only for the sake of children and their families but also for the survival of American society.

Programs need to be philosophically organized to enhance wellness, not focusing merely on lowering pathology. Lip service is often paid to this philosophy in modern human services, but there seems to be insufficient depth or commitment in practice and funding. In searching for informal and formal helping resources, we need to view individuals' service needs as a normal part of the life cycle, with particular sensitivity to the ethnic, social, and cultural origins of their difficulties. The assessment process needs to focus on children's and families' assets and to build on those strengths.

The educational structure needs to undergo broad changes, since wellness is created in a normal, not in a special, environment. Education as merely an intellectual process is not applicable to our large non-college-bound population. Hands-on programs designed for ongoing success and achievement must be created for those who cannot master reading, writing, and arithmetic easily and well. Preparation for jobs needs to be created, involving tasks at which a whole segment of our population can succeed.

Above all, social network support—especially kinship and early life connections—must be preserved and validated. Individuals cannot and do not live in total isolation. These linkages are particularly important for those young people for whom the service systems have to provide institutional living, foster family care, or adoption as alternatives to living with the family of origin.

Funding and monitoring structures need to be designed to validate creative, successful programs along these lines. Programs that work should not be cut off before they can be fully developed by having to respond to continuous pressure by state and federal governments for new, untried initiatives. An integrated array of services designed with an understanding of systemic needs must be put into place.

The public bureaucracy must be organized to provide programs and services adapted to people's needs rather than squeezing these needs into predesigned systems. Even worse, we sometimes arbitrarily transfer people into new and different systems in response to artificial guidelines when their needs have not really changed very much; often some irrelevant milestone, such as reaching the age of eighteen or twenty-one, makes them ineligible for previous services.

There needs to be a national philosophy and policy for the family, if family life is indeed perceived as the primary institution around which our society is organized. A high premium needs to be placed on family, work, and above all the child. Children's nurture and care must be central values, for in them lies the future and the perpetuation of all that we create. If parenting and the care of children are perceived as a privilege rather than as a burden, they will have the highest priority for the family, the community, and government.

NOTE

1. There were 1,727,000 documented reports of child abuse and neglect nationwide during 1985 reported by the American Humane Association in 1986; the reported cases of abuse and maltreatment have increased yearly: In 1975, 36,666 reports involving 72,195 children were received by the New York State Central Register; in 1985, 84,119 reports involving a total of 139,032 children were recorded [Crotty 1988:134, 135].

2

The American Family

The family is the unit in our society charged with the fulfillment of a number of socially desirable goals. The family must conceive, bear, and nurture children, provide some satisfaction for the primary caregivers, and assist its elderly members. Families are intended to be able to function "in sickness and in health"; their members must be more than just fair-weather sailors. Family members must, therefore, be able to give much of themselves and in turn to receive what they need.

The family is an organization that must have rules and structure. But different members have different needs at different times. It is not unusual for the needs of one member to be incompatible or even in conflict with the needs of another member at any given time. Therefore, the family must also have a great deal of flexibility so as to change and adapt continuously to the constantly shifting needs of its members as each individual and the group as a whole move through the life cycle. It must be able to plan for an ongoing, continuously changing, and thus unpredictable future.

The family can provide validation, acceptance, and a sense of well-being for all its members, and readily shift demands and expectations according to the life stage and capability of each individual member. The family as a stable institution needs the ability to deal with and mark such life-cycle milestones as birth, christening, circumcision ritual, confirmation, engagement, marriage, and, of course, death. It must have the capability to care for its members during times of illness, unemployment, and other socially inflicted hardships. At its best the family must be able to provide sufficient income to meet the most basic housing, food, clothing, recreational, educational, health, and incidental needs of all its members.

In the process of living and caring, the family transmits its values and expectations. Older family members look to the next generation, to the children by birth or adoption, to nieces and nephews or even younger cousins, for another opportunity to reexperience those stages of life that have come and gone only too quickly. Some family members see the next generation as a possibility to rewrite or redo a script; other members prefer the scenario to be replayed from memory and by fantasy. In return for what it offers, the family looks to its members for loyalty and commitment. Unhappily, loyalty is sometimes defined as the maintenance of the status quo.

The American family, often perceived to be in danger of extinction, exists in a very complicated social system. Major social and economic changes are occurring in this country and in many other parts of the world, in such rapidly industrializing nations as Japan, Korea, China, and other Pacific Rim countries. Most recently Russia, Poland, Hungary, Germany, and other Eastern European countries have been visible in their struggle to adapt. Economic challenges and social upheavals will affect the welfare and functioning of family units that tend to be dependent on stable economic conditions for their social and psychological well-being. Change in methods of production, the shifting of international markets, and consequent pressures on this country present Americans with a host of new challenges as to who works, how, and at what. Contrasting with these socioeconomic realities are American expectations of a lifestyle and level of affluence that will probably never be seen again.

As American society becomes insecure and confusing, so also do families and their individual members become unsure and confused. National and international conditions already require a rethinking of the roles and functions of individual family members. As both mother and father join the work force, traditional role and task assignments need rethinking and restructuring. Energy is drained from the generation that is just completing the tasks of childrearing as they shift, often without respite, to care for the elderly as senior family members live much longer, or even to taking in grandchildren who cannot be cared for by their parents.

The large number of single-parent families, the high rate of divorce, and growing reports of child abuse and neglect are among the symptoms telling us that the pressure on the modern American family exceeds the coping ability of many families and individuals. We need to look closely at the underlying causes that have made the American family so vulnerable during this major period of change and uncertainty, and at the variety of new, badly needed supportive institutions that must be put in place.

ETHNICITY

The migrant nature of our society compounds the complexity of the American family. Each cultural and ethnic group brought with it a history of its own, a set of rules and norms integrated and passed on to the next generation. Ethnic heritage determines how we value children, how we raise them, and how we program them for the perpetuation of life's tasks.

Ethnicity describes a sense of commonality transmitted over generations by the family and reinforced by the surrounding community. It is more than race, religion, or national and geographic origin (which is not to minimize the significance of race or the special problems of racism). It involves conscious and unconscious processes that fulfill a deep psychological need for identity and historical continuity (Giordano and Giordano 1977). Ethnicity patterns our thinking, feeling, and behavior in both obvious and subtle ways. It plays a major role in determining what we eat, how we work, how we relax, how we celebrate holidays and rituals, and how we feel about life, death, and illness. [McGoldrick 1982:4]

Historically, the dominant cultural group in the United States has been white and Protestant, but even within that group the cultural variations were enormous, among those of German, Dutch, English, Scottish, and Scandinavian origin. There are major differences among the Chinese, Japanese, and Koreans, and between the Pakistanis and the Indians, among Jews of German, Russian, and Spanish origin. The behaviors and expectations of the more dominant groups are often very much in conflict with other ethnic groups. The white Anglo-Saxon Protestants are often future-oriented and openly optimistic, yet many have major difficulties coping with tragic life events other than through denial or repression. Eastern European Jews and Italian Catholics, who tend to have a much freer expression of emotion, are often seen by white Anglo-Saxon Protestants as behaving inappropriately, if not in fact hysterically. Physical punishment of children is acceptable in some cultures, while in others it is perceived as abuse [McGoldrick 1982]. In China, Japan, and Korea, direct eye contact shows lack of respect and trust. It is seen as rude. In the West, lack of direct eye contact is seen as evasive and inappropriate.

These intercultural differences are enough to raise difficulties, but we are also dealing with differences as to when each migrant group arrived and where they are today in the process of acculturation. Groups that arrived intact and set up their own reasonably insulated communities, such as the Scandinavians in the upper Midwest, were more able to preserve their traditions and identity. On the other hand, "families who migrate alone have a greater need to adapt to the new situation, and their losses are often more hidden" [McGoldrick 1982:13]. In the adaptation process there is often a superficial compliance to standards and norms that do not feel right, a price the individual is willing to pay for an acceptance that is also only superficial. The more the pain is repressed, the more superficial and vulnerable the adaptation.

Most migrant groups came in search of a better life. Some wanted to escape societies that seemed too confining socially, economically, or in terms of religious freedom. Others came because coming meant survival in the face of devastating persecution. Still others were displaced by force. In any case, it is instructive to compare migrants as they contrast with those who chose not to leave. Is there something, for example, to be learned about basic differences between those people who chose to risk early flight from Nazi Germany versus those who thought until it was too late that this was only a passing storm that would soon subside? It is reasonable to assume that those who chose to immigrate were less committed to the maintenance and perpetuation of the status quo than those who did not leave when it was still possible to do so. Under the stress of coping and adapting to the new, however, other rigidities may have developed. Hanging on to the known and therefore less frightening offers some respite from the threat of the unknown.

The messages given by migrants to the next generation will inevitably have many double meanings and double binds: "We have left the familiar behind, have uprooted, have tolerated the pain of many losses in order to give you the opportunity for a better life." But this "better life" in the United States is the life of the dominant, white Anglo-Saxon Protestants. Therefore, the underlying message is, on the one hand, "change and adapt so that you can make the grade and pass," but on the other hand, "do not change so much that our system is shaken, and worst of all that we lose you." The theme of parental sacrifice and subsequent threat of loss of their children is poignantly articulated by Maxine Hong Kingston in her book *The Woman Warrior: Memoirs of a Girlhood among Ghosts*, as she speaks of the struggle to leave her Chinese immigrant family.

Do you know what the Teacher Ghosts say about me? They tell me I'm smart, and I can win scholarships. I can get into Colleges . . . they say I could be a scientist or mathematician if I want. I can make a living and take care of myself. . . . I can do ghost things even better than ghosts can. Not everybody thinks I am nothing. I am not going to be a slave or wife. [Kingston 1976:201]

As migrants' original values become weaker in transmission, without either full understanding or absorption by the young, they are left without much to hang on to. The "good life" often becomes synonymous with material acquisition and other outer trappings of the dominant culture.

Creature comforts are nice, but even the thickest carpet and fanciest video cassette recorder cannot compensate for the pain of psychological emptiness. If the sports car, motor boat, or private plane are the unknowing vehicles of flight from self, past, roots, and connections, their acquisition cannot be anything more than emotionally disastrous.

With each successive generation after arrival, the rate of intermarriage with different ethnic, cultural, racial, and religious groups increases. With each intermarriage, conflicting priorities, norms, values, lifestyles, and modes of communication make the search for mutually acceptable mechanisms for stress alleviation more hazardous. When there are two partners and each is the product of parents with a mixed cultural background, the complexities burdening the interpersonal adaptations mount exponentially. To complicate matters, individuals often have little awareness of the origin of these difficulties. Miscommunications become personalized, are perceived by both partners as a lack of caring, and are acted out in the relationship through blaming, scapegoating, noncommunication, somatization, and symptom development. The survival of a marriage becomes vulnerable while the children become symptom bearers of the inevitable, yet often unarticulated, tensions and discord.

Given the industrial nature of American society, the size of the country, and the premium on higher education as the entry ticket at the gate of success, people's geographic mobility is the American norm. Protestants claim the responsibility of good parents is to raise children for self-dependence. In preparation for this, many young people from the middle class are sent to colleges and universities away from home. Going to postsecondary school in your own community is seen as second-best. However, as young people are encouraged to leave home either to go away to school or to advance up the ladder of promotion, family ties may appear to loosen.

When the family of origin is plagued by cultural confusion and discontinuity, the young person often does not have a set of conscious values and priorities as guides for interpersonal relationships that will be strong enough to absorb the normal tensions and stresses involved as new family formation occurs. "During courtship a person may be attracted precisely to the fiance's differentness, but when entrenched in a marital relationship the same qualities often become the rub" [McGoldrick 1982:21]. One might hypothesize that especially those people who work toward changing their own social position may tend to search out a partner based on difference rather than similarity.

Constant geographic and socioeconomic mobility as sources of stress cannot be minimized. In some sense geographic distance seems smaller as transportation systems have improved and the cost of travel has decreased. The telecommunication industry also decreases isolation as a way to maintain connections. Moreover, one can argue that, when roots and connections are healthy, geographic distance allows for the degree of individuation that permits a healthy beginning for the new couple. In some cultures, however, this in and of itself brings much guilt and dysfunction: "If we have done right by you, you should not have left home or moved away."

A major built-in dysfunction inherent in the nature of our society, the emphasis on providing a better tomorrow for subsequent generations, can impact negatively on children. In reaction to the stresses of the Great Depression and then World War II, parents were almost obsessionally preoc- cupied with the "happiness" of their children while raising a generation of baby boomers. This "happiness syndrome" exceeded all reasonable expecta- tions and left many youths unprepared to cope with realistic frustrations. The objective of keeping children "happy" was inflicted upon the educational establishment, which often supported this value, though only ambivalently. Parents project a great deal on the educational system, which is unrealistically programmed to pick up the confusing parental messages while still producing a product acceptable to the parents. Young people, equally confused, respond with low motivation and underachievement. Often the comment is "He is not being sufficiently challenged," while in fact, "He is depressed" might be the more realistic assessment.

Another difficulty with the "happiness" goal for childrearing is that it denies the inherent difficulties that human beings encounter during the life cycle. Childrearing, if it accomplishes anything, needs to teach individuals how to cope with frustration. This goal can be accomplished by setting age-appropriate demands in a consistent, predictable milieu. In Korean culture for example, children are very much indulged during the preschool years but then rigorous expectations are established for the school-aged child. The Korean system works because the design is clear, the expectations of both parents are clear, and the children in the family know what the rules are. The more discord about rules, methods, and objectives, the weaker the frustration tolerance and subsequent ability to cope with stress and the unpredictable.

Over the years Western experts have argued and disagreed as to what is best for children. Every culture has its own childrearing rules. Some wean early; others wean late. Some toilet train early and rigidly; some later and permissively. Some indulge young children; others demand an early ritual conformity. However, people throughout the world have demonstrated that when cultural rules are consistent, clear, predictable, and coupled with security, validation, and love, they do turn out functioning human beings capable of continuing the tasks and goals of their culture. But American society has had difficulty defining these tasks and goals. In our multicultural society, childrearing standards contain many discrepancies and contradictions. Unhappily, when there are no such articulated cultural norms, or when these undergo often unarticulated challenge, there is constant confusion and unpredictability, and a set of performance expectations emerges that is not necessarily the predictable result of a given childrearing environment. For example, the second-generation Jewish parent may still hold the value of scholarship or book learning as an indicator of achievement and prestige. Somewhere, however, the message may come through to the children that material affluence is a better indicator of status and achievement: Children are often indulged with possessions, but given no clear guidelines on behavioral expectations. Then in early adolescence a premium on academic achievement is set, perhaps beyond the innate capabilities of the youngster.

The childrearing pattern often has no built-in, predictable course. More specifically, the tasks and methods are continually canceling each other out. Is book learning a value in itself and rewarded as it was in the small Polish village of the child's great-grandparents, or is book learning and academic achievement valued as a vehicle to financial success, for example as the admission ticket to medical school? The child so unpredictably programmed inevitably becomes confused.

GENDER

Children are not alone in this ambiguous environment. There has been a major shift in the perception in this country of the legitimate rights and roles of women. This is the scapegoat of conservative groups who simplistically look to a return of the old family order, of "Mom at home with the children, and Dad out working to feed them," as a way to right all problems of the nation. In the United States some of the disagreement over women's issues arises from the great diversity of conflicting messages filtered down through generations of different ethnic and cultural groups. But there is no turning back the clock. For one thing, most young families insist that they need two breadwinners to achieve the standard of living perceived as at least minimal in our society. Although in some instances one can argue that the standard of living is a matter of individual choice, most young couples accept this national standard. And the national economy depends on this level of consumption.

However, there are some clear national policies that continue to have an impact on the shifting place of women in American society. As soon as equal education for both sexes became the norm in the United States, basic assumptions began to shift. Many communities are moving from a system of parallel education for the sexes to a truly integrated system that encourages equally both sexes to optimize their talents in any field regardless of sexually stereotyped mandates; for example, auto mechanics only for boys and home economics only for girls. The extent to which this public policy affects life choices by gender varies widely from one community, one family, and one individual youngster to another. How this policy is implemented varies with the value system of each school system, administrator, and educator. If the principal or classroom teacher does not believe that girls should or can be auto mechanics, somehow or other there will only be a few girls taking those courses. Nutrition and sewing instructors who do not enjoy boys in their classes will let this be known. Perhaps the most that national policy can do is pinpoint expectations, monitor implementation, and enforce legislation against outright discrimination. The extent and degree of change in attitude, however, is much more subtle than is sometimes acknowledged.

Prior to the emergence of the latest women's movement, not all women felt discounted, put down, or undervalued. However, many women did. Yet although a great deal has been written about the women's movement in its effect on women, not nearly as much is articulated about the impact of this on men, and on young men in particular. Indeed in the past and even now many family systems abuse men by discounting and undervaluing them. As young women's expectations of equal treatment in the workplace take hold, there has to be a shift in how young women and young men relate to each other and how they choose their partners. The most important change now in the United States is that this entire complicated, vital question of the intimate relationship between the sexes—their roles and expectations with respect to each other—has resurfaced and is being openly discussed. For many men, the change is in the male family role model. There is today a clear expectation at least in some groups that men take on an equal role with their life partners, and that job status and earning power are not the sole or even primary indicator of the husband's potency, competency, and success.

Historically, American marriages varied a great deal in how they distributed power and esteem, and how these standards have been articulated in individual family relationships. In those societies where differential gender roles are still clearly defined, the ability to follow an established model is sufficient. Where there is no choice of lifestyle, adaptation is the only option. However, as women become less and less economically dependent on their marital partners, there need to be other identified reasons for a couple to remain committed to each other during the many periods of stress, tension, and discomfort they will experience with each other throughout their life. All of this is clearly spelled out in traditional religious marriage vows designed to be lifelong. But today these commitments have lost much of their meaning. Therefore, young people committing themselves to each other need a high level of sophistication and know-how in our society.

In the search for equality of the sexes in the workplace, we must not lose track of the obvious: men and women are different biological entities. We know of differences in emotional response, differences in the priorities of certain needs, and, in many instances, differences in the perception of how to deal with particular situations in the family and on the job. A much better understanding is needed not only of the cause of differences, whether biological or social, but of the implications of these differences in the context of equal partnership [Hubbard et al. 1979; Gersh and Gersh 1981]. Both men and women need to take on leadership roles, but leadership should arise genuinely out of individual natures. Women should not have to seek political or industrial success by functioning as "males" following "masculine" role models.

These and many other issues in the realignment of the genders have led to a disquieting sense of disequilibrium in the American family resulting in so-called "threats to the survival of the American family." Much more needs to be done to define the issues arising from the shifts in the primary relationship between men and women. Treating these tensions optimistically and constructively may help a realistic realignment of values and a more productive, constructive social order and human functioning.

Despite the complexity and difficulties in working through the day-to-day challenges confronted by committed marital partners, the heterosexual two-parent family remains a desirable, if not the only, model for the preservation and continuation of our species. The problem is ensuring sufficient knowledge, awareness, and flexible adaptability to make marriage and the family work. The challenge is to seize this opportunity. We must begin a clearer articulation of the crucial family values, no matter how blurred and confusing they become by intermarriage among those of different ethnic, cultural, religious, racial, and socioeconomic backgrounds.

ALTERNATIVE FORMS OF RELATIONSHIP

Whether marriage in the future will be the only lifestyle fully sanctioned is no longer the question. Fortunately the stigma attached to remaining single has largely been removed and overt social discrimination has decreased in many cultural and socioeconomic groups. To what extent subtle pressure still exists is difficult to assess. Given many career options and group and community recreational opportunities, people may choose to seek life satisfactions through remaining single, realizing their need for connections through a variety of friendship circles. The option of a homosexual or lesbian rather than a heterosexual paired commitment also exists.

Some individuals feel that a legal bond is unnecessary and that a private written or spoken contractual relationship between two adults is sufficient.

The lack of formality then makes the dissolution of the relationship much easier. For some, the lack of legal closure makes the commitment less threatening, and therefore more workable. Others find the lack of formal commitment more unsettling in that there is no binding reason to weather crises as both partners change and mature not always at the same pace and not always in a mutually compatible manner. Sequential relationships seem to meet some individual needs.

While these various nontraditional lifestyles are options, they are almost certainly not in the best interest of children. Some studies show that children of divorce do as well as children of intact families [Grossman et al. 1980]. However, even the best statistical analysis cannot take into account the multiplicity of variables involved. Only systematic follow-up research spanning the life outcomes of at least a full generation could begin to do justice to this complicated problem.

Because of the many plausible lifestyles available today, some thoughtful value clarification on the part of people in their twenties and thirties should be encouraged. If these young people are seeking a lifestyle to fulfill their many personal goals and these goals do not include the bearing and raising of children, there are numerous choices. These lifestyle choices do not need to include marriage, although they may. On the other hand, if childbearing and childrearing are important components of a person's aspiration, then the willingness to make a commitment to a secure permanent relationship such as marriage deserves the most careful thought and deliberation.

Childbearing and childrearing are natural human tasks. They are also very satisfying tasks. However, they form a path of adventure with many unknowns along the way. Two people's supporting and caring for each other allows for the sharing of pleasure, insecurity, and pain as children and parents bond together, grow, and change. There needs to be enough cushioning to weather stress and real or imaginary disappointments, and the strength to move on with the tasks of living. Even the concrete tasks of childrearing— provision of economic security, maintaining a living environment, interaction with schools, community groups, doctors, dentists—can more easily be done by two people, and better still by two people with support from two networks of kin, than by one person alone.

Not only do children need these family supports to feel safe; children also need to experience a close and caring relationship with a parent of the same and of the opposite sex. Children need to know a relationship between adults where tension is negotiated, differences occur, and arguments do not result in the disintegration of their world. In our society these interpersonal skills are best transmitted to children through experiencing an intact functioning family. The most sophisticated, skillful therapist can only offer something second-best. Relationships with other people can, of course, be created elsewhere, but no alternative is as meaningful as the role model of a mother and father solving problems together, dealing with tension and stress, and conveying values and behavior expectations to the next generation.

Although this model is in the best interests of children, reality suggests that we should look closely at the many alternative childrearing models that have emerged because of the variety of American lifestyles. Some of these alternative systems have been developed by choice, others of necessity to adapt to a new and different economic reality and sometimes to counterproductive welfare regulations. But many arise simply because of insufficient preparation or coping skills on the part of the original partners who have undertaken marriage without the necessary knowledge, skills, models, and family and community supports to weather its many storms. One can have great respect for those individuals who are engaged in the task of childrearing under less than optimum conditions. Some are doing a magnificent, in fact an awesome, job under very difficult circumstances in a way almost incomprehensible to those who function in closely connected and supportive systems. However, one can criticize American society's failure to move in early with preventive help to alleviate some family dysfunction, compared to the more typical crisis intervention, often too late for effective remediation with the least amount of damage and pain to the people involved.

FAMILY BREAKUP

Given a child's dependence on family functioning for survival, the threat of family dissolution is a serious issue. Family breakup has many different causes. For example, single-parent households exist for many reasons. First is the family who loses a parent due to illness or accident and consequent death; the issues here are clear and straightforward. Even though premature death is extremely difficult and painful for families and growing children to accept, there is a realistic finality beyond anyone's control [Schowalter 1983].

A second category is families of divorce. The high incidence of legal divorce in the United States is a recent development. However, Dr. Thomas Fogarty accurately points out that

In one sense it's a sign of our legalistic, righteous, contentious culture. In another sense, it's really not quite a change, but only a more open manifestation of a thing we refer to as Emotional Divorce which has always and undoubtedly will continue to exist.

Emotional Divorce describes a situation in which people still stay together, and continue to live in the same place, remain legally married but really have very little emotional connection with each other. [Fogarty 1984b:142]

Some divorces occur because the marriage should never have been contracted. The assets in the relationship were so minimal that educational or counseling interventions early enough might have prevented a union clearly targeted for malfunction. Other divorces occur because the marriage took place due to an unplanned pregnancy. Fortunately, many nonviable marriages are being prevented through better teen pregnancy counseling programs along with a decrease in the social stigma attached to abortion and to children born out of wedlock. The extent to which specific ethnic kin groups insist on these nonviable marriages varies, and cultural values need to be much better understood in order to design workable programs for prevention and intervention.

The most tragic divorces occur when stress in the family becomes so severe due to circumstances beyond the family's control that individual members resort to miscommunication, scapegoating, blaming, and even destructive acting out at a time when both partners need each other more than ever and could use the family crisis for growth rather than to inflict even more pain upon each other. Specifically such events as the death of a child, the birth of a malformed or severely handicapped child, or the incidence of mental illness or other severe debilitating illness suffered by a family member are examples of this kind. These events can shatter the relationship of the marital partners but that breakup can place a double burden on remaining children in the family who are already traumatized by the precipitating family crisis. Still other divorces occur because of difficulties in the establishment of appropriate distance and boundaries between the developing nuclear family and the extended kin of either one or both marital partners. The extent to which this does or does not become an issue is directly related to the expectations of each partner's family of origin, the extent to which these origins have conflicting rules, and how these conflicts are articulated and negotiated in the marriage. Early educational and counseling intervention could save many marriages plagued by these issues.

The most common reason given for divorce is the infidelity of one or both partners. Infidelity can only be seen as symptomatic, and needs to be understood on a case-by-case basis. Ethnic origin, conflicting value systems, degree of satisfaction in and commitment to the relationship are, of course, all primary factors. Often issues of sexual dysfunction or fear of sexual dysfunction in one or both partners are critical components in this situation.

Divorce is always a significant crisis. The legal act of marriage signifies an intent to remain bonded. The inability to follow through symbolized by divorce is inevitably seen as failure. One often finds situations where only one partner has been involved in multiple divorces while the second partner is able to form a very satisfying relationship in the second marriage. Often, the partner who has been involved in multiple marriages will then wonder why he or she had not remained committed to the original partner, recognizing that there may have been something unrealistic in his or her expectations of marriage. When they are understood later on in life, these unrealistic expectations that precipitated a divorce or several divorces may lead to regret.

Regardless of the causes of divorce, marriages resulting in divorce are involved in a predictable cycle that has an impact on all family members [Gardner 1983]. Divorce is the culmination of a struggle between two adults in which children often become the pawns, even when there is a conscious effort to avoid this. Issues of child support, custody, and visitation cannot be sidestepped. There is a sense of loss of self-esteem and a period of grieving for the family that was, or perhaps for the fantasy family that never did develop. Anger, bitterness, and regret are by-products that only the most self-aware will ultimately shed. The children's relationship with the kin of the ex-spouse may become an issue, especially the grandparents' relationship to the children. Whenever a system adds, loses, or evicts another person, there is a major shift in the alignment of roles and relationships, accompanied by emotional stress for all parties concerned. The custodial parent is then additionally burdened by the reality of single parenting, difficult household finances, sometimes reentry into the work force, and often the need to shift living arrangements and community.

Divorce in families with children is a task with broad implications. Children of divorced parents can have a very good relationship with both parents. However, tensions exist as each parent struggles with feelings of pain and disappointment about the other partner.

In some instances divorce solves nothing, since both partners leave the union with the same attributes that were inherent in the unrealistic expectations of the marriage and the other partner that were responsible for the failure. The advantage of legal divorce is that it clearly articulates and defines the conflict, while in "emotional divorce" the children are often forced to become the symptom bearers of the unspoken. However, as further events such as graduations, marriages of children, arrival of grandchildren, illness, and death occur in the life cycle of the family, many partners do reconnect emotionally; those who have chosen to divorce lose this opportunity. Clearly a rigid position cannot be taken in as complicated an issue as divorce, for sometimes divorce is the only alternative that seems to make sense at a given time. Unfortunately, neither the parties involved nor the most brilliant therapists have enough knowledge of what the future holds and the quality of the psychological growth over time of the people involved. There are, of course, legal divorces without emotional divorces. Even though the legal ties are severed, the emotional connections are such that the destructive conflict is continuously reactivated through provocation by one former partner and then the other. Wounds are not given an opportunity to heal, and the children are caught in an ongoing parental battle.

BLENDED FAMILIES

The question of family breakup leads naturally to the question of reconstituted or blended families and of families involving stepparents. The blended, reconstituted family is one in which each partner brings children from a previous relationship to the marriage. Life in a sensitive blended family is far more desirable for children than life in an overtaxed single-parent household.

There are a number of possible causes and combinations for blended families. Most remarriages occur after divorce. However, it may mean a marriage where at least one if not both partners has experienced the loss of a spouse through death and chooses to recreate a two-parent family life since he or she has already experienced satisfaction and success in marriage.

No new relationship can ever replace a previous one, and individuals who remarry bring with them not only expectations formulated in their own family of origin but those which worked, or did not work, for them with the previous spouse. Grieving for the lost relationship still continues. In order for the new union to succeed there must be open, articulated recognition that grieving for the loss of the previous partner cannot be taken personally by the new spouse. Instead, if people can use each other to work through their past, an even tighter, mutually supportive bond can be created.

The new marriage will be different. People usually are older, have had more experience, and are much more realistic in terms of their expectations of each other. Other players are also involved, the extended kin of the new couple, as well as the extended kin of the partner or partners now deceased. Then there are the children of one or both partners who may be living with the couple. They may be children who no longer live at home but are important members of the system. The new union includes the two friendship groups with connections to the previous marriages.

In those situations in which either or both partners have been involved in a failed marriage, both wife and husband's articulated or unarticulated fears will be that this might happen again. If, in fact, the dissolution of the preceding relationship is perceived only as the responsibility or inadequacy of the previous partner, then the risks are high. On the other hand, the dissolution of a marriage is an opportunity for both ex-partners' growth and their better understanding of the needs and expectations they brought into the situation and failed to meet. Under these circumstances, the possibility of a viable second marriage is often quite good.

Blended families in which previous partners are alive, and especially when a previous spouse is also the parent of a child living in the reconstituted family, have to deal with a number of issues. If, in fact, the negotiation and conflict resolution skills of both people were adequate, there is reason to believe that in many instances the marriage would have survived. There are, of course, concrete issues for negotiation such as child support, custody, and visitation which can usually be settled with good counsel, and, if needed, the help of family court. The emotional issues and how these are defined and played out both in relation to the children and by the children remain crucial. The ages of the children, their coping competence, and their basic sense of security have much to do with how they will adapt. Besides the challenges of the normal developmental process, a youngster confronted with the complexity of emotions generated by membership in two-family systems is faced with a major additional task. Any child who is further burdened by a physical handicap or other disability becomes extremely vulnerable.

One of the major difficulties current blended families face is that American society has not presented any clear formulas or rules about appropriate connections with extended kin, nor have any clear boundaries between the various past and present families been defined. Even individualists who like to establish their own rules usually find it helpful to know the norm from which they are deviating. The stepparent, unless he or she has the option and chooses to adopt the children of the other partner, has no legal status at all. Adoption, of course, brings with it the complicated issues of voluntary surrender or termination of a birth parent's parental rights. When this occurs, there are many psychological tasks that all family members need to master.

Another area of concern is the expression of anger and negative feelings. People often misconstrue the expression of anger as responsible for the dissolution of the previous marriage and look to keep the new marriage free of such expression. However, if feelings cannot be honestly negotiated and expressed in a system that inevitably holds a substantial amount of tension, children become vulnerable and often assume the unspoken but clearly prescribed role of symptom bearer [Ransom et al. 1979].

During the period between divorce and remarriage all parties have struggled to regain equilibrium. Empty social niches were left, and frequently one or more children have moved into that role. Thereafter, the child is understandably reluctant to vacate that spot to turn it over to someone bigger, older, and more powerful, let alone to someone who is not that well known. Trust builds slowly for those who have been hurt.

Although the new union may be the wish of the adults, most children are rightfully very apprehensive about what is in store for them, and initially experience the new relationships as losses rather than gains. The only solution is for adults to be keenly sensitive to these issues and to give children the time they need to move closer. Permission for cautious distance is important.

The newly married couple, however, needs to present confidently their team position. Allowing children to rock the firmness of their commitment to each other complicates an already difficult situation. The children will grow up and leave the family someday. The intention of the new marriage is to continue on after that. In a first marriage the beginning of bonding was able to occur before the children arrived. In blended marriages not only are the children there, they bring a history with them, often fraught with pain and disappointment. Even in the best of situations, marital partners themselves have had more life experience and are entering the new union with some caution.

SINGLE-PARENT FAMILIES

Whether single women should bear and raise children by choice is a charged issue. Philosophical and ethical questions are involved. Can some single women with good support networks parent better than inadequate or multiproblem two-parent households? The answer to this is clearly, "Yes, of course, they can." However, this is not the specific issue here.

Each child is the biological product of a man and a woman, and he or she will grow to maturity with the capability of producing children who will be the product of a man and woman. It appears better not to tamper with what seems to be a natural order. If a man and a woman together produce a child, they should be available to raise the child they have produced. If they do so, the child also becomes a member of two kinship groups that are the natural vehicle to perpetuate a viable social order.

Moreover, as a child advocate, one can worry about the motives behind a parent's assuming the heavy responsibility of single parenting by choice. Childrearing is a complicated task. It involves the desire and ability not only to parent an infant and toddler, but to facilitate the growth of that toddler into a self-dependent, optimally functioning adult. My own lengthy experience in hiring and training institutional child-care workers indicates that those child-care workers who choose this work only because of their love of working with children do not have an optimum track record. Child-care workers also must be comfortable with working with adults, such as their colleagues and the children's families. Children cannot be owned, and whoever has that intention has a thorny path ahead, whether this person is the child-care worker or the parent who created the child. Some single mothers by choice, and particularly adolescent mothers, are searching for love or to fill an emptiness in themselves by having a child. That motive is a risky one for all involved. Equally dangerous is using children to fill empty emotional spaces in a marriage. Parenting, like marriage, is a life task requiring flexibility. Conditions and needs of growing children are constantly changing. Parental demands and expectations must be able to change also.

It is well known that, through adoption and foster care, many single men and women have parented children who would never have survived in a two-parent household given the complexities of a marital relationship to deal with. Is it all right for single foster mothers to complete the childrearing task begun by someone else, but not all right for a single mother to create her own child by choice? These are questions to which there are no easy answers. Granted that this desire to be a single parent by choice is still rare, only the people looking to be a single parent over time will be able to offer some insight into these issues as they share their experiences.

AGING

Finally, the role and responsibility of American families in the care of the aged must be addressed. Children and youth services issues can only be viewed, understood, and solved in the context of family and extended family networks. With an increase in longevity, these extended networks no longer include only grandparents but in many instances also great-grandparents. In spite of widespread concern over abandonment of the elderly by the modern American family, "recent studies have emphasized the widespread existence of family help patterns" [Pinkerton 1984:6] and estimate "that about 80% of all caretaking needs of the elderly are provided by their families" [Wallace and Estes 1989:66], even though the elderly person may not necessarily be living in the home of a relative. This responsibility, of course, places additional pressure on the nuclear family, often a childrearing couple that must also support a widowed or abandoned parent, who in turn may be caring for a physically declining grandparent. There are now many four-generation families.

The expectations that people have of themselves to provide household support to the elderly varies from one culture to another. Often this can become an area of conflict and tension within a marriage. Each partner's family of origin may have different goals, roles, and expectations regarding responsibility toward aging parents. Children can get caught up in these family tensions, which have to be resolved by the marital couple.

No matter how burdensome life may become, the marital union must not be placed in jeopardy whereby the quality of the marriage suffers so extensively that it becomes a union beyond repair. Just as the burden of a developmentally disabled or terminally ill child can stress the system, so will prolonged care of a declining elderly parent do this. Survival of the total system is at stake. This issue needs to be included as we look at program design and seek to connect the needs of children, youth, their parents, grandparents, and great-grandparents into a philosophically viable service delivery model.

FAMILIES AND THE MOST CRITICAL SOCIAL DILEMMAS

Given the growing national crises of homelessness, violence, drug abuse, and AIDS in some of our communities among adults engaged in childrearing, one may well ask if there is something different about these people. These adults and their children have the same needs and desires as those whose fundamental needs for minimal safety in housing, income maintenance, child and health care are being met. The difficulties encountered by some of our homeless families, which consist predominantly of women and children [Kamerman and Kahn 1988; Gewirtman and Fodor 1987], is more of a reflection of society's inability to provide a reasonable quantity and quality of low-cost housing in which people can live and adequately perform necessary childrearing tasks [Kozol 1988].

Violence easily erupts from overcrowded, stressful conditions. Children naturally become victims. Drug use and abuse is another major dimension in an already complex scenario in the range of choices individuals make in adapting and coping. Yet, regardless of the nature of the often socially imposed difficulties created by inadequate social policies and provision of service, people must also be understood as individuals within the context of their families of origin, and beyond that within the wider context of their kin and broader ethnic communities to understand their choice of coping strategies. This understanding must then be translated into a method to facilitate optimum provision of service in a way that can become useful and acceptable to the consumer.

CONCLUSION

The American family as a social institution charged with the bearing and nurturing of children from infancy to adulthood is not in as serious jeopardy as might be surmised from the often alarming divorce and single-parent household statistics because people somehow cope. On the other hand, the migrant nature of our society and the multiplicity of often conflicting ethnic and cultural norms, expectations, and communication styles, as well as the overt and covert transmission of conflicting messages within any one tradition, have made marital relationships increasingly more complicated as people from different ethnic backgrounds intermarry. Unsupported stress, coupled with lack of understanding of its origin and complexity, frequently leads to blaming and scapegoating in marriage, with consequent breakups that need not have occurred. The ongoing reassessment of the role and rights of women and shifting roles for men often result in alternative lifestyles, such as remaining single, entering homosexual and lesbian unions, living together as couples not legally bonded, or maintaining single-parent and reconstituted families by choice.

I take the position that an intact family lifestyle with two partners committing their energy and effort to both marriage and parenting as all parties move through the life cycle still provides the best environment for children to mature into adulthood even with continuous change and incompatible individual rhythms. Individuals need to think through carefully whether childbearing and childrearing have a high priority in their value system. If they do not, a whole variety of lifestyles are certainly viable and can be very satisfying as alternatives to traditional marriage.

The major challenge is to design social systems that validate assets and strengths. These assets and strengths lie first in the nuclear couple, then in the extended family network, next in linkages to their ethnic, cultural, and religious groups and, of course, in friendship and community groups. We need to remain keenly aware that we transmit values and behavioral expectations by modeling them for our children. Program design needs to be open to new possibilities and devoid of stereotyping. Problems confronted by families must be defined as normal rather than pathological. Coping with adverse circumstances must be seen as challenges to be confronted as people move through the life cycle in an increasingly complicated, ever-changing environment in which there seem to be fewer and fewer rules and less and less rigid models to follow. All of this can be done in a preventive, educational, experiential context.

3

Children and Youth in Limbo

Children and youth in limbo are young people caught in the problems that adults create for them. They do not know who will care for them until they can care for themselves and so have no predictable future. Uncertainty creates terrifying fears, since their dependence makes them equate abandonment with death.

Whereas life preservation for animals depends on instinctive regulation in unfolding sequence, the human being must depend much longer on parental care, and the feelings surrounding the early symbiosis persist as an inspiration throughout the life span. For the sake of approval by the parents and because abandonment has such disastrous consequences, the child will sacrifice whatever ego integrity is called for in order to survive. If the price for acceptance is to absorb unrealities, accept an irrational identity or role assignment, be persecuted, be overindulged, be scapegoated, be parentified or what have you, this price will have to be paid; to be alone or pushed out of the family either physically or psychologically is too unthinkable. [Framo 1970:163]

THE SITUATION

Behaviorally, the child who is constantly teetering on the verge of physical or psychological abandonment makes urgent appeals for help. Striking out, school difficulties, running away, fire setting, rock throwing, stealing, depression, and drug abuse are all familiar to mental health professionals.

Even the best practitioners get sidetracked by children's frighteningly unsafe behaviors and the how-tos of child management. But we need to keep in mind the family and cultural context of the young people in trouble. The child in limbo often is the product of a family in which the father's and mother's life experiences provided them with minimal nurture and with confusing, inconsistent parenting models. The parents may have difficulty in communicating their own needs and in hearing the needs of others. They are likely to be ill-equipped to face the responsibilities and stresses of adult living, may lack judgment in decision making, and often cope impulsively. Selecting alternatives that are programmed for failure, they compound life's inevitable problems. The parents' overwhelming feelings of helplessness and consequent rage are the result.

These are parents who themselves have often been the victims of abuse, eviction, and abandonment. They frequently abuse their children for lack of knowledge on how to identify, understand, and deal with their own feelings of helplessness. It is rare that the abuse is premeditated. But these parents have never known people who look into themselves to better understand their difficulties; what they have seen is eviction or abandonment of a family member as a common, although ineffective, vehicle for the solution of problems [Finkelstein 1980]. Support from kin is perceived to be nonexistent. Often the lack of social resources is based on assumptions passed down from one generation to the next.

Despite what many would prefer to believe, the child or youth in limbo is not necessarily a product only of the lower socioeconomic segment of American society. "Some of the things that happen in poor families even happen in rich families, too. Rich kids are not exempt from random violence, emotional neglect, family disruption, or even despair" [Pittman 1985:468]. "The rich go crazy, commit suicide, mess up their marriages and their lives at almost the same rate as the rest of us, despite what would seem to be their great advantages" [Pittman 1985:463]. Furthermore, since marital commitments at all social levels are far less binding than they used to be, and geographic mobility has increased tremendously, the lack of secure, functioning kinship connections to support a floundering nuclear family is common in all socioeconomic groups.

There are, of course, differences in how various cultural groups come to the rescue of children in difficulty. There are also ethnic differences in whether and how the offer of help is or is not accepted by the family or the child. Some young people feel free to utter a cry for help. Others are so dependent that they will not attempt their own solutions first, but leave it to the family, however noncompetent, to resolve their difficulties for them. Still others will go to great effort to conceal their difficulties from their family because of their perception that they will bring it shame or distress.

Groups differ significantly as to which nonfamily members will first learn that a child or adolescent is in serious jeopardy. There is also a qualitative difference in how quickly and effectively intervention occurs. Among the more educated and affluent, the private physician or family attorney will become involved. Often, of course, the difficulties become apparent in the child's school. Among the poor, it is the local department of social services, the law enforcement agencies, and the community school or day care center that may be the first to know that children and families are in trouble.

For example, in situations that come to the attention of the private physician and attorney, who are selected and engaged by the parents, the child's protection is not always seen as their primary charge. Besides, physical abuse is often disguised as accidental injury, while psychological abuse is even more delicate and complicated to assess. Furthermore, there are all sorts of attitudinal, philosophical, and ethical differences, as well as different levels of competence, in all professions dealing with complex psychological and social problems. There are times when professional biases, blind spots, and specialized judgments fail the best interests of children.

OUTCOME FAILURES

What happens to the child or youth in limbo? Unsure of their safety and survival within an unstable family, such young people contribute to their own unsettled status by provoking their eviction from the family. Among the affluent, the young person is bounced from parent to parent, entangled in divorce and custody battles. Nannies and nursemaids provide unpredictable and inconsistent nurturing. Spouses and others significant in the lives of custodial and visiting parents get involved in what appears to the child an already confusing medley of messages and relationships. Inevitably the kin of these spouses and significant others also get involved, each with his or her own value judgments and management advice.

Attempted solutions vary widely. Occasionally private placement with a maiden aunt or some other relative or a sojourn at a boarding school may be chosen to alleviate the stress on feuding middle- and upper-class parents. Despite the most benevolent intentions, these temporary respites most often neither address the problems nor are designed to solve them. Among lower socioeconomic groups, the youngster, never legally free for adoption, is sent off through multiple foster-home or institutional placements.

Although the foster parents, relatives, or school may intend the best, they too are clearly programmed for failure. Regardless of socioeconomic background or type of temporary placement, the child—through repetitive provocations for eviction—continues to try to master the early trauma of psychological abandonment by her or his parents. These children and youth are uncanny in knowing what will get them thrown out. They break the rules in boarding school, tamper with their aunt's forbidden china, injure a family's best-loved pet, or sexually harass a biological child in the foster family.

The in-charge and caring adults feel helpless in their attempts to break the cycle, especially because their caretaker role has been clearly defined as temporary. These adults cannot give the key message that is so needed: "We will be available to you for as long as you need us. You will grow up here. We will give to you and you in turn will give to us as you grow and mature. We will love you for what you are." On the other hand, young people, regardless of chronological age, usually cannot formulate, let alone verbalize, what is so frightening to them. The young person's panic is expressed through aberrant behavior.

Temporary foster family and children's shelter placements, and visits with well-meaning relatives intended to provide respite for parents and control for the child, are replaced in the crisis by referrals to hospital psychiatric wards, residential treatment centers, and facilities for juvenile delinquents. The focus is on the acting-out child, while the caretakers helplessly look for some magic to cure maladaptive behaviors. The young person is forced to assume the "sick" or "delinquent" role, and behaves accordingly. Thus, the cycle continues. In many families, when one child is evicted to an institution, foster home, relative, or boarding school, there is some temporary relief. Soon, however, another sibling moves in to fill the scapegoat role now left empty. Often the next and then the next child may be targeted to act "sick" and follow in the eviction path.

Joseph Goldstein, Anna Freud, and Albert J. Solnit in *Beyond the Best Interests of the Child* describe children's sense of time as being

based on the urgency of their instinctual and emotional needs. As an infant's memory begins to incorporate the way in which parents satisfy wishes and needs as well as the experience of the reappearance of parents after their disappearance, a child gradually develops the capacity to delay gratification and to anticipate and plan for the future.

Emotionally and intellectually, an infant and toddler cannot stretch his waiting more than a few days without feeling overwhelmed by the absence of parents. . . . For most children under the age of five years, an absence of parents for more than two months is equally beyond comprehension. For the younger school-age child, an absence of six months or more will be similarly experienced. [Goldstein et al. 1973:40–41]

It is, indeed, frightening to think of the length of separations experienced by foster care children. Most human services practitioners have known children seven, six, and five years old, and too frequently even younger children, who have been abruptly separated from their biological or psychological parents for periods of a year, two years, and sometimes forever. Many practitioners have known children separated from parents indefinitely because these children's cases have little or no priority in the court system.

Only too quickly, months and years pass that these children need to grow in a secure setting.

Goldstein, Freud, and Solnit speak about children's need for permanent bonding in order to grow and develop to achieve their potential as fully functioning and contributing members of adult society [Goldstein et al. 1973:40]. Yet we all know that life seldom provides anyone the optimal conditions for such bonding. The human condition is fraught with ambivalence and unpredictability. Luckily, the innate resilience of the human species is amazing, and many losses can be absorbed before any serious irreversible damage occurs. In most instances one has some control over how one deals with the unpredictable. Alternative positive responses to loss can be found. Under too much stress, however, dysfunctional attitudes and behavior often emerge, and coping mechanisms may fail. Victims of loss, some people in turn become victimizers.

ATTACHMENT AND LOSS

The American child welfare system has addressed itself to the physical care and protection of children. Standards in some parts of the country are very high; some may be so high as to operate to the detriment of children. Children in foster families to whom they were bonded have been removed only because the physical living conditions of the family did not meet these standards, or because arbitrary age or family constellation requirements were not met. In fact, our cribs and playpens are seen as caged prisons by some societies. Our standard of individual bedrooms for children can be interpreted as cruel to young children left alone in a darkened bedroom to struggle with nightmares without the reassuring physical contact of other family members in the room. In many parts of the world, infants are physically strapped to the mother's back, sleep on the floor close to the other family members, and grow up to be competent, highly motivated adults.

In any case, children's impaired attachment capabilities are the result of trauma, which can be caused by physical separation from the primary caretaker but also by emotional distance from that caretaker. The pain felt by the young child from separation or emotional distancing is excruciating; although feelings are often repressed, the child's behaviors, skillfully observed, become very good indicators of the impaired condition.

Children are not the only ones to experience pain and grief from the temporary or permanent loss of the most significant persons in their lives—the adults also suffer. When a parent moves out of the home or a child is sent to live away from home, parents often find the loss of the child so painful that they suppress the pain. Parents will distance themselves from the child, appear uninterested, and even cease to visit or keep in touch. This parental grief has not received sufficient attention from the foster care system. Overworked or undertrained child welfare workers often see this behavior as a clear signal that the family doesn't care and that a permanent plan for the child should exclude them. When this behavior is carefully observed, however, the professional can often see all the manifestations of deep grief.

At Parsons Child and Family Center, experience has demonstrated that those children in foster care who have experienced multiple separations during the first year or two of life are the most vulnerable. Because of this early grief, these children are then unable to bond with and relate to the next caretaker, and find themselves evicted by even the best-intentioned foster families.

These evictions have two unhappy byproducts: first, the child becomes more damaged with each successive failed placement; second, failure with a child leaves the foster family frightened, and some who may have much to offer to other children are lost as a resource to the foster care system.

Any child who has experienced multiple losses early in life is a child at risk, in need of very special parents sensitive to these early losses and willing to work with them. Some children successfully conceal their feelings and do not act them out behaviorally in a children's shelter or institution; yet when a child is placed in a caring family, demands for intimacy and attachment by the family will become very frightening to the child who has suffered the pain caused by rejection. We are only too familiar with the pained cry from failing adoptive families who insist that they have asked for, and were promised, a "normal child" only in need of love and stability.

Much more attention needs to be given to assessing where a child has gotten in the grieving process and what kind of help may minimize the long-term damage to future attachments because of early losses. Our challenge is to sharpen the assessment skills of child welfare personnel without making the task appear so hopeless that workers lose the willingness to risk placing children at all.

PERMANENCE IN FAMILY BONDS

Especially in the early most vulnerable childhood years, permanence has to be very firmly established. When rooting does not occur, the child suffers serious damage. Where family connections have been broken or attenuated, individuals must be helped to reach out to members of their immediate and extended family. At times this may require an extended search. While working on the re-creation of natural family ties, community linkages must also be created. Within this context of avoiding loss, we can examine the concept of permanence of bonds.

The need to provide for and bond with the young on a long-term basis is a natural human function in all societies.

> The parent's capacity for attachment to the infant emphasizes the human readiness for numerous attachments over the lifespan. Children develop attachments to siblings, relatives, teachers, and other important persons throughout childhood with whom frequent, continuous, need-gratifying interactions occur. It is this capacity for numerous attachments that allows children to form attachments to the foster family, while maintaining strong attachments to their birth parents as well. The child's attachment to the foster family need not preclude the child's primary attachment and identification from remaining with the birth parents.
>
> Thus, a child's primary human attachment is characterized by his or her capacity to love, to differentially relate to, and to value one person above all others. The relative capacity for intimacy with family members, peers, and significant others across the lifespan is determined by the bonds developed by the infant with the early primary caretaker. [Hess 1982:48]

When bonding with and care of the young break down, one must take a much closer look at the process. How is our society failing, when the number of young people apparently without meaningful social ties is increasing rapidly? Because neither individuals nor families exist in isolation, these problems with bonding warrant examination in the broadest societal context.

"Permanence of bonds" means different things to different people; "permanence" for me is a sense of belonging to and being part of a group of people committed to each other and to solving problems, regardless of internal and external stress. The strength of these adult relationships provides the foundation on which a sense of identity can evolve for a child growing in their midst. The frequent lack of permanent commitment to marriage on the part of adults should not be underestimated in this regard in its impact on children.

The many intercultural marriages in our society are a complicating factor in that they make a clear transmission of values more difficult. The values articulated through Mom's family may be incompatible or in conflict with those of Dad's family. Familial rules and expectations, therefore, are in constant need of reexamination and redefinition. In many families these values cannot simply be absorbed as they have been passed down through previous generations.

Permanence provides a framework within which the young can gradually absorb a value system. As children grow and mature, they incorporate values from those close to them. For certain periods of their lives, they may temporarily reject some of these values; other values they may reject permanently. Each young person grows to become a unique person, but he or she must begin with a firm foundation of values.

Therefore, permanency planning addresses one of the most vulnerable tasks in human development: the parent-child attachment and bonding process. The mother's fantasies at conception about a wanted child are important. With an unwanted child, the circumstances of the conception, the pregnancy, and the decision to allow the pregnancy to continue are equally relevant. As the fetus grows, its movements contribute to the mother's sense of well-being or stress. After birth, the close connection between mother and child in breast or bottle feeding, and her constant availability during the first few weeks, months, or years increase these feelings. Fathers play an equally significant role. In those instances where working parents cannot be constantly available, optimal child-care arrangements are usually those in which constancy and predictability are carefully planned and provided. Erratic absences on the part of the primary caretakers are experienced as abandonment by the helpless infant.

Interference with a normal child-parent attachment process is usually associated with the parent's physical or mental illness, depression, or overwhelming environmental stress. Some young parents are involved in marital battles, financial support issues, and major housing problems. These often do not allow the young parents to provide the emotional consistency and predictability so needed by an infant.

Family "permanence" no longer can be defined in terms of a permanent physical location. Americans are too mobile and our social links too widely distributed throughout the country to permit such a narrow expectation. In many instances, family connections reach to distant parts of the globe. Nonetheless, people can feel emotionally connected to members of their families whom they have encountered only rarely and then only for short periods of time. Emotional ties may even exist among people who have never met. "Permanence" therefore is primarily a feeling state synonymous with a sense of identity, built on the quality of rootedness.

PRESCRIPTION

Goldstein, Freud, and Solnit stress that "physical, emotional, intellectual, social, and moral growth does not happen without causing the child inevitable internal difficulties. . . . Smooth growth is arrested or disrupted when upheavals and changes in the external world are added to the internal ones" [Goldstein et al. 1973:32].

Children need to grow in a predictable permanent environment where they will be accepted and loved and where they in turn can learn to love and care about others. They need an environment that can help them learn how to channel negative and aggressive impulses; they need to learn that appropriate expression of anger and frustration will neither destroy them nor those on whom they depend. If appropriate management of frustration is not learned, the cycle of impulsive, counterproductive behavior will be carried without change into the family system of the next generation.

Although appropriate expression of anger and frustration can be taught in a therapeutic setting, it is taught more easily and better in the family when all members can engage in the effort together. If inappropriate expression of such emotions had been handled effectively by the original or custodial parent, the young person would have learned to manage frustration in normal development and growth. Learning and growing with one's family is easier than learning separately in an artificial environment. The youth in an artificially created therapeutic setting such as a treatment center or therapeutic foster home may learn more suitable behaviors. But these need to be tested and practiced in a permanently committed family, or these gains will be quickly lost on returning home.

SIX CATEGORIES OF YOUTH IN JEOPARDY

Children and youth in jeopardy of loss of permanent roots and connections through foster care placement can be put into six categories for the purpose of clarity in service delivery:

- That set of children presenting difficulties who come from an emotionally committed family, one responsive to helping interventions and with the ability to adjust and cope.
- Youngsters who have committed families and roots, but who cannot live at home because of major disabilities in the child or in another family member.
- Children who have been separated from their families, although neither the family nor the child has requested separation. These children have been removed from their homes because society, represented by schools, courts, or social services, has decided that the parents are not adequately meeting the child's needs.
- Children of families that claim a commitment to the child's return home, but whose verbal protestations are not validated by follow-through.
- Children who have experienced multiple placements, are not legally free for adoption, and appear not to have any roots anywhere.
- Adolescents, whether moving toward independence, or at the other extreme, adult care, for whom permanence has to be achieved differently.

The issue is no longer whether they will live with biological kin, but rather how to strengthen existing roots and connections of any sort so that they can grow toward a connected rather than a disconnected adulthood.

Each of these categories is elaborated below.

Children with Committed Families

Troubled youngsters with families truly committed to them often do not exhibit severely negative behavior away from home—in school, camp, or day care, for example. Yet their families find them unmanageable. Before their behavior does get dangerously out of hand, the intervention of choice for these children and families must be community-based, either in an outpatient clinic or where available an outreach prevention-of-placement program. If youngsters' unsafe behaviors overwhelm the family so that they cease to cope, which should be rare, placement in a foster family or residential setting may be used temporarily. Foster family placement of the child may engage a frightened family in seeking broader solutions. If their child acts appropriately in a foster family, the parents may soon recognize that their own activities and messages need to change.

When the young person's behaviors are too unsafe for a foster family, placement in a residential treatment facility becomes the best course. A youngster who has set fires or has been acting out sexually might fall into this category. Experience at Parsons Child and Family Center shows that these young people are often quite responsive to an institutional structure and routine with clear, consistent messages and behavioral expectations. Unless there is a substantial nonpsychological primary cause, such as moderate to severe organic difficulties, these children do begin to mature.

When intervention targets the whole family, it can be very effective, and separation from home can be limited to a brief period. Excellent results can be achieved in a reasonably short period if the family, rather than only the young person, is perceived as needing help. We assume that all members of the committed family of the youth with difficulties are in pain. One particular member, the target child or youth, has been chosen to communicate this pain, but in a manner frightening to the family and society, and jeopardizing the child's own safety as well as that of others. As merely the spokesperson for the family, this child is the one to be removed. The most effective communicator for the family's distress may thus be scapegoated by the care system; the system joins the family in condoning the family's organization and mode of functioning, pinpointing only the one child as source of the problem, thus maintaining the family's disturbance. Practitioners, therefore, must make every effort to give the message to all family members, including the child, that the child's temporary removal from the family is to provide safety for all family members, and no single member is to be made the scapegoat.

If a child responds to residential or foster family care, the family care system can safely conclude that this child has had positive experiences early in life. These experiences, essential for bonding and self-sufficiency, were in most instances provided by the family now experiencing so much difficulty. We should immediately share that perception in a genuine way with the family. The family must hear from us that they have been good parents, and must be persuaded by concrete examples that we are not saying this just to be kind. If the family had the ability to nurture an infant, clearly there are important ties and connections to be strengthened and brought into play as rapidly as possible. Every needless day of placement in substitute care is a disservice to all involved.

The child welfare system must do more than pay lip service to recognizing families' strengths. Even where we have been effective in dealing with children's behaviors, we have usually been much weaker in changing families, and the children often regress upon return home. If, while in out-of-home placement, we discover that the child is responsive to nurture, caring, predictability, and interventions that enable this child to express needs and feelings in productive ways, we can assume that other family members will be responsive to the same quality of interventions. If we are committed to permanence as an essential ingredient for growth, we will need to concentrate on the entire family as needing change and on serving all family members with the same intensity that in too many instances is provided only to the identified child client.

Children with Roots Who Cannot Live at Home

This category of children will always be with us. These children are fully committed to their families, which in turn are committed to their child: The child is rooted and belongs. Major complicating factors, however—poor health of the parents, the burden of other family members' being seriously ill, or the child's own organic problem, such as severe retardation, autism, acute epilepsy—mean that these children and adolescents temporarily, and sometimes permanently, cannot be cared for at home.

These are not children in limbo. They have family roots and ties with no ambivalence. Since there is no question that belonging and early bonding did occur, these youngsters have the inner resources to continue growth away from home even if removal is the only feasible plan. Small agency-owned and -operated boarding and group homes are often an ideal setting for these children. Some specialized foster homes can also do the job, as long as issues of possible double loyalty or conflict between biological and foster family can be constructively managed.

The child in this situation comes to foster care placement with strong roots and connections. Under no circumstances should these be weakened or be allowed to atrophy. Constant contact and visiting with biological kin and community friends must be maintained, and as many parenting functions as possible should remain with the parents where they belong. These include planning and keeping of medical appointments, clothes shopping, room decorating and furnishing, and signing of report cards. The function of group home staff or foster parents is to care for the child while nurturing and preserving the ties and relationship to the original parents. At times it may seem easier for group home staff or foster parents to assume all tasks, but in the long run this assumption of full responsibility will not be useful for the child, the family, or society.

Children of Committed Families Considered Unfit

Some of the most challenging situations are those involving families who find their child removed from their care by state agencies, even though neither the parents nor their child has asked for this. The adults want the child back; the child did not want to leave and is angry about the inflicted separation. Placement occurred because the school, social services protective workers, or law enforcement agencies did not believe that the child's need for growth and upbringing could be met while the child remained in the care of her or his biological parents. These are children who come to school without breakfast, if they get there at all, are physically neglected, and have serious learning deficits and/or behavioral problems.

The appropriate authorities may, in fact, have enough of a case to seek termination of parental rights on grounds of parental abuse, neglect, or inability to plan. Yet there is an impasse. If neither the family nor the child wants a legal surrender, it is not a viable option. No court, no matter how skilled and committed, can adjudicate emotions. Usually more than one child is involved, and the family is known to many helping agencies. Therefore, every effort needs to be made to offer outreach preventive services. Over a period of time, however, the family has wrapped itself in a frightened cocoon to keep out those whom they perceive as not having much to offer in return for threatening their life and survival styles.

Child-protective measures should be held off for as long as is reasonable. But when there is no alternative to removal of a child to a residential setting through court order to assure the child's safety, the immediate engagement of the family is essential. Foster family care is usually not advisable because it tends to create too heavy a conflict of loyalty for the child. The residential workers from a voluntary agency may have an advantage over public agency personnel because they had no part in the child's removal.

Initially a genuine attempt to engage the family, facilitate change, and return their child home must be made. If this fails, the child and worker need to join together in an attempt to find alternatives. Beginning to develop some trust in the residential staff, the child may express fear, anger, and ambivalence about returning home. This shift in a child's feelings can only happen if the staff has a sophisticated level of self-awareness. Should the staff knowingly or unknowingly show rejection, criticism, or hostility toward the child's family, the child's bonding with staff in search of an alternative to returning home is immediately placed in jeopardy.

Children must sense and later understand, first, that their parents cannot provide what is needed for their safety and growth, and, second, that this is not because the parents do not care. The child is then able to become a more active, involved participant in seeking termination of parental rights and searching for a permanent family through adoption. Usually this situation necessitates a longer process of placement. Ongoing help to both the child and the adoptive family will assist the youngster to come to terms with what has amounted to rejecting his or her family of origin.

Too often this type of child, kept apart from the family of origin, creates a fantasy world of what the family is really like and what it could provide if only the people rendering the child helpless would allow this to happen. This artificial separation then keeps the child in limbo, preventing growth and finding expression in aberrant behavior. Even where it is obvious to the child that the family of origin is unable to provide sufficient nurturance and safety, the child must be helped to begin to work through her or his feelings about their inappropriateness before moving toward a new, permanent situation. Careful timing of legal intervention in terms of the child's psychological readiness is essential. Otherwise, we risk damaging an already vulnerable child through well-intentioned but poorly timed legal maneuvers, turning into disaster what could have been an opportunity to effect change.

Even though this may sound contradictory, there must be permission for future visits with the biological family. Only a foster family that can accept children with empathy toward their biological kin and their past will be able to succeed in both the parenting and reparenting that will need to be done.

Children with Ambivalently Committed Families

The family only verbally committed to a child is one that does not follow through on its commitments. Most often the child is not living with its two biological parents in the same household. Instead, this child is the product of a union in which the custodial parent feels substantial anger toward the absent parent. Toward the child, the parent expresses ambivalence, if not outright rejection. Children who are the recipients of ambivalent messages live with constant threat to their psychological safety, and so they test for what they most fear: eviction and abandonment. As a result, their behavior in the community becomes unsafe for themselves and others. Interventions by school officials, social workers, and others fail, and out-of-home placement appears to be the only alternative.

At an intake interview or conference with the placement agency, the family commits itself as a resource when the child is ready for discharge. If ongoing family interaction is required as the child's entry ticket into the program, the family also agrees to that. Staff may carefully explain that they are not able to change the child but that all family members will have to make changes so that they can live together; the family, although not deeply convinced, will again comply verbally.

As these children adapt to the secure predictability of the treatment milieu, they will attempt to make some changes themselves. They have been assured that their original family is a permanent resource on whom they can rely. Unfortunately, it soon becomes apparent to these children that they have been left with empty promises: Appointments are missed; visits are skipped. In the child's brief visits home, intended for experimenting with new ways of coping and interacting, the parents quickly revert to the well-established and entrenched scapegoating path: "You are sick"; "you're no good"; "it's all your fault"; "if you don't shape up, you can't visit again"; "we will take you back there and leave you." The child's performance in the residential setting deteriorates. As the parents back away, staff are put in what seems like an insurmountable bind: Staff and child know that the stay in the residential center is temporary, but hope for the child's permanent future with the child's own family—the essential ingredient for successful growth—is now gone.

In this situation there is another common pitfall: The parent with custody rights to the child is often destructively critical of the child's other parent. This criticism is at times reinforced by the referring agency. Whatever the cause of separation or divorce, the custodial parent, now rejecting this child of their union, had a part in the difficulties with the child's other parent. To fully understand the situation and intervene effectively, it is very important to engage the noncustodial parent in the process of dealing with the problem presented by the child.

The child needs to connect with that other parent. In many instances, the noncustodial parent can become a resource for the child. Even if this parent cannot be an active resource, a connection is needed so that the child can have a sense of the individuals from whom he or she originated. Growing and maturing, the child will select those parts of the relationship that have meaning. It is always presumptuous on the part of agencies or practitioners to assume that they have the right, under the guise of protection, to deny a young person full exposure to and understanding of the two people from whom that person sprang.

When confronted by family withdrawal from a child in foster family or residential care, action needs to be taken quickly. Every effort must be made to reach out not only to the noncustodial parent but also to the extended families of both parents. Then we need to share our professional perceptions honestly with the family: The family's plan for reunification is not working. The family is doing the best it can; but, given the life situation and emotional makeup of the family members, the family's agreement to take the child home was based on a wish, not a realistic assessment of circumstances. Childhood is a very brief period and one during which the foundation for adult emotional health is built. Too much time has already been lost, and there is now great urgency to set things right quickly. It is a crisis that must not be minimized or extended.

By giving the family permission to think about permanent separation from their child through legal surrender for adoption, we can validate empathically their ambivalence and pain. When we use the surrender option as a potent therapeutic tool, however, the outcomes may vary. For some families it may mean a new commitment to their child, to the child's permanent return home. By making them deal with the part of their ambivalence that wants to evict the child, the surrender option often enables parents to realize their warm and caring feelings toward the young one. As the parents anticipate the loss of the child, they may more clearly want the youngster home.

Some parents can neither easily surrender nor reaccept their child. They may then be offered three very concrete alternatives. One is to revalidate the agreement with the agency for temporary foster placement by demonstrating that they will follow the plan originally agreed to; the second is total surrender of the child; the third is to take the child home. Keeping the child in limbo is not a viable alternative, since the pace of a child's development does not allow for more wasted years.

When, amid protest and rage, the family finds itself pushed to choose the third option—the child's return home—community-based aftercare is absolutely crucial. The public child welfare agency must be an integrated participant in designing and implementing this plan. There are some risks, and child abuse is certainly one of them, which must not be dismissed lightly. Another hazard may well be that if a residential agency designs a careful therapeutic discharge plan for the child that lacks acceptance by the public placing agency, replacement of the child in another setting may occur. There is then no follow-through on the original plan, and the child will continue in limbo, with multiplying negative consequences.

When the child is discharged to the family, regardless of how guarded the prognosis, the agency's intention must be to make the plan work. The family is responsible for the child. If the family wishes to remove the child from substitute out-of-home care, the family must be assisted in every way possible to realize its control over its own destiny. As soon as the decision to return home is made, extended home visits by the child must begin. The child's behavior or misbehavior while still in the residential center or with the foster family should not be used as isolated criteria for determining whether a visit may take place. In fact, children who feel unsafe with their families will frequently misbehave to prevent a visit home. The child's behavior should not prevent the implementation of a plan whose function it is to search out, and eventually assure, a permanent place with people permanently committed to the child.

In many cases, through supportive help during the visiting period or even after discharge, families are able to realize that life with their child is not a viable option. If that happens, the family, child, and worker need to work toward a constructive permanent separation. When the family's surrender—the ultimate rejection— does occur, we fear for the child. However, experience has shown that the child has lived in the shadow of this threat for years.

The child is indeed in pain. Nevertheless, it is still important if ongoing contact of some kind could be negotiated. It is undesirable, and probably impossible, to totally sever even damaged family connections. Children who remember their past, even though it may have been painful, need permission to return, as needed, to check out their feelings and perceptions. We can hope these feelings will change as the child matures in an environment committed to permanent caring. Anger and hurt can ultimately be converted to empathy and understanding for optimal growth to occur, even among people who have been badly hurt.

Children Apparently without Roots

Children who have had many different foster home or institutional placements are often perceived as being without roots by the people who care for them. Some of these youngsters are free for adoption; some are not, because they have gotten lost in the shuffle. These children are artists in their ability to provoke eviction from their own families or their substitute caregivers.

Many of these children are severely scarred in their ability to form meaningful attachments. Developmental arrest may have occurred in the first year or two of life. This set of children is the most severe indictment of the revolving-door foster care system. Time has almost run out for them. In the saddest cases, this has already happened by the time the child is five or six.

As we look at a child's history of multiple placements, we have to wonder how this could have happened. Inappropriate placements occur because of heavy caseloads, inexperienced staff, lack of readily available appropriate foster homes, personal circumstances in a foster family that force the child's removal, and so forth. At times, however, the reason for multiple failed placements seems to lie in either inadequate professional child assessment or inadequate agency follow-through on the assessment. Children may have physiological difficulties or needs not identified early enough to avoid making their care extremely burdensome for a family. A family prepared and willing to deal with a child with special needs might have been looked for. Providing a committed foster family with additional help might have prevented the tragedy of multiple placements.

The reality, however, is that we will continue to encounter these young people at ages eight, nine, ten, and into adolescence. Their placement is a complex and risky task. In the caregiver's attempt to protect these children from their earlier life, they are often denied permission to feel. The children tell us this by their often otherwise incomprehensible behavior. Their feelings are so repressed that their only release from what hurts so badly is inappropriate, often dangerous, behavior. Depending on the physical size of the child, this behavior may be extremely difficult to manage. We need small residential centers or very special treatment families who have the skill and sensitivity to help the youngsters deal with their grief, loss, and anger in ways other than destructive and self-destructive behaviors.

Children who have experienced so many losses need to be enabled to reexperience their life histories. The reinitiation of contacts with siblings in other placements, and with former foster families, and of other previous ties is often useful and concrete. Even those foster homes from which a child was removed, because the responsible agency saw too many undesirable components, have provided some level of investment in the child. Both child and family experienced pain from the removal, and this pain needs to be shared. We often hear children reminisce positively about homes that sound frightening from the case record. In most such cases one should doubt neither the child nor the authors of the case record.

In introducing children who are legally free to an adoptive family, timing is a crucial challenge. It is unrealistic to speak about waiting until the child has finished grieving. Given the magnitude of the losses, grieving is a life's task. One can only hope that, as the children grow in a more appropriate environment, they will learn to deal with their feelings about their many losses in a manner that is neither self-destructive nor destructive of others.

The adoptive family's ability and willingness to participate in the grief process can lay the foundation for a relationship in which rerooting can occur. Integration of a child into a new family means integration of the total child;

this acceptance includes the child's culture, past, and family of origin. We know that no one's original roots can be discarded. In fact, we in the United States do not expect adults when they marry to shed their identities and abruptly reject and terminate all previous ties and relationships. So the adopted child's roots must be carefully transplanted into more fertile soil in which healthier growth can occur.

An adoptive family able to succeed in the integration of a "difficult-to-place" child must be an open family that tolerates differences and knows how to avoid the trap of "family secrets." Often the family is far more ready for the rerooting than is the child. These children are slow to trust, and use destructive behaviors over and over again to check whether the families are truly committed to them. Other families they have known, after all, were in the end not committed to them. The families who succeed are those who do not fear their own emotions, know that they can control them, and above all reach out for help before it is too late. Thus, the placement of this kind of child will continue to be a task with very high risks, about which much more needs to be learned.

For those youngsters who are not legally free for adoption, service planning and their placement are even more complex. Special families must be found whose primary commitment is to allow another human being to grow in their midst without assurance that the bond can ever be legalized. The psychological and social need for legal ties varies from one culture to another. We do have cultural groups in the United States that accept people as kin regardless of legalities. For other cultural groups, however, the assurance of the law is crucial for families to truly commit themselves to a child. These differences among families must be understood and accepted.

Adolescents: How Do We Define Permanence for Them?

Finally we come to the adolescent in limbo. Like that of the younger child who has been a victim of many early separations, this young person's situation is a serious indictment of our child- and family-caring systems. All too often this adolescent is the very same multiply-placed foster child, but a few years down the road. Time has by now almost run out before he or she is an adult. There will, of course, always be adolescents within this group who have lived with their biological families, with one or the other parent, or with adoptive families for some of their growing-up years. However, some sort of crisis has precipitated the need for attention to this adolescent's situation.

Every possible effort should be made to avoid out-of-family placement of the adolescent, even though this may appear to be the best route for some truancy, delinquency, self-destructive, or assaultive behaviors, all of which indicate that adults have allowed the situation to get out of hand. When out-of-family placement of these youths must occur, it should be time-limited in order to assist the families involved to take charge as soon as possible. Effort needs to be put into opening family communications so that people can begin to hear each other and to function as a unit.

When adolescents have been in the foster care system for some time, there is sometimes a serious misunderstanding by child-care workers and social workers articulated as: "We cannot do family work in the Johnny Jones case since he has no family. We will work toward preparing him for independent living." How can this be? Everyone originates somewhere. Where and who are the people who placed Johnny on this earth? They are very important to him, even though he may not necessarily know how to tell us this. If we don't know who and where they are and if he doesn't know, isn't it time that someone try to find out? This may be the last chance to explore Johnny's past with him, and to search out his family linkages and kin connections.

Supportive ties are crucial during the often difficult transition from protective care to self-dependence. When young people without adequate connections leave the foster care system, they are extremely vulnerable. The transition of foster care youth into adult living has recently been receiving considerable attention, and rightly so. Such attention is late in coming. We sometimes expect the impossible from vulnerable adolescents who lack the usual family supports of a young person growing up in a kin system in the community. Having spent their growing-up years in the foster care system, they have been protected in some ways more than many children raised in ordinary communities. The institution or group home has provided for them not only physically, but also psychologically and socially. Suddenly they come of age and are thrust out into the world. Professionals can teach living and vocational skills, but none of this will work without adequate connections and support. We all know youths who, when prematurely thrown on their own, have joined with individuals or groups of people who have led them straight into the penal system.

When it comes to these adolescents practitioners must recognize that there is always need for family work. The strategy must be to search intensively for biological kin connections, reconnections with old foster families, volunteers, and personnel to whom the young person has been attached. No placement should terminate abruptly. As young people move into self-dependence, they need extensive aftercare services involving frequent outreach. We do this for our own children when they leave home for school, work, or marriage. Why and how are the needs of foster care youth different?

Part of the answer lies in the difficulties of caseload distribution and funding. Regardless of need, when young people are no longer eligible to remain in a program, they are moved out and others take their place. Staff do not have endless time or energy.

There are new federal and state independent living mandates beginning to be implemented in some states, albeit very unevenly. Although conceptually sound, these mandates do not yet meet the enormous need. Only very sensitive and thoughtful program design will turn mandates into useful life transitions for the youth involved.

CONCLUSION

Children in limbo are often the product of families in which the parents' life experiences provided them with minimal nurturance and parenting models, and they in turn function unpredictably and impulsively toward their children. The parents, regardless of socioeconomic status, lack adult problem-solving skills, and confronted with life's stress, they often try to blame and "evict" another family member, sometimes a spouse, but often a child. These families also seem to lack adequate kin support systems, or if these exist, do not know how to get the help they need. Thus, the problems continue from one generation to the next.

Children need to know who will care for them until they can care for themselves. Not knowing creates terrifying fears of abandonment, which young children equate with death. Their panic is expressed in behavior often incomprehensible to adults.

If the biological family cannot offer permanent care, a substitute family needs to be found, preferably through adoption. If a child or youth has a family committed to him or her which because of its own or the child's disability cannot offer at-home care, these roots must never be severed or disconnected. Whether or not the child lives with biological kin, the existence of these kin must be validated. Children need to learn as much about their families of origin as possible; connections with extended kin should be developed regardless of who the primary caregiver will be. The pain of losing biological and other early ties will always remain. The sensitivity and openness of caregivers toward these losses will make a difference in the quality of adjustment of the young people needing care.

4

Program Design:
A Philosophic and Practical Response

HISTORICAL OVERVIEW

The historical origins of the institutionalized child-caring system in this country lies in the tradition of the orphanage, created for youngsters who had lost their parents through death or by abandonment often prompted by inability to feed and clothe them. Many children who came into an orphanage brought with them the psychological asset of having been cared for and nurtured by committed parents. Many outstanding Americans were raised in orphanages; others had parents or grandparents who were. Loss of parents through death is excruciatingly painful, but many children can deal with it.

With improvements in medical care and advances in preventive and epidemiological medicine, the number of children left orphaned by both parents' death and who also have no kin to raise them is, indeed, small. Before the current AIDS crisis, automobile or airplane accidents were more likely than illness to create this situation. With the passage of the Social Security Act of 1935 and the implementation of Aid to Dependent Children (later renamed Aid to Families with Dependent Children), children were no longer removed from families for reasons of poverty alone.

Orphanages and children's homes also sheltered children of unwed mothers, of incarcerated or institutionalized parents, and of abusive families during their growing-up years [Maguire 1985]. The institution provided its own subculture and social linkages. Institutions shifted during the second quarter of this century from the large congregate dormitory models to cottage campuses in order to replicate a life situation as close to family living as possible. In the capacity of house or cottage parents, many staff chose as a lifestyle the institutional care of children. Nevertheless youngsters continued to be grouped according to age and sex, and great emphasis was placed on the peer group as a socializing agent [Polsky and Chester 1968; Polsky 1977]. The quality of care ranged from marginal to acceptable to quite remarkable even by current standards. However, by the late 1940s and early 1950s, with the acceleration of the mental health movement in this country, through both the creation of child guidance clinics and psychological and social work services in many public schools, the difficulties encountered by the institutionalized children came to the attention of professionals and concerned citizens.

Children's institutions were often located in suburban residential neighborhoods. Some of these locations were originally rural and became suburban after the children's institutions were built. The advantage of some of these locations was that the children attended more expensive schools with better resources and higher teacher-pupil ratios. The disadvantage was that institutional youth stood out and were considered different from most of their peers. These young people were frequently stigmatized in the surrounding community as "home children." Furthermore, employment aspirations in the United States also began to shift. The live-in position of house parent became less and less attractive. Soon the turnover rate of the institution workers created major recruitment problems.

As more became known about the negative implications of maternal deprivation [Bowlby 1965, 1966] and multiple caretakers for infants and young children, many youngsters were placed in foster homes rather than in institutions. Although neither the literature nor the media have highlighted successful foster family placements, some of these foster family placements were made permanent in order for children to grow and develop in a stable environment.

Gradually institutional care became the choice of last resort. Fewer referrals of children to institutional placement often left the institutions with youngsters not free for adoption yet without any seemingly viable connection to any family. The behavioral difficulties shown by youth in institutional care became more and more severe. They were indeed children in limbo, and acted accordingly. By the 1950s—with the exception of a small group of leading children's institutions throughout the country, such as Hawthorne Cedar Knolls, Belfaire, Pioneer House, the Orthogenic School, and a few others— institutions were not equipped to deal with the intensive psychiatric difficulties presented by the populations needing care. Even those centers that were equipped to deal with these difficulties focused their attention on the child. Those youngsters who adjusted reasonably well often had no place to move on to, and, therefore, remained in the institution with peers who exhibited many difficulties and inappropriate behaviors.

The late 1950s and 1960s were a time when some of the more venturesome institutions throughout the country began to take a hard look at whom they were serving and what their resources were to do the job. Some institutions closed their doors to custodial care and became residential treatment centers, a change that required different organizational structures, program design, staffing, and admissions requirements.[1]

Those who enthusiastically committed themselves to the provision of intensive residential treatment services soon encountered a frustrating problem with no easy solution. They found it very difficult to discharge youngsters when the time seemed appropriate if no acceptable discharge plan with services to the family was available. What were children being prepared for? Was optimum adaptation to institutional routine and structure really an indicator of a child's ability to function in society under less than optimal conditions? If a youngster did return home where no major changes in family functioning and interaction had occurred, regression by the youth was often unavoidable [Allerhand, Weber, and Haug 1966]. This pointed to residential treatment as ultimately ineffective.

ADAPTING PROGRAM: ONE AGENCY'S EXPERIENCE

The evolution of program development and design at Parsons Child and Family Center is a useful example of an attempt to become responsive to the challenges presented. The discharge needs of Parsons' residential population increased the stress and frustration of its competent clinical, child-care, and educational staff. Creative change of agency program and philosophy of care is surely an enormous undertaking. Parsons found that backing into redesign through initial experimentation case by case and on a specialized pilot unit basis to be a less threatening and ultimately valid alternative to redesigning an entire agency program at once. Over a period of two decades, the Center developed eight new program strategies with twenty-one identifiable subcomponents, each of which started as a programmatic response to the limitation of existing programs.

As Parsons staff looked at the discharge needs of youth in residential care, they became keenly sensitive to the artificiality and restrictiveness of campus-based institutional units. There were youth who could handle community living but had no place to go. The development of group homes or community residences, therefore, seemed appropriate. The agency then set up several houses in various sections of the community. Many youth were able to live in these houses and negotiate their way in the community independently and to attend public school. However, for some youth, attending the Parsons' special-education campus school seemed more desirable.

Initially the Parsons community residences were staffed by house parents who made the house their own permanent home. However, as time went on and the emotional and behavioral difficulties of the youngsters referred to community residences became more and more severe, the staffing of these houses required a more highly trained staff, one that could get respite and distance. Non-live-in child-care staff members working discrete shifts were substituted for houseparent staffing in 1976. Now more seriously disturbed youth could be accommodated. On the other hand, the family-type care was lost and replaced by treatment and specialized family foster care, as described in chapter 7.

Thus, for some youth a discharge option from residential care at Parsons was group home placement in which they could remain until they left for adult living, or which they could use as a stepping stone to family living with their own families, new adoptive families, or foster families. As Parsons' experience developed, group homes were used for direct referrals as well as for youths discharged from residential care.

There were children at Parsons whose families demonstrated a readiness for their youngsters to return home even though discharge from the institution seemed to carry very high risk. Much more work was needed with both the family and the child, although progress accelerated when they lived together rather than apart. A discharge option to a campus-school-based day program was developed. Youngsters continued to attend the campus school while intensive home- or office-based services continued for the family. Gradually a fully-staffed day treatment program evolved.

Parsons' new program development led to another set of questions. If, when provided with sufficient help, families are able to maintain their "discharged" child in their own home, was the initial separation really necessary? Should day treatment become another program option at time of referral rather than only at discharge for those youth who were too disruptive to attend community schools?

For some young people at Parsons, return to biological parents did not appear to be an option, even though the children and their parents were truly bonded to each other. This is often true in situations where parents are of very limited intelligence, extremely immature, or handicapped by a variety of physical, social, or psychological problems. Long-term specialized care with foster families able to accept the total child, including his or her past connections and experiences, needed to be developed. In some instances, this meant maintaining an ongoing nurturing relationship with the child's biological family.

Some youngsters had been so traumatized living in their family that only a neutral setting, such as a residential treatment center, could alleviate distress enough to allow them to later risk family living again. For them, the extent to which bonding with their biological family had occurred was questionable at best. Their family's ambivalence, if not outright rejection, left a poor prognosis for future bonding or the maintenance of any constructive relationship, even if the youth were not to live at home. Some of these children were legally free for adoption when referred to institutional placement. For others the legal work had either not been initiated or not completed. In any case the residential treatment task was to help the child or youth with loss and grieving.

An adoption program for older, hard-to-place youth with severe emotional scars had to be developed. In some instances, open adoption—in which contact with the biological family continues—had to be considered. But, of course, the same challenging questions kept surfacing. Was residential treatment always the program of choice for these youth at time of referral?

Other children needed the therapeutic skills and interventions that residential treatment had to offer, but could then succeed in foster family care treatment as a stepping stone to adoption, long-term family foster care, or even return to the family of origin. Staff who work in family treatment must have as much professional training and therapeutic expertise as staff who work in residential treatment. In fact, foster families in which at least one member had professional child-care experience and training were recruited to initiate this vital program by taking residential youngsters in need of this service into their own homes. Eventually such treatment-family care evolved into a program of choice at time of intake.

By the early 1970s Parsons was experimenting with family-centered group care. One residential unit at Parsons began to provide very intensive family services to youth and their families with a discharge goal of return to the family of origin in the shortest time possible. Family participation in the residential treatment milieu became a method of choice. Some youngsters were able to return home within three months.

The inevitable question again arose: If so much progress could occur in such a short period of time, should placement have occurred in the first place? This kind of thinking precipitated the development of an outreach prevention-of-placement pilot project with the Albany County Department of Social Services for youth and their families who had not previously been responsive to traditional child guidance or family agency outpatient services.

This pilot project at Parsons used "kitchen-table" counseling aimed at putting overwhelmed, helpless people in charge of their own lives and those of their children through providing a variety of intensive home-based outreach services coupled with an enabling, supportive, and nurturing treatment approach. The initial results were heartening, and this program was able to take a full-scale place in the array of agency services with the passage and implementation of the New York State Child Welfare Reform Act of 1979. This act provided not only philosophic validation for the approach but viable funding as well. This program today serves the largest number of Parsons clients.

As Parsons began to move from a one-model residential treatment center toward the formation of a multifaceted program of care, the agency's educational services inevitably became involved in a soul-searching process of change. Initially classrooms were attached to each residential unit. Children lived together in one group and remained together in that same group throughout the school day. There were very clear advantages in ease of team communication and in implementing consistent child management. The teacher was an integrated member of the residential staff team.

But there were also many disadvantages. The children were locked into a small group with seven or eight other youngsters without respite from each other. Educationally it was almost impossible to program other than on an individual basis. Although youngsters were appropriately placed residentially, it was indeed rare that the same placement was also educationally appropriate.

The key issue was philosophic. Was residential treatment a cocoon from which troubled children would emerge able to negotiate the mainstream of society, including the community school classroom? By contrast, as residential care at Parsons became a much more short-term method of intervention, targeted to return children to community classrooms as quickly as possible, the educational experience while in residence needed to replicate at least some components of the community school experience. An educational model emerged staffed by special education teachers with training to understand clinical needs. The ratio of children to teacher remains small. However, the grouping depends much more on educational rather than clinical needs. One consequence of this change is that the teacher is no longer able to be as intensively involved with the treatment team, since no teacher could realistically participate in all team decisions affecting six to twelve youngsters, each of whom may be involved with a different treatment team.

As multiple out-of-home care and community-based programs developed, another dilemma surfaced. Should each program have its own classrooms or should children be placed according to educational need? Since the intent was to mainstream the children as soon as possible, which included placement of children in special education classrooms in community schools, educational needs could be better met by using a larger pool of students from which to create appropriate educational groups. On the high-school level, Parsons designed programs so that individuals would move from one teacher to another for different subjects, just as they would in their community school.

There were (and are) those youngsters at Parsons whose needs meant that special program classrooms had to be created for them in the campus school. Specifically, severely disabled children with autistic-like characteristics need special, self-contained classroom programming. However, even these self-contained classrooms are designed to meet the learning and developmental level of the students, not necessarily to match their place of residence. Units that work with youth exhibiting psychotic or prepsychotic behaviors ideally should have special education services on the living unit itself, since the transition even to a campus school is more than some of the young people can manage safely. For them, immediate integration with a whole new group of classmates is out of the question without careful preparation. However, movement to the campus school may be a next step.

FROM RESIDENTIAL CARE TO AN ARRAY OF SERVICES: STAGES OF PROGRAM CHANGE

The process of an institution's program change and redesign from residential child care to a multiservice model can be articulated according to the following four phases:

Phase I

The residential institution is dominant. A series of small program offshoots develop to provide discharge alternatives for youngsters leaving residential care (see Figure 4.1).

Phase II

The residential program shrinks in terms of relative power compared to the other services, although not necessarily in terms of number of beds or budget and staff allocation. It ceases to be the dominant program as other programs take on equal importance in an array of options at the time of case referral (see Figure 4.2).

This transition is usually a very trying time for the once-dominant program. Institutional staff who saw themselves as the creative thinkers in the system and the motivators in the development of a continuum of care now see their own program being considered the least desirable choice for care. Staff fear that their program is becoming obsolete and may even wonder whether their jobs are in jeopardy.

Sensitive administration is usually very much needed, especially to reinforce the message that institutional programs for children will always be with

Figure 4.1
An Institution Developing Discharge Options

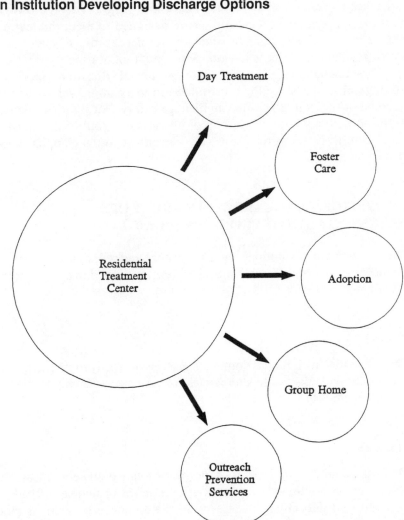

us. The challenge is to redesign these programs appropriately so that children and families in need of these services can receive the best possible help in the shortest period of time. As outpatient and preventive services grow, these new program modules rapidly come to carry substantially larger caseloads than a traditional residential program can ever carry. Nevertheless, the residential components remain much more labor-intensive and require a disproportionate amount of agency administration, plant, and financial

Figure 4.2
An Array of Services with Each Unit Struggling for Boundaries and Autonomy

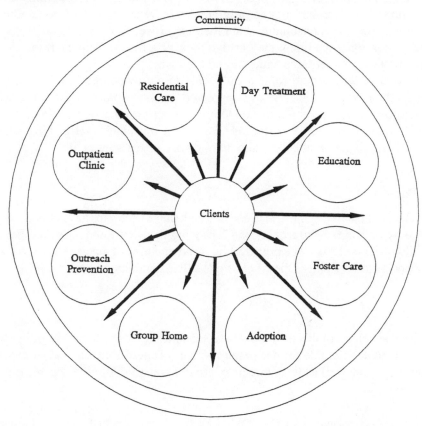

resources. Outpatient staff, therefore, often feel second-best and perceive the agency's primary commitment as being to its historical roots, the residential institution. During this phase, programs struggle to assert their autonomy. Unless much caution is exercised, interprogram competition will flourish at the expense of genuine client-centered collaboration.

The array of services can be visualized as a series of circles of equal size (Figure 4.2). Gaps between the circles suggest how clients may fall between the cracks. This fallout can occur because of blind spots or inattention when clients are transferred from one program to another. It can also occur as programs become rigid in their design and admissions criteria and children or families for whom more imaginative, creative programming is needed are excluded.

As tensions between program staffs develop, morale may easily slip. Much administrative energy must go into facilitating interprogram dialogue and training. The most effective intervention is to encourage interprogram consultation. Staff members of one program can serve as consultants to another program. As these consultants share their expertise, experience, and human and professional qualities, they bridge their differences. This learning is a slow process that requires patience and hard work.

Occasionally there are staff people who do not work well in this type of comprehensive team effort; over a period of time some very competent practitioners may have to move on to practice settings that do not allocate as much energy to team functioning. There are outstanding clinicians who belong in private practice and should not work in agencies at all.

Phase III

The third phase (Figure 4.3) is one in which the service gaps have closed, and an array of programs to meet clients' changing developmental needs has been achieved. The multiservice organization is moving toward maturity. Each component becomes a part of the whole while still maintaining its own integrity.

Phase IV

The last phase of this developmental sequence reaches toward the ultimate service goal: a flexible service system with easy client access to and from the community as well as from one program to another within the organization (Figure 4.4).

The system continues to be far from perfect; no system involving human beings ever will be. However, there is sufficient structure to make the system work. Intensive staff training, ongoing case conferencing, and continuous service assessment are essential. Means must exist for conflict resolution on a case-by-case basis. Quality assurance programs and above all good relationships among program directors are the key. A low turnover rate among management staff is desirable, since with every new program director there is a major system shift that must not be underestimated. Change can be healthy or disruptive; at times it is both, and the costs must be weighed against the gains.

CONTINUING CHALLENGES TO PROGRAM DESIGN

On a national level, the institutional child-caring system changed during the 1970s and 1980s and evolved at varying rates in somewhat

Figure 4.3
An Array of Services to Meet Clients' Changing Developmental Needs

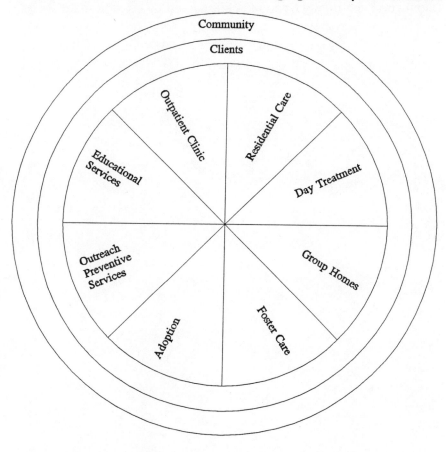

different ways in various places. Program evolution seemed generally to follow the process described here, although not necessarily always within a single agency. The Child Welfare Training Centers initiated and funded by the federal Department of Health and Human Services developed initiatives in their regions that emphasized the need for permanence, prevention of placement, and strengthening of family ties for young people. Staff training workbooks were written, and seminars and workshops, often of excellent quality, were offered throughout the country [*Basic Course* 1977]. In particular, much happened to encourage adoption programs for those children with special needs. There still remains great unevenness in how residential care is used, and the impact of prevention of out-of-home placement programs needs much further study.

Figure 4.4
A Flexible Array of Services Optimally Responsive to Changing Client and Community Needs (as suggested by the dotted lines)

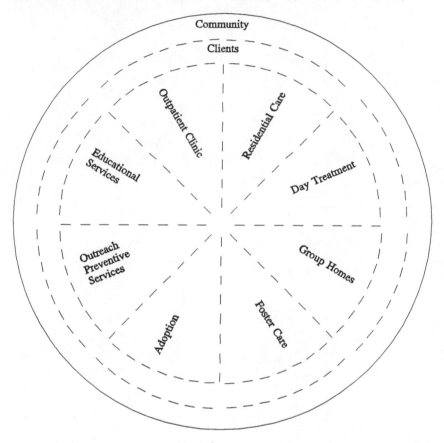

Some of the widest service gaps in services to children and families continue to exist because of the way these services are funded and organized. Mental health services are often organized, staffed, and funded from entirely different sources than so-called child welfare services. Yet children in need of child welfare services including out-of-home care (because they are identified as neglected and dependent) are also in need of mental health services, as are their families. Program segmentation is artificial. When the providers have little contact with or knowledge and respect for each other, a family is often caught, and nothing gets done.

A mental health clinic may provide medication for a depressed parent, but there may be no effort to link the depression with the loss of a child to out-of-home placement. The child may be in institutional placement exhibiting severe acting-out behaviors due to lack of contact with the parent. This is just one of too many examples of the lack of family service coordination under one umbrella.

In addition to the child welfare and the mental health systems, there are family service agencies. In some communities these agencies are very small, struggling with tiny budgets supported by the local United Way, in addition to a sliding-scale fee system. Some family counseling agencies offer adoption and foster care services; others do not. Some offer homemaker services. Some agencies are independent, voluntary, not-for-profit agencies; others are sponsored by a religious denomination such as Catholic Charities U.S.A., Lutheran Social Service System, or the Association of Jewish Family and Children's Agencies.

One of the positive byproducts of fiscal constraints is the need to look more closely at service organization, to see whether there are ways of integrating services to assist the service recipient while at the same time pulling together units that seem to fit administratively. This reevaluation and reorganization can cut administrative overhead, but even more than that, careful analysis can reduce duplication of services, and even eliminate services that turn out to be unnecessary or self-defeating.

This process can occur between agencies as well as within a single agency. In 1978 the Jewish Board of Guardians, which among other mental health and social services provided outpatient child guidance clinic services, court services, and residential treatment services for children and adolescents, merged with Jewish Family Service, which offered family and individual counseling. Both agencies were supported by the Federation of Jewish Philanthropies of Greater New York. The new agency became the Jewish Board of Family and Children's Services, which now offers a wide and diverse range of mental health and social services, with community-based, family-oriented practice at its core, to residents of the greater New York area.

There are other examples of program mergers and integrations throughout the country. The Children's Home and Aid Society of Illinois, a provider of residential treatment, group homes, family foster care, adoption, and child and family counseling services, integrated: the Viva Family Center of Chicago, a neighborhood family resource center, in 1978; the Community Child Care Center of Palatine, located in Palatine, Illinois, in 1984; and the Tom Thumb Day Care Center in Carpenterville, Illinois, in 1990. The Albany Child Guidance and Family Psychiatric Clinic merged with Parsons Child and Family Center of Albany, New York, in 1982.

"NOBODY COMES FROM NO PLACE":
DEVELOPMENT OF A PHILOSOPHY OF CARE

One of the major issues in the development of an appropriate array of child and family services, whether within one agency or among a series of community agencies, is the need for a philosophic belief and value system that all providers can share. Attributes of dysfunctional families have a way of resurfacing among all service providers. Just as our own or client families often come from different cultural and ethnic backgrounds, which require efforts to clarify communications and avoid misunderstanding, so do service providers come from different professional backgrounds and orientations. Some are rooted in the child welfare field; some come from mental health or family services, or juvenile justice, or education. Some are in the private not-for-profit sector; others in the public sector. There are many built-in interdisciplinary differences and biases among the various professional disciplines of psychiatry, psychology, social work, special education, and child care. There are also issues among professionals, paraprofessionals, volunteers, and natural helpers in the community.

The next difficulty occurs with practice philosophy and its implementation. Do we work with individuals only? Or do we work with families? Are we, in fact, family therapists? If so, what and who is a family therapist? People who work with individuals will, of course, also see families. And in most instances family therapists will work with an individual family member, if this seems to make sense in a given situation and time. But is one a Structural Family Therapist, a Strategic Family Therapist, or a Bowenian Family Therapist? What do we mean when we say a children's institutional or foster care program is "family-oriented"? Answers to these very simple questions vary widely.

The general term "work with family" is often mislabeled as "family therapy." "Family therapist" refers only to one who has completed advanced training in family therapy as a specialization above and beyond the required training and certification of a larger discipline, whether psychiatry, psychology, or social work. The training has to include supervised practice by a qualified practitioner in the field of family therapy.

Clients must be seen within their family context, for "nobody comes from no place." Whether looking at a person's problems from a systemic or a psychoanalytic developmental perspective, one arrives at the same paradigm. A sperm and an egg from a man and a woman create another human being. For the most part our society is still organized in families. Men and women who produce children as biological parents each have come from families that can usually be traced for three or four generations back and sometimes much further. The newborn not only inherits genetic physiological characteristics from both parents; she or he is the result of what the "social parents" bring in psychological and emotional development. If the child has spent all or part of its formative years with its family of origin, clearly the impact on the child is massive; the impact is equally substantial on the family. If the child has not spent the formative years with its biological family, the impact is still enormous, but in a different way: "Who are they? Why did they reject me? Why won't they care for me?" When one doesn't know, fantasy takes over. But fantasy about the unknown can be very frightening. Fears can become so overwhelming that they interfere with development, growth, and functioning. Cannot those of us who work with children in limbo, or in jeopardy of being in limbo, agree that there is no youth or child who does not have a family, whether that family is present or absent, alive or dead? Even if children do not know their family, that family is still very much with them in their thoughts and feelings.

Perhaps those of us who work with children and youth in limbo or in jeopardy of limbo can further agree that all human beings need connections, and that these connections occur naturally in the biological family of origin. As a human being grows and matures, the skills learned in family living are then used to develop social relationships and bonds outside of the family, in school, club, community, and workplace. If bonds to biological kin do not appear to exist or are vulnerable, can we agree that this is a major issue in a person's life and must be explored in depth? Can we further agree that, given the often nonverbal nature of our clients, working experientially, such as searching for kin, might be more useful than the so-called talk therapies, which are often only effective as reinforcers of what already has been experienced?

In the development of a usable philosophy of care, it is important to clarify the crucial issue of "permanency" and all the confusion that this term has generated. Permanency planning is a sophisticated treatment concept. It reaches into a person's past and connects that past to a present that is then projected into a future. One cannot do quality treatment without dealing with this very basic human issue. Young people cannot grow and recover unless they are given some assurance about who will care for them until they reach adulthood. In addition, people need kin supports and friendship linkages throughout life. Those of us who have roots and connections work hard to keep these intact. Why are those most vulnerable because of a difficult beginning in life expected to achieve an "independence" that does not need anyone when they are arbitrarily forced to leave an unrealistic system at eighteen or twenty-one? Dealing with and, if at all possible, reestablishing a young person's past ties and biological connections are essential components of good treatment.

On the other hand, the concept of permanency planning has been oversimplified, misunderstood, and implemented only marginally, if at all. Inadequately trained staff, mandated to decide where Johnny or Susan will grow up so an appropriate checkmark can be made on a computer, may make decisions without any professional judgment and skill. Nevertheless, understanding this complex concept remains essential for helping interventions be successful.

Furthermore, most children in the state of New York placed in alternative living arrangements under the jurisdiction of a commissioner of social services have permanency planning as a goal of their treatment plan. This is not true of those young people in a mental health program or facility. In fact, too many children in psychiatric centers throughout the country have no contact with their families. The staffs of the mental health and child care agencies often engage in verbal battle, if they communicate at all. Yet, there cannot be effective treatment without addressing a child's permanence and planning for it.

Conflict among professionals is too often caused by the way all of this is communicated among them. However, just as in families, when there is miscommunication and families get stuck, often the weakest and most vulnerable member of a family becomes the victim. In the human services system, the victim is the client.

SOLUTIONS

There are solutions to these seemingly insurmountable philosophic dilemmas. If the intent of competent, caring practitioners is to provide the best services possible, the first objective has to be to meet client need. This imperative requires setting aside rigid dogma. The search for resolution needs to identify commonalities on which we all can agree. There can still be a whole range of service methods and styles.

"Any person can and must be defined by both the external and internal system in which he exists. Both systems not only exist but are inseparable" [Fogarty 1984a:21]. This dual reality holds true for all people, and especially for those who are particularly vulnerable. Faced with the normal stresses of living—for some extremely harsh—all people do the best they know how to meet their survival needs. If their behaviors are counterproductive, it is due to lack of skill or inner resource, rather than lack of willingness to do better. If we can accept this, resources must be made available to teach new skills and offer new alternatives. Teaching needs to occur within a context of respect and normalization. Clients know more about themselves, their own wishes and needs, than any of the rest of us will ever know about them. It is presumptuous on the part of service providers to establish client goals without their participation. Any goal that clients do not truly set for themselves cannot be achieved regardless of how and by whom it is signed off in a case record. All people have assets, and it is the challenge for the competent practitioner to enable clients to discover their assets and to share them. Families need to be engaged on the basis of their assets, not their liabilities. Within this philosophy, programs need to be designed so that they prevent rather than remediate disruptions of family ties.

Most people do better in small, intimate settings than in large, impersonal ones. Those isolated families and individuals who lack adequate natural support systems need to be able to use the service agency for that support. Some will be enabled to transfer the skills they learn in this way to attach themselves later to more natural helping systems within their communities, such as their church or neighborhood. For others this will not be so easy; it is important not to send them on their way and cut them off when that path may still be too difficult and dangerous for them. In fact, there need to be programs that allow a client to return at times of stress, and even let clients who have begun to cope remain involved in some way, so that help is readily available, just as it is from one's family, physician, friends, and neighbors. Some people may need their emotional attachments to their agencies. Every time a transfer is forced—often to meet program rather than client needs—something is lost; too often it is the client.

PROGRAM DESIGN ALTERNATIVES

No single program can meet the needs of all people. There must be choices. State-operated services are probably essential for some clients, particularly when there are major protective issues involved, as in instances of severe mental illness, dangerous delinquency, or child abuse. For others not-for-profit sectarian and nonsectarian agencies are desirable options. This sector may be able to provide a higher quality of service at a lower cost. Some states have effective purchase-of-service contracts with the not-for-profit sector. This provides good monitoring and accountability while offering diverse program choices usually delivered by small providers. Agencies that can afford not to contract with the public system have even more freedom in creative program design, and they do not subject themselves to burdensome, costly, and often irrelevant auditing mechanisms. There are, however, very few agencies with sufficiently large endowments to be this independent.

Ideally, no socioeconomic group differentiation and discrimination in service provision should exist in either sector. Many states mandate that private facilities such as psychiatric hospitals accept a certain percentage of publicly funded patients and clients.

Two generic options can be offered for providing comprehensive family services involving children and youth. There are obviously many more alternatives. The first suggested here is establishing an array of services within one agency committed to providing services to children and families with special needs. The second option involves organizing a coalition of agencies to provide a similar array of services in one community. The pertinent factors in making each option work effectively are identified.

One Agency's Array of Services

First, an agency seeking to provide a comprehensive array of services must have a clear statement of mission. This statement of overall purposes must not be just a page in a manual to flip open when an accreditation committee visits or a grant application is being written. The statement needs to be actively pursued, subject to constant review by the board of directors and administrative and supervisory staffs, and used as a reference tool for line practitioners involved in day-to-day and hour-to-hour decisions. Clarity of purpose in an organization facilitates focused planning and thinking. From this purpose or mission flow organizational goals that in turn give direction and cohesion to the development of specific program objectives.

The mission of an organization and its philosophy of care in service programs are linked. If the mission specifies assurance of an optimum environment in which children can grow and if the organization is philosophically committed to the view that this environment is best provided in a family, then it follows that the agency will do everything possible to keep children with their families and provide the needed supports and assistance to allow this to happen. Such an agency should operate to prevent out-of-home placement and each situation should be evaluated with a least-restrictive program option as the program of first choice. This approach necessitates an intake or assessment department that will coordinate and monitor all admissions as well as program selection. An assessment department representing all program possibilities can best help families and referring agencies to identify the program that best meets a family and child's needs at a given time.

A true array of services must have the flexibility of moving children and families from one program to another and of using the expertise of more than one program at a time when therapeutically desirable. A treatment team, for example, may consist of staff from an outreach preventive program, a residential or group home program, and an educational program. Program staff must further feel free to consult staff of other programs. Although this flexible approach may sound reasonable, it is in fact quite difficult to implement.

In some ways an agency seeking to work within one comprehensive philosophic approach makes things simpler; on the other hand, it builds in some very real problems in areas such as staff recruitment. Practitioners come from different schools with different orientations, are often highly skilled, and have much to offer. Every time a philosophically specialized agency loses a staff member, it is almost impossible to fill the position with a replacement trained in the same treatment orientation. A more realistic approach is to recruit staff who are flexible thinkers and broadly knowledgeable. Yet the agency practice philosophy, even though it is one that allows for substantial differences in style and method, must be acceptable to the practitioner. Training and formal as well as informal dialogue must be ongoing within and among agency programs.

In order for an array of services to function well, one needs to remember all the basic principles that operate within a family, those that optimize functioning and those that impede and sometimes even paralyze functioning. Crisis-prone families have a way of engaging their helpers to join the crisis and develop the same symptomatic behaviors. These behaviors consist of not listening, not communicating, making invalid assumptions, blaming, labeling, judging what is right and what is wrong, and ultimately forcing the eviction of the client who has "failed"—a dangerous scenario! To prevent this destructive outcome from happening in interprogram work requires a high degree of humility. The professional prima donna, no matter how brilliant, is usually a liability to programs that work with very vulnerable situations. Practitioners who are most successful in this type of setting are those committed not to "the only right way" but to an ongoing search for options not previously thought of. Creative work can only occur in systems where people feel safe to explore, brainstorm, and validate each other.

Interprogram misunderstandings and confusion will inevitably occur among staff working under stress. As in family life there are usually some interprogram power struggles. Practitioners involved in interprogram conflict need to feel secure enough to ask, "What is my part and what can I do about it?" rather than resort to the destructive, counterproductive, "It's all your fault." Supervisory and administrative staff must not allow themselves to become enmeshed in triangles or to be used as arbitrators among programs. The supervisory task is to facilitate the resolution of conflict, just as the therapist needs to be a facilitator in family conflict resolution. Supervisors and administrators must bring clarity to the situation by clarifying the mission of the organization and staff performance expectations, which include mutually supportive and respectful collaboration.

The most effective team building and interprogram collaboration are built on a case-by-case situation. Sometimes agreement seems easier to reach in theory than in practice. At other times, the reverse is true. People can work together but cannot agree theoretically on how a given outcome comes about. As staffs grow in working out their differences and begin to learn to appreciate not only their own but each other's competence, integrity, and commitment, much collaborative integration can happen at the practice level.

The Coalition of Service Agencies

A coalition of agencies is an alternative community approach to comprehensive program design serving families and children with special needs. This is even more complicated than the preceding model, but it may be possible. First, there has to be strong leadership and coordination. The outcome is only as good as the commitment of individual organizations to risk some autonomy as they become a part of this larger whole for better child and family services. In many communities, councils of community services, human services planning councils, and other similar bodies have played very valuable coordinating functions.

Second, there has to be a major commitment by all the boards of directors and chief executive officers to this coordinated functioning as essential and to the needs of the whole superseding the needs of the individual agencies. Ongoing dialogue among key administrators on policy, program design, and funding negotiation is essential.

All staff have to be engaged in comprehensive interagency inservice training programs. Such training has a dual purpose: First, it addresses common interagency philosophy and methods; second, it gives staff members an opportunity to get to know each other, which proves invaluable as they struggle with individual cases.

Upper-level executive and administrative staff must feel secure enough to allow interaction among their staffs. As relationships develop, openness can develop in dealing with one another. The intent is to create a clear agreed-upon goal of improving services.

There will always be a point, however, where coalition pressures step over the boundary of an agency's autonomy. Interagency power conflicts should be monitored carefully by the leadership of the agencies involved, and as needed by a more objective third party, particularly when there is competition for referrals, contracts, grants, United Way allocations, and other limited resources. Some agencies may be perceived as providing a better quality of care than others. Client needs are usually such that it is difficult to prove that only one type of program meets those needs. Different youngsters can benefit from family foster care, group home, or even institutional care depending upon the children's needs and the structures of the programs and the staff skills. Outpatient clinic services, day treatment services, and outreach preventive services share similar boundary problems.

Intake, of course, becomes a key factor. Does each agency maintain its own individual intake structure, or should there be a single intake system with each agency maintaining a veto power on individual admissions? In any case, the simple coalition model cannot realistically be expected to move to the tight integration portrayed in Figure 4.3, let alone to the easy access model of Figure 4.4. Agencies in a coalition need to maintain much stronger boundaries than when all programs are under the same agency umbrella. When interagency boundaries become counterproductive in meeting client needs, the next step in the coalition process might consist of some agencies merging to reduce interstaff conflict over agencies' differences in philosophy of care, client service policies, and personnel issues.

The merger process in and of itself then becomes the vehicle through which these very basic concerns are confronted. Mergers must be done carefully and slowly with the recognition that board and administrative merger is only one part of the process. It often may take several years of hard work for the desired impact of a merger to fully filter down to the day-to-day care of client families.

Interagency consultation can enhance collaboration and mutual respect, as with interprogram consultation in the one-agency model of array of services. Moreover, the movement of staff from one agency to another can be a useful tool for better interagency understanding, although it must be carefully monitored to avoid job-hopping at the expense of quality and continuity of care for clients. No one likes to lose a valuable staff member. On the other hand, if it is clear that a person is ready and in need of another growth step or different professional experience provided by another coalition agency, this move could benefit all.

CONCLUSION

Because of the historical origins of services to children and families with special needs in the United States, program organization and funding is at a crossroads. Many children's agencies come out of a background as orphanages, whereas family work was historically perceived as the province of the family agency. In addition, we have a mental health system, a system that deals with delinquent youth, and a system for developmentally disabled children. To complicate matters, public educational systems are mandated to provide special educational services where needed, but these services often cannot be separated from family issues because learning problems often originate in the family and need to be addressed there.

Program organization is frequently more related to historical origin, licensing, and funding than to the best interests of clients and their needs. In addition to organizational difficulties, there are many different perspectives on theoretical frameworks, philosophies of care, and service styles among service providers. Clients are often caught in the middle, bounce from one type of provider to another, and regress.

Given the complex nature of family problems in our society, there needs to be a program design based on a comprehensive philosophy of care, even though methods and style may vary. This philosophy should acknowledge that "nobody comes from no place." Every human being originates from a mother and father, and therefore does have a family or families of origin, whether known or unknown to that person. Family service practice needs to validate the existence of family and look to create access and networks to whatever extent possible. All youngsters need to know who will care for them until they can care for themselves; therefore, attention to permanency planning, roots, and connections must be an integral part of every helping program. Systems should be designed to validate assets as a way to put people in charge of their own lives.

Those who have experienced difficulties in forming meaningful relationships often do not develop sufficient ability to transfer new skills for living in the community after discharge from a therapeutic program. Therefore, the service agency needs to conceive support programs that can be made available on an as-needed, sometimes an ongoing, basis, to assist people to function in the community.

Two possible models of care can be posited. One is an array of child and family services, from the least restrictive, such as clinic services, to the most restrictive, such as residential services, all provided by one agency. The other is a similar array but with different agencies providing different components. Although organizational and training issues are problems in both options, team training within one comprehensive philosophy of care becomes even more complex in the second model. In reality, these models are never mutually exclusive. Communities benefit from flexibility and consumer choice options.

NOTE

1. Based on the recommendations of a study by the Child Welfare League of America, the Albany Home for Children, now known as Parsons Child and Family Center, made this transition in 1959 [Maguire 1985:61].

PART II

Community-Based Family Services

The second section of this volume examines the need for community-based services to help families maintain their child-caring role in today's difficult world. The section suggests program options to support and enhance functioning family units who need more help to maintain their child-caring and child-nurturing roles, and family units that are finding it difficult even to survive. The purpose is to offer support and service alternatives that will maintain the family as the primary child-caring unit, emphasizing the need to prevent family dissolution with its consequent eviction and abandonment of children.

5

An Array of Community Services: From Natural to Special

As we scrutinize our value system and view economic developments, we can recognize where our commitment to children and families in the United States must be directed in the next decade. If children are to grow into adults who take a productive place in the complex world of the twenty-first century, we must provide the necessary family supports to assure a healthy society. People who are well feel in control of their lives and have some ability to cope with the normal stresses of the life cycle. A well society supports adults responsible for parenting.

In some communities, this job is still performed by the extended family and family friends. Children learn from their parents and grandparents how to live, how to work, how to parent; they learn social rules and expectations. But in many communities and for many families these extended networks no longer work or simply do not exist. If the networks do work, they often do so only with extensive modification, as one traditional family boundary after another is broken due to lack of clear rules and expectations, intercultural and interethnic marriages increase, people move around the country, and new families are created by bringing two existing single-parent units into a reconstituted or blended family.

HOUSING

A crucial entitlement for every family is affordable, acceptable housing. Yet this fundamental entitlement is becoming an issue in our communities as more and more families experience severe crises from overcrowding; some have no housing at all after eviction or displacement. During the past eight to ten years, there has been a marked decline in funds for subsidized low-cost housing. This has left a growing population of homeless women, men, and children in most urban centers and needs immediate attention [Kozol 1988].

Unlike earlier times when the homeless population was mostly male, a growing subgroup of the total homeless population now comprises single-parent, female-headed families. . . . Tending to congregate in urban settings, these families are thought to comprise as much as 75% of the total homeless population in some metropolitan areas. This figure represents a 33% increase over previous years. [Dail 1990:291–92]

This lack of available low-cost housing, often leading to homelessness, has left children at severe risk as they spend their crucial formative years in continuous crisis. "The results of testing 88 children in a family shelter program indicate a possible significant impact of homelessness on both the cognitive and language development of these children, with language more severely affected" [Whitman et al. 1990:516]. These serious implications of lack of housing to the development of children and their eventual functioning in adult life requires study, early program intervention, and above all, prevention.

CHILD CARE

"Organized child care, it has long been argued, is beneficial to children, to working parents and to families. But more and more organized child care is also being considered essential to a healthy economy. . . . [A] national coalition of corporate, union, community and religious leaders and child care experts" has formed the Child Care Action Campaign to advocate a comprehensive child care effort supported by government and employers [Brozan 1988:22]. Its comprehensive report, "Child Care: The Bottom Line," notes that with

a declining growth rate in the population and with an expansion in service industries. . . . "Two out of every three new jobs will have to be filled by women, most of whom are or will become mothers." . . . The Federal Government now spends $6 billion a year on child care, with the Dependent Care Tax Credit accounting for $3.5 billion of that figure. There has been increasing involvement of business and industry . . . [but] the 3,500 employers who provide some form of child care assistance constitute one seventeenth of one percent of the nation's six million employers. [Brozan 1988:22]

Accessible, affordable, high-quality day care for the infant, toddler, and preschool child must be viewed as a national priority. Day care—whether in family day care homes, freestanding day care centers, or centers attached to the workplace—is a necessity for children's optimum growth if parents work outside the home. The need transcends socioeconomic differences, since our society is unlikely to return to a lifestyle in which one parent is at home with young children while the other assumes total responsibility for wage earning. It is also doubtful that older women in the work force while their children were growing up will abandon their jobs to remain at home with their grandchildren while their sons and daughters work.

Day care, however, is more than well-child care. Provision needs to be made for day care of children with routine minor illnesses so that every cold or sore throat will not be a family crisis.

Day-care centers for mildly sick children have increased, according to Jan Paglisasotti, sick-care coordinator for Work/Family Directions, a Boston consultant.

"When we first started looking at this two and a half years ago, we found about 14," Ms. Paglisasotti said. "Now I would estimate there are over 80 in the country." [Libov 1987:14]

Above all, day care service providers need to be carefully selected according to their motivation and ability to care for and nurture young children. Their wages and benefits need to be in line with those of other socially valuable occupations. Licensing day care workers according to specific educational criteria will need to be considered. We do license hairdressers, barbers, plumbers, and electricians, and for good reason. Do our children deserve any less?

THE SCHOOL AS COMMUNITY RESOURCE

We need a different view of the function of our educational system, which has historically addressed only the formal education of children. In many communities adult education programs have been developed. These have given many adults an opportunity to enhance their knowledge and skills, enjoy some leisure activities, and above all make friends with others who live in their community and share some interests and concerns. The more the quality of adult life can be enhanced, the less children are in jeopardy. Parents need to be nurtured so that they can respond to the demands of parenting. Subject matter, whether tennis, photography, knitting, home repair, or ballroom dancing, is never as important as the opportunity to interact and connect with others.

A second critical responsibility of the educational system is child care beyond formal school hours. The latchkey child has become a serious problem in all communities, and this problem is not going to go away. On the other hand, the educational system has an expensive, often seriously underutilized physical plant. Those community schools that have accepted responsibility for after-school programming are providing an important service. Some school districts have accepted the responsibility of transporting children to after-school programs in community centers or churches. Whatever way a community deals with this issue, all-day program options for children need to become a reality across the nation because most mothers are simply not at home when their children return from school.[1]

Some communities have community service programs for high school students. Often, however, these students are not given enough responsibility or are expected to deal with populations beyond their skill to handle. Teenagers need experience with more average populations to experience early some success at service. As we seek to provide care for both the healthy and not seriously ill child throughout the normal working day of parents, day care centers in schools can utilize the capabilities of adolescents from the community. Too little has been done to give adolescents structured parenting tasks, such as after-school clubs for younger children led by high school students with some close adult direction. Such teenage activities supply a sense of purpose to young people, who may otherwise simply "hang out." Community participation enhances adolescents' confidence while offering valuable learning in handling children.

Many senior citizens feel isolated and lonely, yet have much to give. Foster grandparents and senior aides have made a significant contribution to day care and other programs in some communities. But seniors' participation in these publicly funded programs is restricted to the less well-off elderly, excluding many citizens.

We compartmentalize services and thereby unnecessarily separate the generations. That need not be. For example, transportation is a major problem for senior citizens. School buses sit idly for hours while children are in school, or shuttle about half empty while competent senior citizens are confined to their homes for lack of transportation. School buses could transport senior citizens to do work in day care, schools, hospitals, libraries, community centers, even allowing stopovers for grocery shopping. There is nothing wrong with having young people and the elderly on the same bus, and much to be said for its effect on both generations.

How we use or misuse our resources is a major topic for discussion and exploration as we struggle to become less wasteful and more humane in the twenty-first century.

FAMILY SERVICES

Once a community has organized itself to provide essential family maintenance services, we can begin to speak of special services. Too often situations deteriorate to require special services due to a lack of normal resources to support today's lifestyles. "Normal" here means natural supports and facilities to maintain health and optimum functioning. Social connections for people are, of course, built through a variety of community agencies such as the YMCA and YWCA movements, and community centers often linked to special ethnic groups, such as the African-American, Jewish, Italian, or Polish communities. Some private not-for-profit agencies, churches, and synagogues are doing a remarkable job; others do not provide solid preventive services.

There are people who choose not to approach such agencies, nor to belong to churches or synagogues; they must be provided for also. Of course, many individuals and families will always know how to create their own personal support networks outside of any organized, community-sponsored structure.

FAMILY RESOURCE CENTERS

In various parts of the country some very successful family resource programs have emerged. "Family resource, support and education (FRSE) services are community-based services that assist and support adults in their roles as parents, with the primary objectives of promoting parental competencies and behaviors that lead to healthy and positive personal development of both children and their parents" [CWLA 1989:13]. These programs recognize that all families need support to function well. Support may come from immediate or extended family. An alternate social support network may include neighborhood or community self-help and mutual aid groups. Other supports come from professionals or paraprofessionals, are community based, and grounded in a wellness approach that builds on individual and family strengths. Family resource programs use methods that reinforce parental ability to provide an optimal childrearing environment and focus on this primary parenting role regardless of circumstance. Program leadership and participants engage in ongoing advocacy to improve the quality of life for its children and parents. Essential to this advocacy is a focus on adequate income, shelter, transportation, health care, and employment opportunity.

Such programs are operated under a variety of host auspices, which may include social services, education, health, and mental health agencies; religious, self-help, and mutual aid groups; or the workplace. Family participants' ongoing involvement in program design, implementation, and modification is essential. Community advisory boards with a variety of community representatives and participants perform this function. The process must be open and fluid to assure the maximum responsiveness to family and individual needs.

Some of these programs are merely referral agents and facilitators, but programs that have a physical location can often provide a variety of much-needed special programs. Attention should be given to creating an informal, comfortable, welcoming environment. Centers ought to be open during hours that meet the needs of the participating community, which usually include both evenings and weekends.

Outreach to parents becomes an important function, since membership drives need to begin with aggressive recruitment, using traditional and nontraditional approaches. These include standard agency referrals but also use of staff and community members for door-to-door recruitment and presentations at local schools, churches, and other neighborhood organizations and functions. Pamphlets and brochures can be distributed at supermarkets, laundromats, and other gathering places.

Funding is a major problem for these programs, and each community deals with it differently. Seed money often comes through special project grants; once grants run out, however, finding funds to continue the program is difficult. In some instances, organizations such as the United Way or Junior League are able to help. Membership dues are feasible at times; but, more often than not, they are not an option. In-kind contribution of space and services by schools, churches, and public housing developments is one approach; community centers, mental health clinics, and family agencies may be able to contribute staff time. As programs evolve, volunteers can supplement staffing.

Programs may include parenting education, skill development groups, nutrition, and health education. Much teaching and learning, however, occur through interpersonal relationships and modeling. Participation in a process, more than program content, assures human relationships and well-being. The objective is to structure an alternative supportive community in those situations in which the family or extended family is no longer intact or unable to help young parents looking to meet their responsibilities while struggling with a variety of conflicting tasks and roles, such as those of parenting and the workplace. However, the essential approach is to reinforce people's strengths.

MENTAL HEALTH CLINICS

Community mental health clinics—community family clinics, as I prefer to call them—also need competent preventive programs. Progress in preventive health care has now led to these services being attached to insurance policies provided by many employers. Preventive mental health care, however, is lagging in providing a broad enough range of services and making these services affordable. Activities such as special groups for employees with alcohol problems are too often directed toward already existing difficulties rather than prevention. Preventive mental health care programs include enabling people to better understand themselves, and to live with those around them: their families of origin, their extended kin, marital partners, children, and others significant to them. Constructive, self-aware communication skills have to be taught. People need to learn how they influence others, not only how others affect them.

Collaborative arrangements between mental health professionals and schools, community centers, churches, and family resource programs can work well. Some clinics have developed contracts with employee assistance programs in industry and other work sites. Mental health practitioners can be attached to obstetric units in hospitals to assist families with the normal issues of integrating the new member, the baby, into the family. Even though hospital stays are very brief, initial screening can identify people to whom posthospital follow-up should be offered. Staff in pediatric units need to help families with a severely or terminally ill child deal with the impact on other family members. The loss not only affects the parents but has major ramifications on the future lives of the family's other children. Outreach programs are necessary for people who need help but often struggle on their own rather than ask for help. Where family members and kin support are lacking, these networks or their substitutes must be created. In fact, estrangement or divorce is not unusual among couples who lose a child through death.

Family mental health clinics need to provide a whole array of special services designed to prevent family dissolution from this and other preventable causes. Marriages usually do not break up when communication is open and constructive. When family dissolution does occur, much skill is needed to minimize damage to the next generation. One can assume that marital dissolution puts adults and their children at risk. Many children are caught in destructive custody battles, parent visitation issues, and the management of relationships with mothers and/or fathers and with the rest of their families. Support groups are helpful. Some people, however, are not at ease in groups, find them frightening, and do better when seen individually by counselors or therapists. In any case young people and their families are entitled to help as early as possible.

Work with the reconstituted family can be very gratifying for family workers, as two adults, each with children from a previous marriage, merge their households and share their lives. This requires forming a whole series of new relationships, each family bringing with it the scripts and experiences not only of the family of the present partner but also of the absent partner. Often there is much hostility toward the children's absent biological parent, especially if the previous marriages have ended in unhappy divorces, yet the children are bonded to these absent parents. So often feelings and concerns go unspoken only ultimately to surface in damaging behavior. Group work can be very useful when it is preventive: Members of the newly emerging family must learn to feel safe in articulating their fears, to feel heard and understood.

Adding a new member through adoption is an exciting family venture that brings with it new tensions, new experiences, and new configurations. Agencies that provide adoption programs, especially those for older children and for children and adoptive parents of different racial and ethnic backgrounds, do better if they offer adoptive families much preparation and a close relationship with a family clinic staff knowledgeable and sensitive about the special issues of older-child or interethnic adoption. Early support and educational group ties between families undergoing this experience prevent future difficulties.

Intensive services are often needed by families in which one or more members have experienced traumas early in their lives. The lingering pain experienced when young often has a strong effect on adjustment later in life. Young families in which a member has been raised by parents with alcohol issues, lost a parent early in life, experienced multiple out-of-family placements and loss of connections, or been a victim of physical or sexual abuse may need and are entitled to assistance during the many later transitions and central events during the life cycle, such as choosing a marital partner or career, beginning a family, or losing a family member. A community clinic helps clients understand the origins of their own behaviors and actions and clarify personal values and goals. It also teaches some skills for taking responsibility and making decisions. How to know one's feelings and how to express them so as not to interfere with everyday functioning often need to be taught.

Helping systems that offer an array of services can get clients into support groups, and help provide access to normalizing community activities. Nonetheless, clinic staff need to be available for some families over a long period of time as needed, if only by telephone, to prevent crisis and regression.

Clinics that offer intensive assessment and short-term services for a family crisis can be very effective. In many situations, however, the crisis model is not as useful as intensive intervention for a specified period, with a planned decrease in contact. This is much more effective than clinic reinvolvement on a crisis-by-crisis basis.

One child's difficulties are often the focus for initial intervention. An intensive assessment should be done of the target child whose symptoms initially communicated family problems. Psychological testing will often reveal perceptual difficulties that have contributed to the child's lack of skills needed to escape the scapegoat or victim role. No matter how severe a disability the child may exhibit, different families cope differently. These unique coping patterns need to be understood and those that are constructive, enhanced. Programs that concentrate on the interactions of the whole family within the historical context of each family member are more effective than child-centered clinic programs. Working with the whole family to the extent possible, we prevent the isolation of a targeted child.

An effective model engages the family in working out a family map or "genogram," with dates of significant events such as marriage, birth, adoption, death.

The use of a genogram in the study of a family is now as basic a piece of information as the family surname. It is a structural framework which enables the student to diagram in simple terms the general information (names, dates, etc.) and the complex information (triangles, repetitive family issues and scripts) about a family in concrete and easily understood terms. It also has the advantage of allowing a variety of facts to be read at a glance, instead of a wordy treatise that would require a periodic review to refresh a student's memory on what has been previously learned. It is a simple, but completely organized, "road map" of the ongoing life in a family across three generations. [Pendagast and Sherman 1984:101]

Besides identifying factual information about the extended family and its members on the genogram, the nature of relationships by marriage, by adoption, and so forth needs to be clarified. How people label family members by nicknames tells how roles and aspirations are projected onto different family members. The genealogical map points out the quality of linkages and connections—who connects with whom and how closely, and which relationships are close, distant, or conflictual.

For people to construct a genogram, family members need to join together. This often involves extensive search for relatives. Many people today simply do not have information on the whereabouts of their family of origin and relatives. Individuals are dispersed throughout the continent, have moved about a lot, and have often not been in touch for years. Such knowledge is obtainable, though it may require much hard work. Identifying, searching out, and creating linkages is therapeutic for all involved. The person looking for connections often also responds to the isolation and loneliness of others in the family, and is soon perceived by them as performing a valued function [Low 1984]. Indeed, as networks get formed, all participants begin to perceive themselves differently. Once the ties are formed, the path to self-understanding is easier. Choosing or rejecting values, expectations, and patterns becomes conscious, rather than seeming to be a predetermined matter over which the individual has no control. The therapeutic and educational encounter is then well on its way.

Families in need of help are very often isolated. If, in fact, they are not alone, they nevertheless position themselves to be isolated and therefore perceive themselves this way. The objective of the therapeutic encounter is to open options and possibilities. To do that effectively, actually connecting with others is far more valuable to people than just talking about such possible connections. Creation of the family tree or genogram fosters that possibility [Low 1984:37].

Because of the migrant and immigrant nature of our society and the size of our country, separations have been both geographic and emotional. Some of these can be avoided. Others can be acknowledged, their ramifications understood and dealt with. Migrant parents and grandparents have left their homes, their families, their communities, and their pasts. Regardless of the outcome of that exodus, whether the migrants came voluntarily or not, did or did not realize their hopes and their dreams, they endured much often-unarticulated pain. To bury the pain and actualize the dreams, the next generation was given the message to acculturate to the dominant group. Often families have changed their names—Gennaro became Gerald, Feinstein became Stone—or suffered silently the indignity of being given a new name by an insensitive immigration officer or an indifferent slave trader. Some families believed that their offspring would not be able to get ahead if their names identified them as from a particular ethnic group. Parents and their children often no longer share a common language; this is even more common between grandparents and grandchildren.

Because of these generational breaks, Americans developed the idea that family life centers on the creation of nuclear families, denying the fact that we are all linked to previous generations in who we are, how we function, think, believe, and behave [Pendagast and Sherman 1984]. This has led to many painful and unnecessary breaks between family members and to widespread isolation and loneliness.

One of the key ingredients in systemic work is practitioners' flexibility and creativity. Mature, competent practitioners adapt their method, style, and timing to the pace of each family and its individual members. Adaptability is the crux. There are families that cannot be seen as a group until later on in the process. There are families so involved with the symptoms of their child that early work on their genogram would be counterproductive; we would quickly lose them. Of course, whatever way we begin with a family, the clinical model described here is intended for families who can and do get themselves to appointments.

Working with clients effectively and creatively is related to the therapist's ability to tune in and not be distracted by her or his own family agenda and scripts. A family therapist trained to work effectively with this emotionally taxing model needs extensive training. At present this training is provided by only a few centers throughout the country, and it requires extensive work by the therapist on his or her own family. Only this kind of self-knowledge avoids "contamination" of the therapeutic process by the therapist's personal agendas.

SPECIAL EDUCATION

In the United States the school is a normal environment in which children grow, learn, and work. There are families with children who cannot function in ordinary community schools without special attention or classes. The ability of school districts to meet these special needs varies greatly. Many communities have done a remarkable job in providing special education, through resource rooms and special classes for moderately retarded, learning disabled, emotionally disturbed, and sometimes hearing and visually handicapped youngsters. In general these classrooms are monitored to assure as much mainstreaming as possible for each child. The extent and effectiveness of these programs varies according to the values of the community and the commitment of their administrative and educational staff.

Whether a special education program can function in a community school depends on the perspective the school provides all its students about those who may have markedly different physical and behavioral characteristics. Children with special needs are often ridiculed and teased on playgrounds and school buses. A constructive, accepting, enabling message needs to come from the community to the school board, to the district administrators, to the professional staff, to the bus driver, and to the children. Early teaching of empathy and caring to our school-age population could pay handsome dividends in a society that is often sadly lacking in these attributes.

Community school mainstreaming is educationally sound. But special needs students who can be integrated into normal classrooms for homeroom or individual subjects should be given high priority. When youngsters with special needs are excluded from a course because the course is completely filled by others and they are not given an equal chance or even priority in the initial registration, this is patently unfair. Teachers should be carefully chosen for their interest and skill in meeting the extra challenges posed by these children. Reading specialists and individual instruction time must be made available, and hands-on learning must be encouraged.

Where special classrooms are called for, they should be located in places that demonstrate a commitment to mainstreaming. When a special classroom is stashed away in a dingy basement corner of a leased building because there is no "extra" space in the regular school, the community sends a clear message about its seriousness in this service.

When a school district simply cannot provide an adequate education for a youngster in need, or when the young person's behavior is such that she or he jeopardizes the safety of others, education may have to be purchased from a private school that offers a day treatment program.

DAY TREATMENT PROGRAMS

In some situations a family-oriented psychoeducational team must intervene because the children's difficulties in school are so deeply rooted in their family lives. Only a very comprehensive program targeting family issues can alleviate destructive classroom behaviors sufficiently for learning to occur.

There are three types of day treatment programs: One clearly identifies the child as the "patient" and focuses on providing intensive clinical services to the child in a classroom milieu.

The second is family-focused and seeks to provide optimal education services for the child in a classroom modeled after a community school, but is staffed by highly trained special education teachers with behavior management skills. Intensive clinical help is directed primarily to the family. Group work with the children and intensive communication and collaboration with the education staff provide an optimum learning milieu while many changes are encouraged in the youth's home environment.

The third model, a combination of the first two, assures intensive, highly integrated individual and group clinical services for the youngster, a carefully structured clinical-educational milieu, and highly coordinated intensive family services. This model is extremely helpful for youngsters who exhibit behavior difficulties, often because of specific learning disabilities coupled with a family situation in which, for example, two biological parents are not living together and/or are in continuous conflict. The child's learning and perceptual deficits keep him or her from adapting constructively to the stressful home environment, and he or she becomes the conveyor of the family's anxieties and tensions, using the school environment to act them out.

The school district is frequently the primary referring agent. Teachers have given their best, but they are burned out. Not only are the children not learning, but they often put their own safety and that of other students and teachers at risk. The school seeks relief from what has become an intolerable situation. The youngster is referred to a private program for which the schools are often financially liable, so that the youngster's behaviors can be sufficiently modified to allow reintegration into a community school.

In these situations the school district is legally responsible to provide education and, therefore, needs an answer quickly as to whether a day treatment program will or will not accept the child, so that if need be the district can look elsewhere. But the transfer even when authorized and supported by the district leaves a residue of failure for everyone involved.

Not only have the child and the family experienced failure, the community school, too, has experienced failure. All parties—the education staff, the children, and their families—have done the very best they know how. But their efforts have not succeeded. Now each party has its own agenda.

Families who have had to struggle with a child with borderline neurological attention disorders or minimal brain dysfunction often feel blamed for their child's nonperformance. If the family does not perceive the same level of difficulty at home, the parents are confused. Often they themselves have had major difficulties in school while growing up, and some of the disappointments and hurts inflicted then hang on. The family, in turn, blames the school because their child is not learning, is repeating grades, and sooner or later presents massive behavioral problems. If the education staff were competent, the parents argue, the school would not experience difficulties with the child. So the school, too, is on the defensive. Teachers also feel blame for the child's nonperformance. School and teachers are often under excessive and unrealistic pressure to produce positive test results from all their charges. They cannot afford too many children who lower the curve. Scapegoating inevitably results, with the child caught in the middle. With their parents complaining about their teachers and their teachers critical of their parents, children are left confused and helpless. They often express this confusion and helplessness through aberrant classroom behaviors that get them thrown out.

When a child and family are referred to a day treatment program, the needs, wishes, hopes, and fears of the child, the family, and the school staff must be understood by the day treatment staff. This understanding must be integrated into an assessment-engagement approach by the professionals, building trust while learning about each other. If, for example, the family were aware of its own contribution to the problem, it would be engaged in counseling, and the child's community school attendance would be more manageable. The family must learn about the day treatment program, understand its role in the program, and be given a choice as to whether to participate. That participation becomes a requirement for their child's admission to the program. In a sense, therefore, family members are in control as to whether the program will admit their child. Sometimes families need to be given time to think about whether they do or do not want to participate. Several visits with staff may be needed to work through fears and ambivalence. For day treatment to be effective in these situations, the family needs to be engaged in working with the program, perhaps initially on behalf of their child. Over time, they may learn enough about themselves that family feelings and interactions can change. Once initial engagement and admission have been accomplished, the youngster may be placed in a therapeutic educational environment. The child can then grow and learn at an appropriate pace for him or her, without the need to divert energy into maladaptive and counterproductive behaviors just to survive.

Unhappily, this family engagement and decision-making process is often in conflict with the needs of the school searching for an educational program for a child they can no longer maintain. The ideal process has been described above. At times this requires careful adaptation so that legal educational mandates can be met while assuring optimal family participation. The outcome is dependent upon the collaborative, mutually empathic effort between the community school and the day treatment staff.

Just as the youth's educational program must be carefully and individually designed, so must the family work be carefully tailored. Initially family work may focus on the youngster's school behaviors and learning issues in the classroom, but as these become manageable, other home and family issues surface. Often the way the youngster is positioned and perceived in the family is crucial. The family may be delegating symptoms to the child, with Mom, for example, in the rescuer slot, at least in the beginning. As the child begins to experience some classroom success, other much more pertinent family issues can and must be addressed.

Sometimes it is difficult to engage the whole family. The mother is often more ready to involve herself in the process than the father. For the program to demand that all family members attend every meeting is too rigid. But the byproduct of a family approach is that, as changes take place in any member of the group, others are affected. There is no more powerful incentive for a family member to get involved than the need to protect one's turf and the threatened status quo. Family members who choose not to involve themselves initially begin to experience change in other family members over which they have no control. At that point the nonparticipating family members will want to become engaged also. The therapeutic function of the day treatment program is to validate all family members.

Problem-solving and negotiation skills, avoiding blame and put-downs, are some of the most difficult relationship tasks to master. But when teachers, clinicians, and families work together to work out their differences and apprehensions, a great deal of teaching through modeling goes on. As people begin to feel better about themselves, they begin to feel better about each other. This aspect of the day treatment program can then free children to learn and function appropriately without constantly needing to test the system's limits.

All people need to feel accepted and valued by the people with whom they live and work. They also need to feel safe enough to be themselves. When children experience success in a program carefully designed for their real level of ability, they can prepare to return to a regular classroom or a special education classroom in the community school. Since their community school experience in the past has been negative and fraught with tension, the thought of returning brings with it apprehension and often regression to earlier counterproductive ways of coping. The careful preparation of the school, the child, and the family is crucial. The availability of a specialist who can carefully and skillfully effect this transfer is important. Many children who have successfully moved on from Parsons' Day Treatment Program would not have succeeded without the help of a special community school coordinator to provide immediate practical consultation during the critical adjustment to the unknown from the known, and to monitor the child's performance.

Services to the family may need to continue after the young person has returned to a community school. It is best if these services can be provided by the same practitioner who was involved with the family while the child attended a day treatment program. Often agency caseloads and program design require that a client be transferred to another worker or even a different department at a time when the family is under the greatest stress. Caseloads are always a problem, but people's needs often are not compatible with routine case assignment patterns. The return to the community school where everyone concerned had experienced so much failure and pain places all parties at renewed risk of failure unless familiar supports continue. As people begin to settle in, contacts can decrease, although staff need to remain available as needed. If the family still needs long-term family work—even though the youngster can function in the community school—referral to an outpatient program should occur.

RETURN TO COMMUNITY EDUCATION AND
PREPARATION FOR WORK

While families work to reduce tension and stress so that day-to-day living tasks can be performed better, the youngsters need to be offered a variety of training and experiences in daily living and coping. Communities, however, often lack activity programs for young people with special needs. Even schools that have ably provided for the classroom needs of the special education child have been much weaker in providing for the social needs of that child. Special education classroom youngsters usually do not get invited to parties and informal gatherings, on picnics and trips. They do not have the social skills to seek social entry. Even when parents of other youngsters encourage their children to include a neighborhood special-needs child in their social activities, this rarely works, because the child forced upon a group will soon provide a valid reason for eviction. Children and adolescents usually do not reach out for help in making social links, and these children quickly find themselves excluded.

Special education programs in community and private schools would do well to create buddy systems to encourage their young people to bring students with special needs into club and other social activities. These activities work best when not limited only to special-needs children. If they provide an opportunity for mixing all kinds of students, they not only help the special students to be reintegrated into the community but establish for the young people some ongoing friendships in the community after the special club or program has ended. The development of a brother/sister program between a community public or private school and a special education private school can also be invaluable, as can activities, such as dances, roller skating parties, and picnics.

Many young people somehow manage to stay on in school even though they continue to fail year after year. They are chronic nonreaders whose vulnerable self-esteem keeps deteriorating under what can only be described as a system of academic negligence, if not outright abuse. Some young people respond by intermittent or constant truancy. Others become dropouts. This educational failure is a tragedy of wasted lives and human potential. The challenge has not been sufficiently met in many communities. The families of the youths are often the politically weakest citizens. If they had power, our educational programs might be quite different. It might be helpful to include these families in designing programs to better meet their children's needs.

Some young people do not do well in classrooms that are academically oriented. These youths need smaller teaching units that use hands-on and very concrete learning. The learning environment needs to follow the model of a workplace. Apprentice job assignments can be extremely valuable, in which a young person can learn to develop job skills. In a hands-on experience with success, many a nonreader has learned to read to be able to follow directions. Learning for the sake of learning has not worked, but learning in the context of a success-related experience with an employer can have impressive results.

A SPECIAL VOCATIONAL PROGRAM

Hands-on and technical education need strengthening in many school districts. Much emphasis is often placed on academic subjects for students programmed to fail in them. No young person can be subjected to daily failure without being seriously scarred. Much more work needs to be done with the non-college-bound curriculum with more supervised field experience, in which students can succeed. These critical issues are addressed by a few isolated sophisticated programs. Some involve education–private industry partnerships.

For example, in Lexington, Massachusetts,

More than 300 students at Minuteman Regional Vocational Technical School were directly involved in the construction of a state-of-the-art child-care center on the school's 65-acre campus.... The $500,000 building is the result of a partnership between this public school and Lincoln Laboratory, a high-technology research laboratory run by the Massachusetts Institute of Technology. The laboratory, located about a mile from the campus, wanted to provide child care for children of its 3,500 employees. [Walters 1990:C–8]

This effort engaged not only youth at all levels of construction but involved early-childhood-education students in design and choice of materials. Students will continue to maintain the building. The possibilities of a venture like this are limitless to enhance skills, self-image, and motivation of non-college-bound youth. The future of vocational education is in projects like these.

Parsons Child and Family Center has had some excellent results with an after-school vocational education program for youth who are not succeeding in the regular schools, have histories of truancy, and are not doing well even in the Parsons special school for troubled youngsters. These programs are run two or three afternoons a week for two hours. Youngsters check in, sign time cards, and are paid for attendance as if they were in a training program with an employer. Some time is spent on necessary remedial reading. The remaining time is spent on particular skills training, like carpentry, food services, maintenance work, or computer science. The youth are highly motivated, attend consistently, and perform well. Instructors emphasize appropriate behavior for employment and function as quasi–job supervisors rather than teachers. As soon as a youth demonstrates the ability to function appropriately, she or he is matched with outside employers for an after-school job. The vocation education liaison staff remain closely involved and monitor adjustment to the job situation.

This vocational program has worked not only with youngsters who have had difficulties with the law but also with emotionally troubled youth. The reason for success is that the program is highly individualized, and expectations are individually tailored for success. The time youths spend in this program is limited, and the monetary reward is concrete and attractive. The youth know that they are being trained for real life, namely work. They experience skill, success, and confidence—primary factors in motivation and managing frustration.

As the work force crisis increases nationally, and employers are not able to fill their positions, there is hope for movement toward valuing all our people and what they have to contribute. As we develop volunteer networks, there could be partnerships in which competent but retired senior citizen volunteers work in a supportive relationship with a young person who requires one-to-one monitoring in the workplace. Other volunteers could include owners of small businesses, such as garages, laundries, small restaurants, and shops, to provide invaluable hands-on learning. Sometimes large industrial establishments can provide excellent supervised jobs. Often such placements are provided with the support of a manager or union leader who has experienced the pain of a family member in need of special help.

Families and youth in need of apprentice training placements can network in their own extended families and communities in search of such supervised work training opportunities. Too often families with youngsters who have special education needs are discounted as resources. These families often have much to offer if engaged as partners. Their inclusion, however, must be genuine. If practitioners are apprehensive about the partnership and provide lip service only, the attempt will fail.

CONCLUSION

All families need support as they embark on the challenge of childrearing. If extended family support networks are available for an intact two-parent household, that is certainly optimal. However, with the dramatic increase in families with both parents in the work force, single-parent households, and reconstituted families, plus the challenge of continuing geographic mobility, these conditions do not describe the majority of families. An array of community systems, from the natural to the special, acts on the belief that all human beings are valuable, and that a society must adapt its systems to support changes in the primary child-care provider, the family.

Support should begin with wellness programs for all, to prevent people from feeling alone and abandoned. Family resource centers, adult education programs, and community programs, sponsored by churches, ethnic community centers, YMCAs, and YWCAs, can perform these functions through imaginative programming. The needs, skills, and resources of our often still healthy and energetic retired population can assist in many childrearing and family support tasks. Day care, after-school programs, and special programs for children not seriously ill but who temporarily cannot be in regular programs are part of the natural continuum.

Available community resources need to be better utilized. The use of school buildings and community school bus systems, especially during idle nonschool hours, should be carefully considered. Older adults who have no other easy way to move around their community could also be in contact with children in this way.

Besides normal wellness supports, we need to include mental health clinic and counseling programs, and day treatment programs for populations with special needs. Regular and special vocational education is needed to assure productive participation in society for all people. This participation is essential for the individual; but it is also essential because the skills and contribution of every citizen will be needed in the decades to come as major skilled and unskilled labor shortages arise in our effort to maintain our standard of living and a competitive edge in world markets.

NOTE

1. As of the fall of 1986 there were 978,924 children of working mothers in the United States five to fourteen years of age caring for themselves. During August 1986 when school was not in session, the figure exceeded 2.5 million children [U.S. Bureau of the Census 1990:371].

6

Outreach Preventive Services: Families at Risk

Associated with the massive changes in American society, there are families in every community who fail to provide the housing, nutrition, medical care, and child care required to assure success for the next generation in family living and in the workplace. Due to longstanding histories of family and individual difficulties, many of these people are unable to use the support services described in chapter 5; they are well known to their communities and to all helping community agencies.

These families show little progress for all the effort invested in them. They consume a large share of the social services and Medicaid budgets of their communities, often because of needs and illnesses that would be prevented by healthier, more productive lifestyles. This affluent society is only beginning to get a grip on situations that generate child abuse, domestic violence, and family member eviction. The victims too often are children who as adults become the populations of our penal systems.

FROM CHILDREN'S SERVICES TO FAMILY SERVICES

With the passage of the Social Security Act of 1935, federally funded Aid to Dependent Children was established to discourage out-of-home placement of children merely because of family poverty. The 1939 White House Conference for Children and Youth emphasized that it was wrong to remove children from their families for reasons of poverty alone.

But the latest milestone in family social legislation is the federal Adoption Assistance and Child Welfare Act, Public Law 96–272. Enacted on 17 June 1980 with the overwhelming support of both houses of Congress and a commitment to its philosophy and approach coming from a broad range of federal, state, and local officials; interested professionals; foster parents; adoptive parents; and children's advocates . . . [The act] reflects the belief that a piecemeal approach to child welfare reform . . . will not work. [McGowen and Meezan 1983:120]

The issues are no longer just families' financial need, as with Aid to Families with Dependent Children (AFDC); the issues are family dysfunction and dissolution. One of the major accomplishments of PL 96–272 is a redirection of inappropriate foster care and institutional placements by providing clear financial incentives to states to develop prevention of out-of-family placement, as well as family reunification for children in placement. The act provides adoption subsidies for children who cannot be returned to their biological kin but are considered difficult to place with adoptive families because they are older, there are several children in a family who should not be separated, or they are members of minorities, and/or they have other special needs. This law is the first comprehensive piece of legislation to support family permanency for children and accept the hypothesis that family living is the best possible childrearing environment in our society. Now there are some fiscal incentives for a state to invest in prevention alternatives to the destructive, unmonitored placement of children.

Nonetheless, the law still addresses these problems as child welfare issues rather than making family preservation the primary issue, with the welfare of children its natural byproduct. This emphasis is understandable from a historical perspective. The children's advocacy movement began with the necessary and purposeful removal of children from adult almshouses. While an advocacy system for children may remain politically necessary, a comprehensive family advocacy approach comes closer to current needs.

Preventive services discussed in this chapter address what is called "tertiary prevention," in that they address the needs of people who have not been able to use the usual supports and services in their communities. Because of the act's restrictive mandate in its funding mechanisms, preventive services are often deliberately aimed only at populations that have at least one member at a high risk of placement.[1] Such an approach raises problems—often we are able to provide too little too late. When funds are appropriately allocated, however, other children in the family who are not at imminent risk of placement may benefit.

Families at risk are often referred to as "multiproblem," "disorganized," or "underorganized" families. They are families in perpetual crisis who are unwilling and frequently unsuccessful users of the smorgasbord of human services, draining the financial and personnel resources of a community. Working with these families is very frustrating, and the outcomes are difficult to measure [Kagan and Schlosberg 1989a].

Families in need of preventive services are often those whose children were historically removed to foster care. As a child got into difficulty, she or he was removed from the family. After the first child was removed, another usually took on the job of expressing the family's pain and dysfunction by acting-out, destructive behavior. This child was then also removed, and the process continued. Such families felt helpless and hopeless. They withdrew from contact with their children; and when they did not keep family appointments with the placement agency, they were labeled as "resistive." To the extent that states have not implemented or have been weak in the implementation of the mandates of the new Adoption Assistance and Child Welfare Act, these families are still families of children in foster care.

These are serious child welfare issues, but the problems and their solutions lie with the adult family members. The adult difficulties are so entrenched and repetitive that the needs and potential of the family members must be assessed and defined differently in order to avoid the high human costs of disconnecting children from their kin. Whether disconnections are temporary or forever, they always cause heavy damage to the affected and to future generations.

FAMILIES IN TROUBLE

The adult members of families in need of preventive services have experienced little success or validation. They have had minimal and usually inconsistent nurture, structure, or predictability during their own growing-up years. Adult relationships frequently lack legal bonding, and the children in the family may have different fathers. Welfare regulations often require that fathers of children remain out of the house for the family to be welfare-eligible.

Some families in trouble are multigenerational, with a grandmother just barely holding the family together with minimal emotional and financial resources. Such a grandparent may be a constant critic of a daughter's lack of control over her own children in the family. Some of these families are strongly committed to their children; some are ambivalent; some seem outright rejecting. But no matter how they feel, the noise level in the family is often such that any positive interaction or expression of caring or concern is quickly drowned out by the next crisis or episode of destructive behavior. Their lifestyles give them little respite from chronic day-to-day hardships and no sense of accomplishment.

Law enforcement agencies, such as police, probation officers, family court judges, and child protective workers, are all well known to these families. For years everyone has been trying to change some part of their behavior so that its destructive, negative aspects do not impinge on society. School officials are inevitably involved because the children are often truant, have learning difficulties, and behave disruptively in the classroom.

Behavior is impulsive, and the outcome expected usually does not go beyond the immediate gratification it is to provide. "Drinking makes me feel good for the moment." "Having a baby could be fun; the baby will be my very own and will love me." These are familiar attitudes to family workers. Many of the adults are very young emotionally, yet the problems with which they must cope call for good judgment and a high level of frustration tolerance. Above all, these families are chronically resentful and feel unfairly victimized and misunderstood. When asked about the kind of help they want most, often they say they want to get the department of social services or the probation officer "off our backs."

These clients are frequently unemployed, sporadically employed, or underemployed. Work histories have been inconsistent. Job training efforts have varied in success. They may have been incarcerated. They usually have had poor school histories and have often been school dropouts. Many adults have marginal intelligence; they may have neurological problems that add to their impulsive and unpredictable behavior. Some have had extensive contact with mental health agencies because of depression and assaultive or self-destructive behavior. Many have been foster children for at least part of their lives. Most recently the incidence of drug abuse has surfaced as a critical concern.

These families are disconnected. Individuals often lack knowledge about their extended family, and they do not seem to be connected to others. They lack the skill to develop their own support network. Therefore, they reach out through their negative and destructive behavior to such community agencies as the child protective system, police department, and the court; only in this way can they feel actively engaged and alive. At least there are these negative networks; there is action; and they do experience some structure, limits, and concern.

WORKING WITH FAMILIES IN NEED

Fragmented services, funded by a number of state agencies in conflict with each other, are seldom useful. Andrew Selig suggests that the service system creates "multiproblem families" through the fragmentation of services by multiple providers who work at cross-purposes and do not communicate with each other. Often they do not even respect each other, each taking full ownership of the client and offering advice that cancels out the plans and strategies of the other providers [Selig 1976]. Providing an array of services each targeted to alleviate only one particular symptom—alcoholism, risk of teenage pregnancy, drug abuse, domestic violence—is probably wasted without ongoing directed, skillful coordination. When there is no coordination, one service provider with the best of intentions may offset whatever the others are attempting to do. Participation by the families, when it does occur, is often merely compliance with attendance requirements rather than true engagement.

These in-need families do not ask for help, and often refuse it. When ordered to receive help, they cooperate marginally or not at all. With the nature and history of the client populations, an official command is often necessary for them to accept services. If this were not so, these families would already be clients of voluntary clinics and other nonmandated community services. The mandate to accept services usually comes from the child protective agency or the court. These families have long histories of involvement with the public agency, often for more than one generation. Since they move often, some families are known to the department of social services in more than one county or community.

Many of their contacts have been negative. Too often workers lack the professional training necessary to handle the stress and complexity of working with these families. Department of public welfare staffs are chronically overworked, which leads to excessive staff turnover and repetitive client failure as the inevitable outcome.

The service delivery system has to understand this stonewalling. When dealing with multiproblem families, well-tried methods of verbal counseling are useless. The principles are helpful, but methods and work styles must be adapted to these families' particular needs and conditions. Programs must reach out. It is unrealistic to expect these clients to come to child guidance or mental health clinics and adapt to the staff's nine-to-five working day. The old social work practice principle that one needs to begin where the client is still holds true. These clients, though well known to providers, often barricade themselves to keep people out, lest they get hurt. The pain is intense, but for good reason they have never learned to trust. These people have been programmed for failure and disappointment.

Whenever possible, protective or law-enforcing action should be separated from therapy. To this end, the public agency can subcontract with a voluntary provider to do the family work. Subcontracting allows separate implementation and monitoring of the necessarily tight legal mandates to assure permanent parenting of a child. With this separation the voluntary agency worker can establish goals with clients that they can own. Often this means allowing clients to take charge of their lives and to eliminate what they perceive as interference by the public agency. To successfully mix this therapeutic function with a protective or legal mandate is almost impossible.

The public agency protective worker or probation officer should have a good relationship with the voluntary agency staff. The objectives and strategies of working with and on behalf of the family need to be negotiated among them. Everyone needs to be clear as to his or her role and to know who is responsible for which functions.

The intensive involvement of one family services worker is usually preferable to the confusing involvement of many agencies. Of course, this does not preclude individual family members having special needs. If a child wants or needs to join a recreation program, the worker's task is to help the parents assume their legitimate role of inquiring about and visiting the program, discussing the possibility with the child, and finally deciding whether the child should consider enrolling. The worker's task is never to act on behalf of a parent or unwittingly usurp the parent role. If day care, after-school programs, or day camp is called for, the worker's responsibility is to put the parent in charge while assisting the parent in gaining program access. The constant message must be, "These are your children; only you know what is best for them and what you want for them."

The client and the worker can develop a partnership early by recognizing that the worker is mandated to help the client family so that a particular acting-out child will not have to leave home. Together, worker and client need to outline what has to change. The family must be included as part of the team so that discussion occurs with the family, and not just about the family; if family members are excluded, they are left helpless, distressed, and legitimately paranoid about others' plans for them. This model of team effort and mutual respect can be very helpful to a struggling family that is trying to understand what some of the benefits might be if it were to change its operating style. They are asked to do things differently. These families have a style they know; the known may be unsatisfactory, but the unknown is frightening.

The parent, often developmentally an adult child, is desperately in need of success, structure, and predictability. Tasks to be accomplished have to be concrete—"Bill will be home at six for supper every night." Global objectives, such as the parent "will help her or his child improve self-esteem," are too vague and too confusing for the client.

Furthermore, the adults themselves must experience nurture, caring, and the value of constructive communications. Assistance with concrete tasks may involve helping a parent to negotiate with the public systems. Johnny may need a bed; Susie may need a public school placement that allows for some success; Mother may need help with grocery shopping, menu planning, and money management. Help in getting a turkey for Thanksgiving, for example, can be very important.

Family group work is often best done during sessions that provide food— lunch, dinner, snacks. With some families it is best to begin in their own home.

With others, sessions can start in an agency or community building, but then transportation and child care for very young children are usually necessary.

During the earliest assessment phase, the social and psychological assets of each family member must be identified. Family group work can begin by asking family members to list each others' assets, things a person does well, such as throwing a ball, shampooing hair, cooking spaghetti sauce, fixing the plumbing. Helping families think this way is not easy. They often use only negative language. Validation of all family members must occur before any change can begin.

Many preventive services clients see themselves as victims. This attitude needs modification for any progress to occur. Families need coaching on their rights with the housing authority, the department of social services, and with the landlord. But people have to know how to communicate in a way that will get them the response they need. Teaching effective communication is often the first step toward placing power and authority in the hands of the family's adults where power and authority belong. The social worker is simultaneously reparenting to redo early inadequate parenting, teaching skills, and doing advocacy so that the adult clients can negotiate important concrete issues that will improve the family's quality of life. As people experience some success, they become more confident.

Many preventive services clients are very much alone even though they often live in congested areas. They do not belong to anyone, and no one belongs to them. Once some concrete tasks have been accomplished, human connections must be built. With some families, work on a family genogram is possible. Some family members do have relatives with whom they could connect; it is worth the effort to try.

With some families group work is too disruptive, and it is helpful to divide the family for family sessions. For example, a worker may work with the mother and some preschool toddlers on house maintenance issues while the other youngsters are in school. If there is a father, some sessions may involve both parents without the children. Salvador Minuchin and Braulio Montalvo, who are well known for their interesting work with explosive families, support this approach.

Disorganized families from low socioeconomic populations require adaptations of traditional family therapy and therapeutic style that take into account their specific characteristics of communication, cognition and ways of experiencing affect. Rather than treating the members of one family as a single unit, we have found it effective to treat various subgroupings by first working with the family's natural subgroupings. [Minuchin and Montalvo 1967:887]

In this article they describe imaginative teaching of self-awareness in a family where two older daughters met with one therapist, while the mother and another therapist watched through a one-way mirror. The mother was seen as an equal in that relationship with the therapist, and learns to observe her children, their interactions, and emotions as she was unable to when in the room with them, since her authoritative style immediately brought forth conflict. At the same time the therapist available to the mother was able to be a model for useful attitudes, and coach her in them. However, with many families this phase may have to wait until some concrete services have been offered.

Jobs, of course, are a critical issue. Which family members work outside the home? Is their pay reasonable? What are the family attitudes toward work? Has anyone ever had a positive experience in the workplace? The acquisition of vocational skills and assistance with job search may be needed. Sometimes sheltered employment is appropriate. Attention to these crucial concerns must be carefully timed.

Therapeutic interventions open options and extend hope that things can be different. When there are options, there are decisions to be made. People who make decisions have power. This needs to be repeated over and over again. What is simple common sense to those who have always managed their own lives is not at all simple for people who have neither seen nor experienced real decision making during their own growing up.

The physical environment in which families live is often unsafe for young children. Although all young children have accidents, these families are more accident-prone, both because of hazards in the home environment and because the adults tend not to think or act preventively. Crisis anticipation, prevention, and management are major tasks for them in the therapeutic process.

Ongoing crises in a variety of forms will inhibit or delay constructive change. Constant crisis has been the family's style of operation for years. The baby is rushed to the emergency room of the hospital late at night with a temperature of 105 degrees. But a telephone call to the doctor and perhaps an office or clinic visit when the child first showed signs of illness could have prevented the high temperature and possible complications in the first place.

Parent effectiveness training has been very helpful to highly motivated, articulate parents who cope well in other areas but feel ill at ease with children and are interested in learning how best to function and communicate with them. Moreover, the group aspect of training can be very supportive. With families who need preventive services, however, parenting education is best done through coaching and modeling in a one-to-one relationship. The adults in the family must themselves take charge of their lives and of their children. For this to affect the children, the worker must model respect and esteem for the adults. As we carefully nurture these families, they can begin to experience and perceive themselves differently, and their parenting improves.

Messages given to children can always be improved, but that is only fine-tuning. How people feel, not what they say, is vital. Affect and emotions cannot be taught. Clients served by preventive services programs are usually not ready to benefit from parent effectiveness training.

It is always emotionally stressful when a worker who is both advocate and mentor for a family must report them for child abuse. Even though reporting is necessary and can be used constructively and therapeutically, staff often personalize these episodes and see them as therapeutic failures.

STAFF SUPPORT

The fewer different workers involved in preventive helping initially, the better the result for the family. But prevention workers need their own built-in support structure. A very small caseload is essential, with no more than ten cases per worker, fewer if financially feasible. A skilled supervisor must be available to assist in creative planning and implementation, and above all to support the worker during inevitable periods of crisis and discouragement. Client progress is very slow; at times the worker may find the situation frightening. Many families in need live in unsafe neighborhoods, and adequate security protection for workers must be provided. Some situations require that two staff members make a home visit together. Given the crisis-prone behavior of families, a supervisor often needs to pick up on a case quickly and knowledgeably when a worker is absent or unavailable.

Psychiatric and psychological consultants can play an important role. They, of course, contribute to the initial assessment and treatment plan, and to ongoing reviews. Those consultants who are willing to join a family worker on-site are particularly supportive. Team consultants who do not hesitate to go to a client's home do best, but they are hard to find and hire. In-home assessments often give a better understanding of a family much more rapidly.

Seeing the client's actual environment can help in the development of concrete, creative intervention strategies and methods. Seeing a laundromat half a block away from the family's apartment may suggest to the worker that one of the teenagers assume responsibility for doing the family's laundry; Mom can share some homemaking responsibilities while offering an older child status and the opportunity to learn skills for future self-dependence. Visiting the client's home and neighborhood makes it easier for the worker and the consultant to understand the family's crisis-prone behavior. The suitability of the home for a family with children and whether the location allows for ties with others or is totally isolated from neighbors can be quickly assessed on a home visit, as can the family's ability to organize their living environment and therefore their lives. We often begin by assisting people to organize their living arrangements.

Peer support is another necessary ingredient for workers engaged in outreach prevention. In contrast to the clinician who works in an office where there is constant professional peer contact, the outreach worker often feels very much alone while struggling with difficult situations in a threatening community. The client family initially reacts with suspicion and overt or covert anger. This hostility can be frustrating; at times it is outright frightening. Then, when clients begin to engage in the helping relationship, they become tremendously needy, which is also very draining. Knowing that back at the agency there are peers who will empathize with them makes a real difference in staff morale.

The location of the outreach program is an important consideration and often an agency dilemma. If the program is one part of a system of services, it is a good idea to have the outreach staff at the same site with staff of other agency programs. Yet the outreach program should be accessible and seen as part of the community. Under the best of circumstances, outreach staff should be in a facility within the client community that also offers other services, such as day care for children, and has adequate space for a variety of group activities and classes. A public housing project, for example, is a natural setting for preventive services, or they can be set up in local churches, schools, community centers, or even in empty stores.

PUBLIC MANDATES AND REGULATIONS

Non-agency connections are essential and must come from the family's relatives and social system, because this is natural and normative. Only when the socially defined biological kin cannot provide nurturing child care now and will not be able to do so in the future should permanent alternative arrangements be considered and implemented. The federal Adoption Assistance and Child Welfare Act (PL 96–272) provides stringent criteria and guidelines for how this is to be accomplished. Above all, deadlines are established against children's lingering in limbo. Permanently severing a young person's ties to sociobiological kin has many serious and potentially damaging implications, although sometimes ending this relationship is by far the least detrimental alternative. Since temporary removal of children from their families may become permanent, the separation requires cautious, careful consideration.

The state of New York developed a philosophic commitment to permanence for children just as the national mandates were being legislated by PL 96–272. The New York State Child Welfare Reform Act (CWRA) was enacted by the legislature and signed into law by the governor in 1979, and we have had more than a decade of experience with it. An "Evaluation Report to the Governor and the Legislature on Impact and Implementation" was completed in October 1985 [NYS Division of the Budget]. It speaks to much progress in permanency planning efforts for children, including the allocation of funds previously used for children's institutional placement:

Six years after enactment of the CWRA, the number of children in care has been reduced from 44,000 to 25,000; the average length of stay in care for children discharged has been reduced from 3.2 years to 2.5 years; the number of adoptions from foster care has increased as the foster care population has declined; and, preventive services are being provided statewide to over 30,000 children annually. Costs within the child welfare system have been redirected and their growth has been contained. As we envisioned, preventive services expenditures have risen since 1981, but these increases have been more than offset by reductions in foster care maintenance costs. [NYS Division of the Budget 1985:iii–iv]

The report notes further that foster care placement has been averted for 80 percent of the children receiving preventive services [NYS Division of the Budget 1985:4]. Many people throughout the public and voluntary child-care sector have worked with great dedication to accomplish these results.

It is still too early to assess the quality of care being provided; only major longitudinal studies will give us the information needed to assess the effectiveness of these programs on the adult lives of the recipients of preventive services. For example, there is legitimate worry whether we risk too much neglect or abuse of children just to avoid their removal from their families; these are difficult judgments at best.

In order to monitor the quality of care, New York State has mandated a particular case record format, known as the uniform case record (UCR), for all providers of services funded through the Department of Social Services for children in foster care or at risk of foster care. The UCR is designed for two functions: as a tool for supervising and training staff and as a monitoring tool to track children's movement in the system to assure compliance with the law. For training and supervision, the format reflects the philosophic intent of the Child Welfare Reform Act and addresses specific issues of permanency planning. Furthermore, it gives the knowledgeable record reader an overview of the quality of care a family receives. How family and child assets and liabilities, goals and objectives, and the worker's practices are articulated reveals a worker's attitudes, understanding, and intentions. Reviewing this document quickly reveals whether the worker adheres to the timeliness and casework activities mandated by the Child Welfare Reform Act.

The mandated format, however, is accompanied by a system of fiscal sanctions implemented through a record audit mechanism that measures adherence to timeliness and task performance, such as the number and frequency of home visits, but lacks capability to evaluate the quality of care. Therefore, providers can be in complete compliance with Child Welfare Reform Act mandates, although their quality of care may be questionable or even extremely poor. On the other hand, agencies providing high quality care may find themselves penalized for being out of compliance on some minor recording requirement. Moreover, if an agency loses funding because of sanctions, the quality of care can come into jeopardy. Agencies are hiring their own record audit staff to protect themselves, sometimes at the expense of caseload reduction or salary increments needed to retain skilled practitioners. The time needed to maintain these records also reduces a social worker's direct practice time.

County departments of social services are required to use civil service rosters to fill their positions. Yet a person can do exceptionally well on a test without having the values, motivation, or personality to perform well in providing highly skilled case work services to families on the brink of family disruption and child eviction. For some county departments, contracting with voluntary agencies that meet with the standards of national accrediting bodies such as the Council on Accreditation of Services to Families and Children, Inc., provides assurance that the training and experience of the direct service and supervisory staff will provide the care the Child Welfare Reform Act mandates.

A PUBLIC-PRIVATE COLLABORATION IN SERVING FAMILIES

In spite of many inadequacies, there are outstanding examples in the state of New York of collaborative efforts between the public and private sectors to meet the challenge of the Child Welfare Reform Act. The Albany County Department of Social Services, for example, was committed to preventing needless institutionalization of children even before the Child Welfare Reform Act. It has a long history of constructive collaboration with voluntary child-care agencies in Albany and adjoining counties. The department's Children's Division has worked consistently with collaborating agencies to resolve differences in methods, philosophy, and perceptions. The result is a working relationship based on mutual trust, respect, and confidence.

Excellent preventive services programs are now operating in the county, and the providers are members of a coalition. In addition to information sharing, the coalition works to familiarize county legislators with the rationale and financial requirements of preventive services. Such community collaborative efforts, as well as trust between public and private providers, is necessary for effective services.

To move the client population out of isolation, the service providers also must be connected. The public agency worker takes on a heavy responsibility when she or he decides to contract for preventive services rather than mandating placement. When children are left in a home even after several warning calls to the child protective service from concerned community citizens, we all fear for the children's safety. Many of our preventive services clients have been the victims of child abuse themselves. Under stress, they impulsively mishandle their children. In the short run it is easier to rescue children and place them in a protected institutional environment with toys, hot water, adequate food, and separate beds. In the long run, however, we know the serious and often irreversible damage that occurs when children, particularly young children, are removed from their families for any period of time. These decisions require sensitive judgment, and public sector workers and supervisors are entitled to support in making them. For public workers, the ability to share these burdens with trusted and trusting staff of the voluntary agency is very important.

High costs plus the difficult and sometimes even antisocial nature of the clientele in need of preventive services mean that these programs must have community support. In New York's Schenectady County, an active Advisory Council to the Commissioner of Social Services, made up of representatives from community agencies, interested citizens, and service recipients, meets monthly and reviews preventive services, day care, and Title XX proposals for service contracts. The council makes recommendations to the commissioner and offers an opportunity to engage community representatives in a dialogue about needs and priorities. Over a period of time, council members become knowledgeable about the needs of the social services department and can share this insight with other citizens in the community. Similar advisory councils exist throughout the state. Just as loneliness breeds family disruption, so isolation among those responsible for services creates dysfunction. Networking and support are important to both service recipients and providers.

PROGRAM MODELS

Both government and private foundations have funded replicable, innovative practice programs to prevent out-of-home placement of children and the dissolution of our most troubled families. The Edna McConnell Clark Foundation *1986 Annual Report* speaks to their commitment to innovative family preservation programs that provide in-home assistance to turn family crisis into family growth through the empowerment of its members.

The Foundation currently funds ten family preservation programs across the nation. Regionally diverse, the programs are also in a wide variety of organizational settings. Perhaps the best known is Homebuilders of the Behavioral Science Institute of the state of Washington, which has achieved an 88 percent success rate (the percentage of families still intact one year after the termination of Homebuilders services) in working with 2,360 families since 1974. [Edna McConnell Clark Foundation 1986:9)]

The Homebuilders approach of timely, short-term, intensive in-home services, by workers with very small caseloads, has had major influence in many states where similar models with a range of adaptations have been instituted.

There are many small progressive programs throughout the country [Kaplan 1986]. An example is the Parsons Child and Family Center of Albany, which has organized itself to meet the challenges of providing preventive services to three counties: Albany, Rensselaer, and Schenectady, comprising urban, small-town, and rural farming communities.

Preventive services at Parsons evolved gradually out of the realization that children able to be discharged from out-of-home placement back to their families within a reasonable length of time should probably never have been separated from their families in the first place. If the same kind of outreach family services that allowed for the return of the child after placement had been provided to the family before placement, perhaps the separation need not have occurred. A pilot program to test this premise was developed in 1974 with the Albany County Department of Social Services, using county funds, Parsons endowment income, and a United Way grant. Parsons assigned staff to the County Department of Social Services children's unit for both child protective services and long-term intake services. Project staff—an advanced professional social worker and a psychiatrist with a specialization in family therapy—were responsible for determining, in collaboration with county staff, whether family preventive services or a child's removal from its home was more appropriate. By the same process children in an institutional placement were evaluated for early discharge with in-home services. During the first year, 58 families were referred for consideration; of 32 cases, consisting of 101 individuals receiving services, only 5 children required placement away from their families. The alternatives pursued were assignment of the family to a Parsons Prevention Project worker or to a public agency worker with project staff consultation.

With the passage of the Child Welfare Reform Act, funding improved substantially as money was moved from the foster care budget into the preventive services budgets [NYS Division of the Budget 1985]. The voluntary and public agencies had by then enough knowledge and experience to refine the program and develop new approaches. We all recognized that too many youngsters were removed from their families by the courts. Concerned judges who had no alternative program resources available to them rendered decisions that resulted in children's placement. Even though the Department of Social Services had had no part in the decision, the Albany county commissioner immediately became financially responsible. In response to the concern shared by the courts and the Department of Social Services, a collaborative program evolved with the County Department of Probation. A Parsons worker was assigned to the probation department to read referrals and to make recommendations for outreach preventive services as an alternative to placement in addition to offering direct services for some families. During the second year of operation, a total of sixty-seven youth at risk of placement were diverted from placement. Six children required placement, and eight children returned home from foster care placement.

Building the necessary sophisticated teamwork among the Parsons staff and the social services and probation departments required considerable care and energy. Differences were openly negotiated, and extra effort went into identifying who could best do which job. Cases were indeed volatile and difficult, but there was no permission for scapegoating or blaming. All team members did the best they knew how; however, at times the work with families did not proceed as hoped. Then team members truly needed each other. This same teamwork was then replicated with clients. When professionals know how to trust each other, clients have a better opportunity to trust themselves and the professionals.

The Family Activity Learning Center (FALC)

As the preventive services project gained experience, it became apparent that many families responded to this constructive outreach team effort, but would quickly regress soon after discharge from the program. This was not surprising, given the nature of the client population. Lacking meaningful, supportive human connections in the community, the clients became attached to the agency as a substitute family. Termination of the relationship, therefore, was equivalent to rejection and abandonment. On the other hand, maintaining people as active counseling clients forever was not the solution, either.

Recognizing this, Parsons created a Family Activity Learning Center (FALC) modeled in part after the archetypal settlement house that served immigrants so well. Families that need attachment and a place to belong are referred to FALC. The program focuses on the family's assets. Clients share

their knowledge and skills, teaching each other cooking, furniture upholster-
ing, mending, and much more. There are clubs and support groups. FALC
provides children's activities, while adults meet their own needs together.
Clients run a thrift shop to which the community contributes items for sale.
These items are then nominally priced for clients and other neighborhood
residents. The proceeds are allocated to the program. FALC offers an opportunity to share holidays such as Thanksgiving. When a client parent is ill,
others assume responsibility to provide food and care for the children. The
participants do together the things that go on in neighborhoods among
connected people who care about and for each other.

As outreach in-home preventive programs evolved and prevented out-of-
home placements, court-ordered placements to institutional thirty-day assessment programs became a concern. It seemed that too many of these youth
ended up in long-term placement. These children's behaviors during this
assessment period in the thirty-day placement program demonstrated that
they were a danger to themselves and to others. This outcome is not surprising. The youth perceive themselves as the targeted "bad" persons deserving
punishment, and they are in a frightening new environment with people who
want to "study" them. These youngsters have learned to deal with their fears
through assaultive, aggressive behavior, so they resort to what they know.
The families feel supported in the perception that their sons or daughters are
beyond their capability to control and need "experts" to manage them.

The CRY for Help Program (CRY)

In reviewing these cases we at Parsons wondered whether another approach with the youth and their families might bring different results. These
difficult situations do not develop overnight. Many youths who come into
the court system have had previous histories of institutionalization. Often
their parents had such experience also. The cycle needed to be broken. At the
same time concerned and responsible judges needed an alternative to institutional assessment when the tensions were so high that the youth could not be
discharged to his or her parents without a better understanding of the risk to
the youth, the family, and the community.

The CRY for Help Program (for Court-Related Youth) was a response to
these concerns. CRY was designed to provide family court judges with an
effective alternative to institutional placement when a young person could
not remain at home. Under the program, judges were offered the option of
referring a youth for an immediate "emergency" placement in a family foster
home for up to thirty days. The primary function of this placement is to keep
the youth safe while agency workers assess with the family whether they will

engage with agency services so that its members can gain control of their lives and of their youngster's destructive and self-destructive behavior. When it is not possible to return the youth home within thirty days, he or she may be considered for continued placement in the foster home rather than being moved to an institutional facility. Nevertheless, the key factors remain: a family assessment and engagement of every member of that family to solve the problems that had led to temporary family separation. Families in the CRY program are seen as a necessary resource for change and as a much-needed source of help to their son or daughter, rather than the cause of problems [Kagan, Reid, Roberts, Silverman-Pollow 1987].

The CRY program has several unique features. For one, it accepts families who have earlier rejected help from other preventive services. The program includes an option for long-term involvement. Above all, CRY seeks to empower the family by giving its adults the message that they have been good, competent parents. At the time of initial crisis, however, the program recognizes that they are exhausted from their efforts to help their youngster. They are entitled to respite in order to gain some perspective on the issues and get some well-deserved rest.

That the young person has gone into a foster family and is able to function there when not targeted as "the bad one" gives pause to parents. An appropriate sense of rivalry quickly develops: "Why is our kid making it in this foster family? They're no different from us." With placement in an institution, this opportunity for parental engagement is lost, for the staff are viewed as "experts," and the problem is perceived as no longer the family's.

Another major asset of CRY is that the program is a collaborative effort between two separate programs in an agency offering an array of services. The foster care department recruits the family and supervises the youngster's daily activity. The outreach prevention team works with the youth's family. In these highly charged and often potentially dangerous situations, this division of responsibility is very useful because it is very natural for foster families and foster care social workers to want to protect the youth from her or his family rather than encourage necessary ongoing exposure.

The collaborative work by the team is the key to success. Every youth referred to CRY would otherwise have gone into institutional assessment programs. Based on county projections, 85 percent of these young people would have ended up in institutional placement. The follow-up study done on twenty-nine families in this program by Kagan and others [1987] found that 55 percent of the children who were removed returned home following the initial assessment. Through the follow-up period, with a mean length of ten and three-quarters months, 52 percent remained with their families and an additional 10 percent left the family but were able to avoid institutional placement. Given the relatively late intervention and the severity of the problems, these figures are quite remarkable. Even if it is too late to help the youth in difficulty, other children in engaged families have benefited.

There are occasions when the symptoms of a child are such that removal from the community school is necessary. In those instances the same methods of preventive intervention can be used with the family while a slot is found for the youngster in a day treatment program. Family work is done by the day treatment team itself in cases of direct referral to such a program.

However, when referral of the youth occurs after a close relationship has been established with the outreach preventive services staff, an interprogram treatment plan can be developed with the best interests of the individual in mind. If it appears that this plan may involve long-term day treatment, full transfer to that program may be advisable so that intensive school-clinical communication can be maximized. In some instances a case transfer may be clinically unadvisable, particularly if the needs of several other children in the family are being served well and a constructive relationship with the outreach preventive staff has been formed. Interprogram team effort is often time- and energy-consuming. Its success requires flexibility, mutual respect, and effective communication. The same program design can occur when a coalition of community agencies work together as described in chapter 4. The task of collaboration and communication for optimum outcome requires even more care and energy than in the single-agency service model.

Vocational Training/Prevention Team Effort

The vocational training program described in chapter 5 is another collaborative option for the outreach prevention team. Adolescents in trouble become school dropouts. Many adolescents with a history of truancy, and of academic failure, often manage to hang on in school without ever learning how to read. These concerns led Parsons to utilize the agency's school building in the afternoon for a prevocational program. Transportation to and from the school and pay for classroom attendance are offered, just as with industrial on-the-job training. Youths use time cards to punch in and out. They are taught basic skills in auto mechanics, food services, maintenance, secretarial work, or computing, and they are counseled on how to behave at work. They are then placed with carefully selected employers where one-to-one supervision is provided. As these young people begin to experience success, they readily engage in remedial reading, offered by the program. Coordination with the family remains with the prevention worker.

WHEN FAMILY REUNIFICATION IS NOT AN OPTION

Even with the prevention team's most committed efforts, a youngster sometimes has to be placed away from home permanently. Sometimes placement is finally arrived at by a family willing to consider voluntary legal surrender of parental rights to their child. A move for the young person into a neutral setting such as a residential treatment center can be invaluable during such difficult periods.

Yet during these times, the staff too experience much stress and pain. Inevitably tensions between residential and outreach prevention staff surface. Values, objectives, even language seem to differ, often causing major misunderstandings. The residential team is particularly sensitive to the prevention worker's implied, if not always articulated, message that residential care is to be avoided if at all possible. Prevention workers see residential treatment as "placement" and "failure." A sophisticated residential treatment team may feel the word "placement" devalues their professional competence; they resent their program being seen as a "failure." Such a team, not surprisingly, defines residential treatment as a desirable program of choice. They resent having residential treatment relegated to the "underdog" position in the continuum of care. "If, in fact, they were doing their job right, they would be discharging all their children," the prevention workers seem to be telling them.

Prevention workers are very vulnerable and in pain when they and the family have to work through termination of parental rights or voluntary child surrender. They may look to the residential treatment staff to provide support to them in working through this painful transition. Yet residential staff responses may seem slow or insensitive.

The residential staff are caught up with a multitude of issues unique to residential care, such as the problems of ensuring twenty-four-hour, seven-day-a-week staffing in the face of vacation and staff sickness, and how to handle the dangerous acting out of youngsters in the group. Indeed, residential staff problems may be increased because, with preventive services providing alternatives, the children actually referred for institutional care are now particularly difficult to handle.

Staff negative feelings quickly escalate. The responsibility for quick, open, and direct communication must be placed on all parties concerned. Such problems require constant programmatic review and adjustment. Even though each program comes from a different subculture with an apparently different value system, perhaps with different language and terminology, the human needs of both staffs and their vulnerability to stress are the same. The administrators responsible for the supervision of both these programs must work energetically, or the quality of care can quickly deteriorate. Clients must be allowed to trust both systems, and should not become victims of inter-program conflict at a time when they are hurting most.

Differences among professionals with different schooling and of different disciplines are inevitable. Yet these differences can in fact provide a tremendous amount of professional stimulation and excitement. With excitement comes energy. In an agency with an array of services, differences can and must be dealt with through a variety of structured arrangements, such as regular interprogram meetings, case review conferences, quality assurance programs, interprogram case conferences, and inservice training. The agency philosophy of care must be clearly articulated. If, in fact, the least restrictive alternative and maintenance of young people in their family systems have the highest priority, all programs must be designed to acknowledge these priorities.

CONCLUSION

The passage of the Adoption Assistance and Child Welfare Act (Public Law 96–272) has brought new government incentives for developing out-reach preventive services to maintain children with or return them to their original families at the earliest possible time. When this is not possible, adoption as the next best alternative should be considered. The implementation of this law has varied from state to state. However, many exciting programs are being developed throughout the country that deserve attention and study.

Families in need of outreach preventive services have long histories of difficulties. Client families are usually isolated and frightened. They feel victimized by society and its systems, and experience themselves as having neither options in nor control over their lives. The family members need a great deal of validation, tightness of structure, nurture, modeling of produc-tive behaviors, respite, and fun. They need to learn to appreciate their own and each other's assets and those of their family as a whole. They need help in discovering that they have ties and connections to others, or that they can create them.

The fragmentation and duplication of services in many communities has hindered the delivery of effective assistance. Families need tightly integrated programs in which one staff person delivers most services while tightly monitoring and controlling those services that must be obtained elsewhere because of family members' special needs. There must be efficient ongoing communication between the primary care provider and others involved in services. Although their basic principles are useful, traditional counseling approaches need constant modification. Knowledge about integrated methods and programs that work is available throughout the country.

Programs need to be located where they are accessible, preferably in the communities where client families live. Agency service hours should meet the needs of the clients. Programs work best as collaborative efforts between the public and the private not-for-profit sectors. The public sector has the resources and state's mandate to provide family services. The private sector, with only some exceptions, is not usually connected to protective agencies. This separation can be very useful in the services' engaging clients who have had long negative histories with the child protective agency or the court. Some of these histories can be traced back over several generations. At the same time, the legal mandate presses the family that needs a tight structure to get through the difficult initial phases of involvement. Small caseloads are essential in order to provide the intense effort needed.

How the public and private sectors perceive each other and work together in a community is critical. Preventive services coalitions and citizens' advisory councils can be of great help to the public agency in meeting these difficult mandates. The public agency staff should have support and understanding from the private sector as well as the community. But understanding can only come by allowing the involvement that in turn brings support. Active, involved team membership by the public worker assigned to carry a family receiving services from a private agency is crucial. Case plans and methods should be discussed and shared to avoid fragmentation.

Outreach prevention of the need for foster care, as part of an array of services offered by a private agency, can be a very useful program model. These service options offer the opportunity to develop special program combinations, such as working with courts to offer alternatives to placement, which become more difficult to implement when more than one agency is involved. Interprogram collaboration is fully possible, but sharing, trust building, and adherence to an agreed-on basic philosophy of care are important. To be sure, a philosophy of care is more easily designed and implemented within a single agency.

Recruitment for preventive services staff and prevention of rapid staff burnout and turnover will always be of concern for those who manage these programs. To assure preservation of experienced leadership the agency must keep the caseloads of experienced practitioners at a level that does not preclude their taking on supervision and consultation assignments. Regular work hours for staff are often difficult to schedule. The crisis-prone nature of the population served almost guarantees that calls will come in at any hour, certainly during the family's early phases of involvement. Structured on-call systems can give respite to staff during their off-hours. The agency must organize the workweek to allow for predictability and assure compensatory time off even though work schedules may not be Monday through Friday, nine to five. However, most people cannot tolerate the stress of this type of professional work for more than a few years if they continuously ignore their own personal needs.

The provision of outreach preventive services requires an effort to recruit, train, and avoid rapid burnout of staff. Only longitudinal research studies will give us a measure of success for this model. We have, however, enough highly successful demonstration programs throughout the country to continue work with this approach.

NOTE

1. In New York State, under the mandate of the Child Welfare Reform Act, a 75 percent state reimbursement to counties is available if a child is at risk of placement within sixty days. Only a 50 percent reimbursement is available when a child is at risk of eventual placement but not within a specific time frame.

PART III

Alternative Family-Based Services

The third part of this volume addresses those situations in which the biological family is unable to care for its children either temporarily or permanently. Several models of family foster care are presented as resources for children who need to be removed from their families of origin, temporarily or permanently, yet are able to function in family living. Then the many complex issues unique to those children who are legally free for adoption are examined. A variety of models is offered to support the special service needs of these children and their families.

7

Family Foster Care:
A Multitude of Possibilities

Group living or foster family care for children who cannot live at home with their families: which shall it be? This debate has been going on in the field of child welfare since the recognition that an almshouse was undesirable for children. Charles Loring Brace set a powerful example by taking groups of children out West to place them with farm families who would step forth at each train stop to choose them [Brace 1872]. A foster family was, and often still is, considered to be a more humane alternative than a large institution. There is in fact a refreshing and challenging dialogue in the literature on how to combine the advantages of both institutional group and foster family care [Lewis 1987; Maluccio 1987; Arieli and Feuerstein 1987a, 1987b; Polsky 1987; Whittaker 1987].

Over the years family foster care has come under severe attack in the American media. However, it is not the model that deserves attack but rather the indiscriminate use of family foster care without providing adequate screening, supervision, and training of foster parents.

If family foster care is considered as part of an array of services, there is room for both institutional and family foster care. Just as institutional care has to identify those services best provided in an institutional setting and find solutions by developing specialized programs to meet the many different needs of the children and youth requiring care, so family foster care needs to develop a range of models and options. The various models of family foster care will share many similarities. Each model, however, has some unique features.

All family foster care programs share certain characteristics. These are described as well as unique program designs to meet needs of specific families, children, and youth. This discussion draws on the major contributions to the literature on family foster care [Fanshel and Shinn 1978; Festinger 1983; Jones and Moses 1984].

UNIVERSALS IN FOSTER FAMILY CARE

Of course, our commitment today is to maintain children with their biological families. In the United States, since the passage of the Social Security Act in 1935, children are no longer removed from their biological families because of poverty alone. Aid to Families with Dependent Children has allowed children to remain with their biological families, to be removed only if the family is unavailable or unable to cope. As already discussed, cutting off a child's biological connections is dangerous and to be avoided if at all possible.

An isolated, overburdened family can prevent its own breakup by allowing willing members of the wider extended family to help. The primary task of the helping system in a family crisis, preferably in anticipation of the crisis, is to explore the assets among relatives of both parents. Asking the family to contact all their relatives to see who might be willing to assist with the care of children can yield amazing results. Even if an unrelated foster family is needed, the child or youth continues to live in what is considered a normal community environment, to interact with other community children, and to attend a community school.

Children who must be removed from their biological family should remain as close to them geographically as feasible, with as much contact as can be arranged. They should, of course, also remain connected to their social network of aunts, uncles, cousins, and teachers if possible to avoid needless losses and disconnections [Lee and Nisivoccia 1989].

Removal from the biological family is traumatic for any child, even if life at home has been difficult. The foster family, related or unrelated, must be able to view the child's family as worthy people experiencing difficulties. Support and respect for them by the foster family is essential. Anything short of this accepting attitude puts the child in a searing conflict of loyalties with destructive side effects. At best foster parents should see themselves as a second family available to support the child and its family during a difficult time.

In the event that a foster family placement has to be long-term, the foster family needs to work actively to help a young person maintain his or her family ties. Parenting can be shared by the biological and the foster parents, although this is usually not possible in the more concrete tasks of feeding, clothing, and day-to-day supervision. But even if such responsibilities are not shared with biological parents, it is important to consult their wishes, opinions, and advice. At no point must the foster family see itself as a "replacement family."

A foster family, like all families, has its own family and community connections. Life has pattern and rhythm. Not all nuclear and extended family members, neighbors, and friends are necessarily supportive of the family's foster care role and function. There may be other children in the family home; sometimes there is an aged parent. At times the foster mother is very committed, but the foster father only tolerates rather than fully supports the venture. The reverse situation is more unusual, given the more traditional lifestyles of many foster families. Today, of course, there are also single-parent foster families in whose lives friends and others play a role.

The introduction of a new member upsets the equilibrium of the family. This added stress receives too little attention. Each new person who enters a household has an effect on the family's functioning and alliances; each time a person leaves a household there is a further impact. There is no way to protect foster children from these realities at a very vulnerable time in their lives. But the child can learn to relate to all the others within the foster family and those outside the family connected with it. Under the best of circumstances, the foster parents are on the alert for these potential difficulties. They need the skill to help a youngster deal with the questions, attitudes, and feelings of other people. Protection is not always the most effective path—education for coping is usually more beneficial in the long run.

For many children a good foster family experience can be a model for creating a successful, effective family lifestyle that they can carry into adulthood. It teaches values and attitudes toward work, education, care of possessions, use of money, and so on. It offers an opportunity for a youngster who has lived under chaotic conditions to structure time, take on responsibilities, and enjoy leisure.

Foster children often lack positive earlier experiences in constructively resolving conflicts and differences. In many of their homes, disagreements or mood swings of individual family members quickly escalated into fights that veered out of control. Living in a family that knows how to negotiate its ongoing differences is invaluable.

Along with these advantages of quality foster family care come some potential dangers. When an event causes stress that exceeds a foster family's coping ability, such as severe illness, loss of employment, or death of a loved one, the foster child is immediately at risk, often evicted and moved to a new home. In many instances a foster child has committed itself to a family, only to find that the family, facing personal crisis, is no longer able to reciprocate. There is no permanent commitment built into the design or intent of foster care. Yet foster children often cannot understand this lack of permanence, which in some situations becomes counterproductive or even destructive.

The schools' attitude toward foster parents and foster children must not be overlooked. Many foster homes are in suburban neighborhoods—although some are in the inner city and some in rural areas. Foster children often come with behavior problems and special educational needs. The very fact that they are in need of foster care indicates that their earlier home life has been troubled. Many have also had difficult school experiences.

The timing of foster family placement, too, often does not follow the rhythm of the school calendar. Foster children suddenly appear at the school at inopportune times, and require a great deal of attention. Not only is their arrival a burden to the staff, but it often creates difficulties for the other children. Furthermore, peer groups have already been formed and may be closed to a newcomer. These added difficulties must be dealt with.

Ideally the foster family should live in the same school district as the child's biological family so that a change of school does not become necessary if not warranted for educational reasons. But practitioners know that these options often do not exist.

When differences and counterproductive communication between agency staff, biological family, and foster family exist in any or all combinations, children can easily be caught in the middle. Relationship and loyalty demands become too complex. Social workers leave agencies or cases are transferred to other workers without considering the needs of a given child or family. A change of family worker, regardless of the reason, requires hard work dealing with loss and establishing a new relationship. Perceptions often change, as a new worker brings a new and sometimes different understanding to the situation. The desire to move a youngster to a potentially better situation must be carefully weighed against the damage created by another loss for a vulnerable child. A youngster's perception of the placement is often quite different from that of the responsible adults. These different perspectives need to be heard, respected, and understood.

Foster family care has traditionally been seen as less expensive than institutional care and has become at times a preferred option for financial reasons alone. There is always a danger when decisions are driven by financial motives. There are situations in which outreach preventive services and brief institutional respite care, for example, can be even less expensive over time and more desirable in outcome than foster care. Program choice must be based on the immediate and long-term needs assessment, which includes permanence as a goal.

Skillful foster family selection is essential for placement success. Foster children who are thought to be well adjusted are often expected to adapt to the foster family, taking their place in the family configuration; more often than not this expectation is fallacious. A careful review of a youngster's past history, including the number of placements, disruptions, and transitions, will quickly provide a more accurate assessment. Foster children, regardless of how they behave, are usually deeply troubled and require careful, sensitive work.

When a foster child is placed in a family with younger children, some built-in dangers exist. The foster child, although chronologically older, may be emotionally younger than the biological children; although manageable in family living, this situation requires special sensitivity and skill. Often foster children will select a younger child in the foster family on whom to vent their pain and disappointments. The threat to hurt the family's biological child is the fastest route to eviction for a foster child. Careful placement practice needs to guard against this kind of outcome.

A family foster care program that is part of an agency array of services offers some unique features. This structure allows for consideration of all program options before a decision is made. Other program choices within the same philosophic framework are available if a shift is needed. A high quality of interprogram work is possible should the services of more than one program within the agency be required in order to best meet the needs of a given family.

UNIQUE FAMILY FOSTER CARE PROGRAM OPTIONS

Family foster care is provided by a wide variety of foster families from different sociocultural and economic backgrounds, each with a unique family composition and individual needs and wishes. In that sense, the number of program options and the type of program design know no limit. A highly specialized situation can be created to meet the individual needs of a youngster and family. But the placing agency must remain flexible and creative in its search for and supervision of the very special family that the child needs. These individual program options can be characterized for discussion purposes as Emergency/Assessment Foster Care, Treatment Family Care, Long-Term Foster Care, and Parent-Child Care. The important issues of parent-child reunification will then be addressed.

Emergency/Assessment Foster Care

There are family crises that require immediate removal of children from their parents' household. These may be precipitated by a parent's mental or physical illness, injury, hospitalization, or incarceration; by violence in the home, including physical or sexual abuse; or by the parents' inability to control dangerous or antisocial behavior of their children. The objective of emergency/assessment foster care is to provide safe child care during the family crisis. Agency efforts focus on alleviating the crisis and assessing the ability of the family to resume its child-care function. If return to the family is the plan, needed supports must be built in. If return to the family is not an immediate goal, a viable long-term plan for the child must be developed.

A child facing removal from his or her biological home is very frightened, regardless of the precipitating cause. This child's very existence seems in jeopardy. Moreover, the family's behaviors are often difficult to deal with, let alone understand. Foster home placements are frequently made because of problems experienced by the parent and not by the child, yet the child inevitably bears the burden, and often feels the blame, for removal. If at all possible, the parents must be helped to let the child know that he or she is not the cause of the difficulties that have led to the placement. Furthermore, children beyond the toddler age should be included in discussions about where they may live temporarily and should certainly be given a chance to contribute their feelings and ideas.

While family assessment and case planning occur, contact between the child and the biological family should be maintained. This may mean visits to the hospital or jail where a parent may be. Siblings should be kept together. The temporary loss of home and parents is frightening enough without the added loss of brothers and sisters. Siblings often are separated because it is either difficult to find a home that will take them all or family workers perceive the sibling relationship as problematic. Separating siblings just because there are relationship problems does not make the problems go away. Siblings provide safety for each other, while experienced foster parents can usually deal with the problem behaviors their interactions may create.

Emergency foster families are those willing to take a child into care at any time without a specific plan and without any commitment that the child will remain with them for any specified length of time. Of course, people who have the flexibility and desire to make adjustments for children to move in and out of their homes are difficult to find, particularly in urban communities.

Those who do well as emergency foster care families usually have large extended families with many people coming and going at all times. They have active, busy lives and are not inclined to overinvest in a particular child temporarily under their care. For some very frightened children, this lifestyle does not give the degree of structure needed to weather the crisis. Others do well because they do not want closeness and cannot tolerate a burdensome, emotional investment by their foster family.

On the other hand, there are situations in which an emergency foster family would like to become a long-term placement for a child or children. If this is compatible with a child's best interest, program boundaries should be sufficiently flexible to allow this to happen, even if the agency thus loses an emergency home. To allow for this individualized approach, an agency operating an emergency family foster care program must do active ongoing foster family recruitment.

Assessment Foster Care for Court-Referred Youth

Youth who come into the court system either as Persons in Need of Supervision (PINS) or because they exhibit delinquent behavior have historically been placed in institutions for assessment of their behaviors and needs. But this approach is too limited, since all family members should be observed. The foster family's responsibility is to care for the young person while intensive assessment of all family members takes place.

Usually placing the young persons in foster family care with a clear message that the whole family is experiencing difficulties, rather than identifying the youths themselves as the cause of the distress, will engender behaviors quite different than those in an institutional placement. The objective of the foster family placement in this type of program is to allow youth to function in a normal family environment. Information about the youth's ability to handle community living along with information gathered through an outreach team's intensive work with his or her family helps the court and the service providers to formulate a workable plan with the family and child. Institutional placement usually does not yield as much information because the youth see themselves as scapegoats and respond to a frightening situation with the same counterproductive behaviors they exhibit at home (see chapter 6 for a description of the CRY for Help Program).

Assessment Foster Care for Long-Term Permanency Planning

Children who require intensive medical and psychosocial assessments as part of long-term permanency planning need a second type of foster family home. For some, adoption may be possible if enough knowledge is available so that an appropriate family can be found. For others, long-term foster care or institutional placement may be the answer. The most destructive alternative is frequent and haphazard transfer. Foster home and even institutional placements are often disrupted because the people or facilities selected lack the knowledge or the resources to respond to the special needs of the children involved.

Children born to mothers suffering from drug addiction, for example, present special medical difficulties and management demands that families and child care staff often are not equipped to handle. Some of these youngsters require twenty-four-hour-a-day awake attention and supervision.

Some are diagnosed as having not only symptoms of retardation and neurological impairment but also mental illness. Children who have experienced such severe psychological deprivation early in life, often coupled with physical abuse, are difficult to evaluate. A family home with enough respite for the primary caregivers is often the best possible environment for these children. However, if there is danger of constantly changing placement because of family burnout, a specialized institutional unit may be able to do the job better.

Treatment Family Care

The concept of treatment family care has evolved from recognition that there are many young people in foster care who have been seriously scarred emotionally. These youth may end up in institutions that may not necessarily be best for their continuing development. Even in the best institutions these young people are in a peer environment difficult for them to manage; usually there are no appropriate role models from whom they can learn productive behaviors.

These young people need skilled, carefully trained adults who know how to create and manage a therapeutic reparenting milieu. These treatment parents are usually professionals such as nurses, teachers, social workers, counselors, or child-care workers who understand human development and have the knowledge to implement a treatment plan. Treatment parents need to know how to deal with young people, each at different and often incongruent levels of emotional, intellectual, and physical maturity, and requiring different expectations, limits, and interventions.

For some youth a treatment family can provide a more growth-enhancing environment than an institution. This requires exceptional families and a youngster who can tolerate at least the minimal demands that a family environment inevitably presents. The young person in the treatment home cannot be expected to adapt readily to the family's lifestyle. Often major changes in the family's routine and way of operating have to take place. Family treatment is best done through an agency that has supportive resources, such as psychiatric consultation, respite for the family, and structured day treatment and education for the youth if needed.

Treatment families must have the ability to function as agency treatment team members. Treatment issues are usually complex. Ongoing review involves line professionals, sometimes consultants and the funding agencies, and above all the youth and the biological or adoptive family. The parents' potential for and role in resuming care of their child must be understood by all parties.

The family of a youth in need of care may find it easier to understand the role of a treatment family than that of a foster family. After all, treatment parents are experts needed for the child's care. The treatment family, however, must willingly and skillfully engage the biological family, which otherwise may find comfort by withdrawing. This often happens after families have institutionalized a child. Treatment families are not magicians. Children in care need permanent linkages if they are to understand and accept who they are. Growth cannot occur without ongoing contact. The role of the treatment family is intended to be temporary. The youth, permanent family, and treatment family will need to redefine this short-term contract over and over again.

Treatment parents are selected because of their exceptional skills, but they also have lives in the community. Ideally one parent should be at home. Often, however, one or both are employed away from home, and daytime arrangements for the child must accommodate this schedule. Therefore, certain types of difficulties cannot be handled in this environment. Youngsters who easily become assaultive and destructive of property cannot be maintained here because their behavior requires a readily available on-call support system that such a family usually does not have. A young person who is likely to set fires cannot be kept in the community. Excessive running away during which the young person sets up dangerous situations is not viable, either. Some youth exhibit these behaviors in institutions in order to conform to peer pressure, but with help are able to change them as they observe and learn other alternatives.

Treatment parenting is a difficult task. Some agencies have developed cluster-home models. In this model, several treatment families are supervised by the same social worker, meet regularly in support and training groups, and share resources. Cluster family parents know each other well and know all the children in placement. Families provide respite for one another by having children visit overnight on a planned basis or when one family is experiencing too much stress. A child-care worker is often available to offer another relationship option, to take one or more of the cluster children on outings, to supervise after-school activities, and to help in other ways.

Treatment families are frequently used effectively as the first aftercare stage for youth who have been institutionalized in a residential treatment facility. Initially remaining in the campus school may be helpful, with a carefully timed and monitored transition to a special program in the regular community school. Often a treatment family is well equipped to work with the young person's biological or potential adoptive family. The treatment family can teach and model behavior management within a context of realistic expectations. Sometimes a treatment parent can establish rapport with a biological parent more easily than a more youthful child-care worker can. The treatment family parent can share ways of dealing with multiple family demands that are often in conflict with the care demands of a child with special needs.

Long-Term Foster Care

Long-term foster family care is a model providing a family for young people who cannot live at home with their parents. Some children are bonded to their parents, as their parents are to them. Some youth may be legally free for adoption but a family has not been found. Sometimes children in long-term foster care are youngsters whose adoptions have been disrupted. When young people spend their lives in long-term foster care by default rather than by plan, destructive "foster care drift" may result. Children who experience multiple placements get hurt, and many bond only marginally. Agencies must change poor practices, so that long-term foster care does not occur by default, but can remain a valuable, necessary component in a comprehensive array of care.

Long-term foster families who have done excellent work are those whose family systems are very open and whose lifestyles easily allow for the addition of one or more children in their homes. Children in need of long-term foster care are those for whom a careful permanency assessment indicates that they cannot live with their biological family but are so closely bonded to that family that commitment to an adoptive family is not a viable option. These young people need a place in which to grow up, but they want and need to maintain their own family identity and connections. Often these are young people who have benefited from early nurturing. The family may have experienced disruption later on because of severe illness or death of an adult family member, and the parent left alone was not able to provide a home for one or more of the children.

War orphans brought to this country after World War II, and more recently children from Vietnam and Cambodia, were children who already had deep roots, loyalties, and commitments, and they have benefited from long-term foster care. Some young people feel that they need to carry on the family name. Some have relatives in the old country or this country who cannot care for them but to whom they are bonded.

These young people have the capacity to bond with a foster family, yet they appreciate not having to deal with the loyalty conflict that could occur in adoption. With the help of committed foster parents, they often grow into very productive citizens. This model of care must not be tampered with.

Some children have committed biological parents who unambivalently want to parent but lack the emotional, intellectual, and/or psychological resources to do so, and these children often do well in long-term foster care. There is the example of a very young widow left with twin girls to whom she had given much love and nurturance. But because of her own intellectual and emotional limitations and the needs of the children as they grew older, she could not parent them alone. Any attempt at breaking up the siblings or breaking the parental bond would have been most destructive. The solution in this case was a foster family who was able to take both children into their home. The mother visited regularly on weekends and in a sense became the "teenage" daughter to this very unusual foster family. As the children grew, they were bonded both to their biological mother and to their foster family.

The ability to integrate both foster children and their parent is very unusual, but people exist who can do this well. For some foster families the appreciation of the child's biological family is intuitive. With other valuable long-term foster families, a great deal of work has to be done so that they can learn to understand and feel the young people's need to be in touch and at peace with their roots and origin [Lee and Nisivoccia 1989].

Often biological parents are unpredictable and appear hurtful in their perceived indifference and inconsistency toward their child. At other times the foster family feels assaulted by biological parents as they project their disappointment in themselves onto the hard-working, well-meaning foster family. To prepare foster parents to handle such responses constructively, carefully designed training programs, using experiential rather than didactic teaching approaches, can be implemented in agencies providing long-term foster care.

Sometimes the foster family that asks the least from an agency may be in greatest difficulty but is overlooked by workers with heavy caseloads. Too often the worker-family ratio is very high, leaving professionals to do the troubleshooting and crisis intervention rather than the planned preventive work that enables the optimum growth for youth in care. Suddenly and seemingly unpredictably comes a request for removal of a child that might have been averted earlier with intervention. Excellent foster families can easily be exploited by an overworked agency staff, because these families are so ready to care for children in need of a home at a moment of crisis or disruption that they can overextend themselves. Foster families deserve agency attention so that unintended neglect or involuntary abuse does not occur.

After extended placement in a long-term family, a young person's situation may sometimes change. A family's commitment to a child over its whole future life span may be needed, and if the child is legally free, permanence through adoption may become the plan of first choice. There is no question that if bonding has occurred, the foster family should be given the chance to adopt the child. The foster family has certainly earned this right. The young person, of course, should contribute to the decision. If these children want to be adopted by their foster parents and the foster family seeks to adopt them, agency staff should make sure that their personal biases do not interfere as they assess the suitability of a placement.

Rigid placement criteria are often harmful. There is the case of a six-year-old boy who had been in long-term foster care with an older couple. The child was biracial and the family Caucasian. This child was bonded to the foster parents, and they to him. With the new mandates to provide permanence for such children, he was listed and placed for adoption with an out-of-state black family. The foster family was devastated. They had wanted to adopt this child. He was a member of their family. His removal from them was equally devastating to him. The worker clearly was looking for a younger family of the same ethnic background. Even though theoretically this made good sense, the child was not able to make the transition. He quickly deteriorated by badly regressing. The new family was able to get competent professional help, who advised that the child, now badly hurt, be returned to his foster family. Brief but intensive residential treatment was necessary before the child could go back to the family, from which he should never have been removed in the first place. They were ultimately allowed to adopt him. This is only one example of many in which a serious misjudgment occurred, even though the decision appeared to be sound theoretically, met new mandates, and was certainly well-intended.

A long-term foster family in some cases can and should be used to prepare a child for adoption with another family. However, this may not always be the case. If the child and family are bonded to each other, but because of some unusual circumstances the family is not able to adopt the child, it may find itself in competition with the planned adoptive family. If the foster family placement is not working out, the foster family may not be the best place in which to work out the preadoptive placement issues with the child. Under either of these circumstances a move into a temporary, more neutral setting such as an institution might be more desirable.

In the event that a child does have to leave a foster family because adoption is needed but is not possible for the foster family, we must be sensitive to the child's bonds with the foster family. These bonds should never be arbitrarily severed. This child and family have shared a part of their life together. Even an experience very brief in terms of time can be very important when measured by its quality. Children and families must not be expected to say arbitrary "good-byes" to each other. The possibility of reconnecting in a different context with different expectations must be left open. Children should be encouraged to write to former foster parents, visit them if needed, and introduce their new families to them. As new relationships are formed, the need for contact will diminish; on the other hand, when children and foster families get together even years later some will pick up where they left off.

A frequently overlooked issue in foster care is how the extended family of the foster family views the presence of long-term foster children in the home. There are foster families that have done this for more than one generation. For these families, which include children neither born nor legally bonded to them, fostering is part of their family culture. These families usually have a built-in support system in the event that the foster parents are temporarily incapacitated through illness or other family crisis, or are simply in need of respite. Foster children are then cared for by the extended family, just as biological or adopted children would be.

There are situations in which the courts are very reluctant or downright unwilling to terminate the parental rights of the parents of a young child, especially where biological family attachment does exist, even though they are in all likelihood not going to be able to take care of the child. Foster family custody over the child may be an alternative option for more stability for some of these youngsters. In those situations, a foster family custody agreement requires more commitment from the foster parents. This avenue in fact can provide an assessment tool to readily identify committed foster families and disqualify those who may more easily disrupt their ties to the child.

When the courts can deal with the more limited issue of custody disputes between biological parents and foster parents, the interests of the child may sometimes determine the outcome. In these situations, courts are relatively free to recognize the importance of an established, positive relationship shared by the child and the foster parents. In custody, unlike adoption, residual parental rights are not disturbed. . . . When there are important family ties, permanent foster care could steer a course between the instability of the usual foster care situation and the harsh either-or choices in adoption of older children where, typically, one set of adult contenders legally banishes the other from the child's life. [Derdeyn 1977:609]

In the literature, the rights of long-term foster families are discussed in relation not only to possible adoption, but also to foster family visitation, should children either be adopted or returned to their biological family. If bonding has occurred, foster families should not suddenly disappear from a young person's life—particularly if they wish to remain involved and if this is in the best interests of the child. The issue of foster family visitation rights can best be addressed if it is seen in the same context as the rights of grandparents; for example, in the case of a divorce when the parent other than the grandparent's son or daughter becomes the child's custodial parent. This raises an issue with major legal consequences; arbitrary cutoffs from foster parents to whom children have been bonded are destructive.

Parent-Child Foster Family Care

The separation of a child from a parent, in instances where a single parent is still in need of parenting, can be averted if the parent and child are placed in a foster home together. The removal of children from parents is burdened by so many disadvantages and risks that the alternative of parent-child foster care is often talked about. A few such programs do exist in this country, in Great Britain, and in some other countries. In Israel the kibbutz with its communal childrearing practices demonstrates this approach as the norm rather than the exception.

There are parents, usually young, who lack the ability, maturity, and social supports to engage in effective parenting. They are usually the product of very difficult life experiences themselves and are in need of nurture and protection. Many of these young parents are highly motivated and very much want to raise their own children. Their desire to parent, however, is often not clearly articulated and may not even be perceived by an intervening agency. Progress has been achieved in developing teenage pregnancy programs and parent-infant foster home placements, but there is still considerable room for creative program design and dissemination.

Parent-child foster care programs might best be referred to as "shared parenting" programs, since they are based on the assumption that the young parent is not ready or able to assume full parenting responsibility but could learn, grow, and succeed if the responsibility were shared with older, more mature adults who do have the knowledge and emotional resources to be parents. In many societies, and even in isolated pockets of our own society, parenting is often, without stigma, shared with grandparents. Shared parenting programs can be particularly useful in preventing child abuse and neglect, which usually occurs in households of young parents who have themselves been the victims of abuse and neglect. These young parents feel overwhelmed by adult living, and the demands made by young children often become the last straw. Usually no extended kin or community supports are readily available to offer help and thereby reduce the danger of parental failure and physical as well as psychological harm to the children.

Nayman and Witkin [1978] describe a program of parent-child foster placement designed to meet the needs of potentially abusive parents in Tompkins County, New York, that is based on the following premises:

a) The most effective method of evaluating parental skills is through direct daily observation, in a sheltered environment approximating a normal household.

b) Abusing and neglecting parents usually exhibit . . . a history of intergenerational abuse, neglect or family pathology.

c) The healthy, functioning family is the most effective agency for socialization, role prescription, and the instruction of parental skills.

d) Society's long term social and economic goals will be served best by the strengthening of relationships between a child and his or her parents, provided that the child's safety is ensured, and the parents' motivation, abilities and efforts are directed towards positive behavioral change. [Nayman and Witkin 1978:251]

Parent-child foster placement or shared parenting programs may need to include vocational counseling and training, recreational and respite opportunities, as well as the teaching of home management and child-care skills for the mother. Models that allow mother and child to have their own quarters adjacent to a foster family might work well. Other young people do better by becoming more fully integrated into the foster family's living space and life, depending upon the young parent's level of maturity.

Some young single mothers remain with their own parents during their child's early years and gradually assume more and more independent responsibilities. Usually these are single mothers who are fortunate enough to have been raised in functioning families. Social agencies hear very little about these natural support networks. In families such as these, which often include extended family members, people feel a strong commitment to each other. These families know how to cope. They can be a supportive and valuable consultative resource or even a peer system for clients and agencies.

Semi-independent living apartments for mother and child, with supportive shared parenting assistance, are another possible component in an array of services. The cost to society of abuse and neglect of children is too severe to continue offering isolated programs only. Shared parenting programs can be funded through already existing mechanisms in most communities by using the foster-boarding home rate for the child and grants available for adult tenants or boarders under the Home Relief or Aid to Families with Dependent Children programs for mothers. Other creative ways to adapt existing reimbursement options must be explored.

REUNITING FOSTER CHILDREN WITH THEIR BIOLOGICAL PARENTS

Our premise is that permanent connections are of primary importance, and that these are originally based on biological ties, but may be established by adoption. The quality of care and nurturance a child receives is far more important than material comfort or possessions.

The reunification of family foster care children with their biological parents remains a major and troublesome issue in this area of service. Professionals worry that foster families will be competitive and destructive with regard to the biological family. They also worry that foster children will reject their biological family because it cannot or has not been able to provide for them in the same manner that the foster family has been able to do. These concerns point toward the work that must be done in recruiting, selecting, and training of foster parents.

Good foster family placement requires the development of a realistic discharge plan at the time of placement, with provision for ongoing services, review, and plan changes as required. When appropriate services are provided to the family while their child is in foster care, the necessary circumstances may be created so that the child can return home. Services usually must include careful attention to the parents' vocational education, employment, housing, health care, recreational activities, and life-skill training. For most families that need to place their children in foster care, counseling services are insufficient. Counseling can be helpful in teaching people how to alleviate stress and tension and to sensitize them to the many life options and alternatives available and how to use them. At no time can counseling replace often badly needed practical services. A variety of services is often available in a community for these families, but the different agencies may not communicate with each other. When agencies are able to offer an array of services within one system, the task becomes easier and more focused.

If, indeed, the primary goal is to reunite the family, then all other services are linked to the accomplishment of this objective. Any agency philosophically committed to the need of permanence for children has the incentive to keep things moving. Whatever the administrative structure, interdepartmental pressure is necessary to keep all aspects of work focused on permanency for the child.

Case management may be provided by the agency with primary foster care responsibility, provided that programs with an outreach capability to families are available. The agency must not wait for its clients to keep scheduled office appointments while years go by during which confused children grow up in foster care. Some agencies offer outreach programs for prevention of foster care. These programs often can provide reunification services as well as case management. Another possibility is a clearly identified family services department or mental health clinic in the agency providing a foster care service. When there is no distinct family component attached to the agency providing foster care, the staff can easily lose track of the placement objective. When this occurs, agencies fall into the trap of only providing rescue services to the child, which renders the family more and more helpless and incompetent, until the parents themselves lose hope and withdraw from the struggle for independence as a complete family unit that includes their child.

FOSTER FAMILY RECRUITMENT, TRAINING, AND SUPPORT

Foster family recruitment needs to be an ongoing program component. The number and variety of children in need of services require a wide range of foster homes of different ethnic compositions, religions, and lifestyles. The traditional foster family of father, mother, and biological children is not easily available nor is it always the best choice. Sometimes single people will do well with an individual child. Many foster children are so needy that they cannot tolerate sharing a parent with another child or a parent's spouse. At times a foster family in which the child can be the only or the youngest child is the best situation.

There will never be enough foster families, nor foster families that are available for the children who come into care at a given moment. Institutions usually accept children regardless of age, sex, race, or ethnic background, providing the child meets the eligibility criteria and there is an open bed. Foster families expect to be able to choose whether they will accept any given child. Moore, Grandpre, and Scoll [1988] have done a valuable three-year study of foster family recruitment in Hennepin County, Minnesota. Smith and Gutheil [1988] present an interesting approach to the increasingly difficult problem of successful foster family recruitment through financial incentives and the use of foster parents themselves as recruiters.

Foster parenting is often best done by people who have already raised their own children. Usually these are people who have come in touch with their own imperfections as parents and have developed the needed humility. They know that there is no such thing as perfect parenting, and they have developed a higher level of tolerance for the many inadequacies presented by the foster child's biological family. These foster parents will not need to look to the foster child to validate their own adequacy. Children enter foster families with many hurts and many needs. Their emotional and psychological development has often been quite uneven. They are very much in need of parenting. Progress is often painfully slow, and foster parents must be able to tolerate and accept this.

The placing agency and foster family must have open, mutually trusting communication. Foster families need ongoing support from the agency, not just in times of crisis. Foster children need the opportunity to speak alone with the agency worker. However, family sessions including foster parents, foster children, and other family members who live in the home are necessary to work on issues and deal with problems. At times meetings involving the biological family, child, and foster family are indicated to discuss goals and the methods to achieve them. Working together helps those most affected to understand and internalize both goals and methods.

Support groups and training sessions for foster families are important. With the best of intentions, these agency training sessions are often difficult to implement. Cluster-home models usually build training right into the program. Some foster families prefer to meet at each other's homes. Others are willing to come to the agency as long as the travel distances are manageable.

Sometimes an agency must be willing to provide transportation, child care, and meals. For many foster families these meetings provide a much-needed opportunity to leave their home and socialize with people around shared interests.

The participants' contributions to training sessions can be valuable, such as presentations by group members with discussion. The discussion should flow from the issues of most relevance to the foster families. The agency responsible for providing foster care has a mission, and with that mission comes a philosophy of care; training sessions convey both the mission and philosophy to the fostering families. Foster parents are members of the agency team, and they need to know and contribute to the philosophy of care. To assure the accomplishment of a very difficult task, this kind of clarity is essential.

Titterington [1990] speaks of foster family training as empowering to foster families and cites the literature [Boyd and Remy 1978] to show positive correlation between foster family training and stability of placement for the children. He further describes an interesting training approach using "a nonformal educative model as a vehicle to facilitate networking" [Titterington 1990:164]. He sees this nurturing, supportive approach as having educative, recruitment, and retention potential for family foster care.

Foster family recruitment is best done by other foster parents by word of mouth and through groups to which they belong, such as their churches, unions, jobs, social clubs, and parent-teacher associations. This does not eliminate the need by agencies for broad efforts through the media. Television and radio programs, automobile bumper stickers, newspaper advertisements and stories, all contribute to foster parent image building. This publicity can help give foster parents badly needed prestige for their invaluable contribution.

Foster families, like other child-care workers, have become vulnerable to accusations of child abuse. Many states now have a child abuse hotline and carefully regulate child abuse reporting procedures. Foster families in some states must have clearance to assure that they do not have a past history of demonstrated child abuse. The dilemmas here and the potential for misunderstanding are considerable. Some individuals are afraid of becoming foster parents lest they later be accused of child abuse. Many young people placed in foster families have been victims of abuse and are, therefore, masters at provoking abuse. Sometimes what may appear as abuse is the result of self-defense or protective maneuvers by a foster parent. The abuse of a foster child may result from a biological child's hostility toward the foster child coupled with insufficient supervision. These serious complications to recruitment and retention of foster families require a great deal of careful attention.

Foster family training directed toward the physical management of children, and, even more important, toward the prevention of physical intervention with children when they become destructive of property or hurtful to others or themselves, is essential. The placing agency has a responsibility not to place potentially dangerous youngsters in foster families, taxing these families beyond what can reasonably be expected of them.

CONCLUSION

Foster family care is an important component in the continuum of family care best provided by an agency with a variety of other program resources that can be used in many combinations. Foster care should be seen as family care for young people for a short or longer period of time in the home of a family other than their biological or adoptive family. The foster family must never be assumed to substitute fully for the young person's biological or adoptive family, and must only be viewed as an additional supportive parenting team. Foster families must be empathic and knowledgeable about the young person's permanent connections and do everything they can to strengthen these connections.

Within the concept of foster family care, we need a whole array of specialized models including emergency care, assessment care, treatment family care, long-term foster care, and parent-child foster care. These foster care programs are designed for a range of situations, from temporarily providing care in an emergency to evaluating a family's ability to take charge of its youngster at home or assessing a child who presents major emotional and physical problems. Treatment family care is conducive to the provision of very special treatment services in an environment with professionally trained foster parents. Long-term foster family care is a community alternative for children who are bonded to their biological families or are not otherwise free for adoption, but cannot live at home. Parent-child programs are used to avoid separating young children from single parents, often involved in child abuse and neglect, to help the parent to function without inflicting the trauma of separation on both parent and child.

Given the histories and needs of the children requiring family foster care, we are asking a great deal of these families. Adequate financial reimbursement for at least one family member is essential so that family foster care can become an alternative to working outside the home for one parent. Regardless of financial reimbursement, these families can never be remunerated for the true value of their work and contribution. Their rewards must lie in the knowledge that they are making a major difference to the life of another human being, which may affect future generations as well.

8

Building Families through Adoption: Multiple Roots

Adoption of children by someone other than the biological parents is as old as the existence of the family. Historically it has occurred for many reasons, although it has usually been to meet adults' needs rather than those of the children: People might adopt a child because there was no heir in the family to carry on the family name and traditions. Some people adopted children because it provided them with more labor to tend their fields or trade.

In some parts of the world, adoption occurs within the family; when, for example, one brother does not have children but another brother has several. In many cultures, family planning is uncommon or nonexistent, and the many children of some couples are distributed widely within the clan. In Japan when a family lacks a male heir but does have daughters, the heirless family may adopt a son, who, by marrying their daughter, would then take the father's family name and occupation. This assures the family's continuity. Some cultures have no difficulty with the adoption of kin but will not adopt outside their own blood line. This is the case in Korea, although it is now slowly changing.

A HISTORY OF ADOPTION IN THE UNITED STATES

In nineteenth-century America adoptions developed out of altruism and concern for orphaned children. Orphans who roamed East Coast city streets were transported to the local and Midwest countrysides; adoptive families came to the train station to select children. Some of these placements were only temporary, but others bonded, became permanent, and resulted in adoption. Many of these adoptions worked out well; some were disasters and would be termed child abuse by current standards in the United States. Massachusetts in 1851 became the first state to establish laws governing adoption; others followed [Spencer 1980:15]. Adoption laws assured the adoptee's rights of inheritance as well as the assumption of the family name. Because of the hit-or-miss nature of adoption placement, the use of orphanages and children's homes became much more acceptable for children who lacked their own families' care.

Adoption during the first half of the twentieth century was limited primarily to infants born out of wedlock. A number of adoption agencies were founded throughout the country with strict, clearly defined standards and procedures. Adoption practice became child-focused. Quite specific parent eligibility requirements were set with respect to the adults' marital status, age, health, and family configuration. Medical documentation of infertility was requested because adoption workers thought that the birth of a biological child into the family that had adopted a child would be detrimental to the best interests of the adopted child. There were occasions when a child who had been placed in an adoptive home was removed when the mother became pregnant prior to the legalization of adoption, even though the adopted baby had begun to bond to the family and the parents did not want to lose their to-be-adopted child.

The purpose of adoptive placement was for the infant to become a full member of the adoptive family, one who was as similar as possible to a child who might have been born to them. "Matching" by agencies even went so far as to find a child who would have physiological characteristics similar to the adoptive couple's—race, hair and eye color, physical build—based on the appearance of the biological mother and (usually her description of) the biological father. Matching the child to the adoptive family in terms of physical characteristics validated the family's desire for the adoptive infant to become truly their own—in fact to substitute for the child they could not have themselves. The adoptive child was thought of primarily as filling a void left by infertility.

The adoptive placement of an infant was often shrouded with secrecy so that the family and child would be protected from the outside world ever learning of the relationship. Gradually, however, it became common to tell the adopted child of the adoption. But this was often only pro forma, and did not meet the child's need to know about her or his family of origin.

During the first half of this century and as late as the 1960s many children faced barriers to adoption. The focus of adoption practice was "to match the race and religion of the child to the race and religion of the [adoptive] parent. Few agencies extended themselves to a religious or racial group different from their own and a pattern of sectarianism and racism prevailed" [Billingsley and Giovanni 1972:23]. Children who differed from the characteristics of available adoptive parents were frequently not placed, and ended up living in institutions or foster homes.

Furthermore, couples who were of two different religions or races found it almost impossible to adopt a child. Some couples who very much desired a child had to move from one state to another in search of more liberal adoption requirements. Adoption agencies came under attack by frustrated potential adoptive parents. Throughout the 1960s some loosening of these requirements began to occur throughout the country. In some states biological mothers were able to sign waivers so that the agency could place a child with a family of another religion if a family of the same religion was not available.

During the late 1950s and early 1960s, adoption agencies faced a rising number of infants born out of wedlock, adding to the pressure on earlier restrictions. By the later 1960s, in many parts of the country, there were almost no waiting lists for parents who wanted to adopt an infant, and adoption agencies worked hard to have a sufficient pool of families available when a child needed a home. Early placement was seen as both desirable and necessary. The accepted practice of keeping infants in foster homes to be observed and studied prior to placement began to decline. In fact, these study periods were no longer seen as desirable, and placement in the adoptive home directly from the hospital maternity ward became quite common, with emphasis on early bonding between infants and their adoptive parents.

The late 1960s and early 1970s saw a sudden and abrupt reversal of supply and demand in infant adoption. The contraceptive pill took hold as a method of easy and acceptable birth control. Liberalization and legalization of abortion followed.[1] Now babies in need of adoption again became few and far between [Lindsey 1987]; those who needed adoption often were handicapped or of minority-group parentage. The social stigma attached to out-of-wedlock parenthood has declined. Many young women chose to keep their babies, who in the past would have looked for adoption because of family and social pressure. Reacting to the decline in healthy Caucasian infants needing adoption, many families and agencies turned to other countries and continents in search of healthy infants.

RECENT ADOPTION DEVELOPMENTS

The dramatic decline in the number of young women seeking early adoption for their infants had far-reaching ramifications for American adoptions, especially for couples seeking to adopt healthy Caucasian infants. Many single mothers with available family support have done well with their children. In the best of circumstances the child grows up in the biological family, preventing the trauma of loss for both parent and child. However, many young people lack adequate support, or misjudge their capability to parent, and the child comes into foster care later after major trauma, including neglect and abuse.

A great many children in need of adoptive placement today are handicapped, members of a minority group, or older children. These children often have had very difficult and damaging life experiences. The needs of these children have challenged child welfare agencies to rethink adoptive placement practices. Badly needed changes have been stimulated by the recognition that children need permanent family connections, that children carry their past family ties with them in memory and in fantasy, and that most youngsters in need of adoption are physically or emotionally handicapped or members of minority groups. Adoptive and potential adoptive parents have also contributed considerably through adoption support and advocacy groups. Research in the field, too, has brought change [Kadushin 1970; Nelson 1985; Kagan and Reid 1986; Reid et al. 1987].

Child- and family-care professionals have come to realize that restrictive adoption policies and practices have prevented children from finding families. Many people have much to offer to children in institutions, but do not meet traditional adoption eligibility because they are older, have large families of their own, or have already raised their children. Some may be able to have more biological children but choose to expand their family by adopting. Single men and women sometimes want a child in their lives. Members of minority groups who have been labeled as unwilling to adopt youngsters, in fact very much want to when approached in other than the traditional ways [McKelvy 1981:3; Washington 1987].

A large set of potential adoptive parents are already giving foster care. Many foster families have nurtured children and bonded with them, but in the past have been denied the right to adopt them because the families did not meet the traditional eligibility requirements or because this possibility was not included in the original agency contract with them.

Economic barriers have been largely removed by providing subsidies to families who adopt older children or children with special needs. In 1980 subsidizing special-needs adoption became national policy with the passage of the Adoption Assistance and Child Welfare Act (PL 96–272), which provides for federal matching of states' subsidy costs and for Medicaid coverage of special-needs adoptive families' medical expenses for their children [Waldinger 1982; Nelson 1985:4]. The result is that many children who were labeled as "unadoptable" are now finding families.

With a new philosophy of care and practice has come a change in adoption vocabulary, pioneered by Marietta E. Spencer, program director of postlegal adoption services of the Children's Home Society of Minnesota:

Choosing emotionally "correct" words is especially important in talking about adoption. For example, when a social worker speaks to new adopting parents about "your daughter" or "your son," he or she is validating and strengthening the cognitive process by which parenthood becomes a reality. If, instead, the social worker used the phrase "the child you are adopting," a very different message would be conveyed. Both phrases are correct, but the first conveys the emotional reality of parenthood, while the second merely reflects the technical procedure of adding a child to the family. [Spencer 1980:21]

Spencer offers many examples of destructive negative terms: "adopted out," "abandoned," "given up," "relinquished," "surrendered." More suitable words are "arranging for an adoption," "making an adoption plan for the child," "arranging for the transfer of parental rights." It is preferable to speak of "birth mother" rather than "real mother," to assure that psychological parenting is given the same weight as biological parenting [Spencer 1980:23–25].

Social workers no longer try to match families with an appropriate child. Instead, families are recruited by reaching out into the community through education, information sharing, and a variety of media. Agencies seek access to groups that include potential adoptive parents, such as churches and parent-teacher associations. They no longer hesitate to educate, advocate, and advertise for adoptive parents in newspapers, through press conferences, and on television programs. Booths are set up at fairs and in shopping malls; bumper stickers are placed on automobiles. They want people to think about adoption who never thought about it before.

As people come forth with an interest in adding a child to their family through adoption, the agency worker tells them about the kinds of children in need of adoption and what the adoption process entails: from family application to study of the home, acceptance of the family, choosing the child, placement, prelegalization family supervision, the legalization process, and postlegalization activities when needed. The worker then needs to get to know the potential adoptive family well. Even though the agency remains unquestionably responsible for every placement decision, we believe today that the family knows best what kind of child they will be able to parent, and they are usually given the opportunity to view videotapes or pictures of the children along with vignettes of their histories before actually meeting a child. After the meeting, if both child and family's reactions are encouraging, additional meetings, then overnight and finally extended visits can take place, until the child and the family are ready to begin life together.

The pace and momentum of the adoption process varies greatly for different families and children. The process needs to be individualized. Variables of age, past attachments, and disruption traumas must be taken into account. There are times, however, when more pressing factors affect the timing, such as the need to move a child out of temporary care within a given time and the desire to avoid another temporary adjustment. Out-of-country adoptions are affected by special circumstances that differ from country to country and placement to placement.

Current practices are still controversial, and they vary tremendously. The fate of children who "drift" in foster care without long-term connections has generated so much indignation that agency workers may have moved too far in the opposite direction. Some individuals believe that any family placement is better than no family placement, even though inappropriate and then disrupted placements are very painful to both children and families, and cause damage to both.

Some children may never be able to function in family living because of the degree of trauma they have experienced. When we place these children in families and they are not able to adjust there, we add to their difficulties and disappointments. Of course, some children are able to learn from a disrupted placement and to move successfully into the next placement. We do not want to deprive the latter group of children, when one placement does not work out, of the chance to try again. A balanced, cautious approach is best, especially if it leans toward taking a risk on adoption when there is even a modest chance for success. We need longitudinal follow-up studies to assess these practices.

Certain questions are raised in all adoptions. First, is the adoptive family willing to accept the child's roots? The acceptance of a whole human being with all his or her previous ties and connections is crucial. What differentiates human beings from other animal species is possession of memory, conscious planning abilities, and fantasy. We all have a genetic past, and we need to be allowed to think and wonder about it.

Regardless of the age at which children join a new family, their past must be validated. They must be helped to understand and accept the past in spite of the circumstances that surrounded their parents' inability to provide for them. Whether a child is adopted in infancy or at a later age should make no difference in the adoptive family's acceptance of the child's need and right to know. Adopted children have two sets of roots, of equal importance: the genetic roots given to the child by biological parents and the social and cultural roots provided by the adoptive family. If the biological and the adoptive parents were to draw their family trees, this child would be included in both. The important task is to validate that reality [Spencer 1980:13].

Second, all adoptions involve risk, in fact a very high degree of risk. People who find risk difficult should be discouraged from adopting children. Adoptive parents often criticize adoption agencies for providing too little information about the child's past. Workers who search for an adoptive home may be reluctant to share too much that is negative about a child's past. Or the adoption agency may not have a great deal of information. Just as many of us lack relevant genetic knowledge when we create our biological families, so too there will always be gaps in knowledge when someone adopts a child. Often the agency has given information the adoptive family has failed to hear in their eagerness to adopt, so they are, indeed, honest when they say "nobody told us." Adoptive families who need to know everything will quickly be disappointed. Life and growth are shrouded by the unknown and unknowable. To some, the unknown becomes a nightmare; for others, the unknown becomes an exciting adventure of ongoing discovery.

Health issues and adjustment problems will arise that cannot be foreseen. A new member entering a family has an impact on all other members. Family configurations shift. Some families feel better adopting an infant; however, even an infant can present challenges not anticipated before placement, such as minimal brain dysfunction or other neurological problems that affect learning. Many young mothers who ultimately choose adoption were not able to take good care of themselves during pregnancy. In some instances, prenatal and birth history could give some clues to potential difficulties. However, while some of the records are very complete and comprehensive, others are sparse or lacking altogether. With older children there is often information available on how they have progressed physically and developmentally, but many unknowns exist about the quality of the caring the children have experienced during their most crucial formative years.

Adoptive families do best when they are willing to take risks and do not need a high degree of predictability. They want to add a child to their family because they want to be parents. Often potential adoptive families are seeking a sense of completion for themselves and their family unit; at other times the motivation is to help a child who needs a home. Whatever the motive, families that find it easy to add others to their intimate circle have an easier time than families who come from backgrounds where it was difficult to include new family members. Families with extended kin relationships and active community involvement usually do better than more isolated families.

Achievement expectations can be a major issue in adoptive families. Families that emphasize their children's academic or professional achievement are disappointed if achievement is average or below average. This disappointment is inevitably conveyed to the child, especially one with learning deficits [McRoy et al. 1985], and the deficits are often blown out of proportion because of unrealistic family expectations. These families would have the same difficulties with a low-achieving biological child. However, when learning disabilities occur in an adopted child, inordinate disappointment may be projected onto that child. The more flexible a family is in its acceptance of a wide range of potential, the lower the risk for the child.

The child, particularly a very young child, does not participate in the adoption decision. The philosophy of practice has changed to allow families to make their own judgments of which child would be best for them. Yet the child's needs and rights have to be protected by the placing agency, which ultimately is responsible for representing her or his best interests. Not only does the family take a risk by adopting the child; the child also takes a risk. The agency, therefore, remains responsible for the child's welfare in every placement decision.

CATEGORIES OF ADOPTION

Beyond these general issues that affect all adoptions, specific issues are unique to infant, special-needs, older-child, minority, and intercountry adoption. They deserve separate attention.

Infant Adoption

Infant adoption programs in the United States have declined significantly with the popularity of birth control, abortion, and lifestyles that allow single mothers to keep their babies with less stigma. Nevertheless, there are an increasing number of families and individuals who would very much like to adopt a healthy Caucasian infant.

In most instances people have three options. The first is to apply to an infant adoption agency, often connected with a program for pregnant women in need of help in planning for their baby. The waiting lists are usually long; the religious affiliation of the couple may present a barrier if there are few infants of their particular faith in need of homes. Cross-religious placements do occur, however, and couples looking to adopt an infant should explore every available resource. People who become discouraged by the long wait have the second option of adopting an out-of-country child or an American child with special needs.

Inevitably some individuals with the necessary financial resources will choose the third option by seeking a physician or attorney to assist them in finding a baby and circumventing the child welfare system. There are families whose needs have been met and babies who have found good nurturing homes through this route, but the process offers the child little protection. Physicians and attorneys—however well-meaning and competent in their own practice—are not trained in the complexities of building families through adoption. Families do not receive the counseling necessary; above all, infants do not receive the protection to which they are entitled. The money exchanged often exceeds legitimate expense reimbursement and fees for service. In some states the courts may ask a bona fide social agency to do a home study prior to legalization of these adoptions. Inevitably the professional social worker is placed in a bind. If the placement is at all questionable, the damage done to the infant by interrupting bonding versus approving the placement must be carefully weighed.

Just as physicians and lawyers need to be licensed to practice their professions, so adoption should be handled only by those who have the appropriate credentials to do so. Stringent state licensing and enforcement structures are essential to protect children from high-risk gray- and black-market placements. The ability to pay high fees for a child is not a measure of parenting potential. We owe children this minimal protection.

Some interesting figures on individually arranged adoptions are cited in Victor Flango's report [1990]. The percentage of individually arranged adoptions varies from zero in those states where individually arranged adoptions are not permitted (as in Connecticut, Delaware, Massachusetts, Michigan, Minnesota, and South Dakota) to a figure as high as 80 percent in California and 83 percent in Georgia. The breakdown by source of placement, however, is not available for all states [Flango 1990:273–74].

Special-Needs and Older-Child Adoption

Older children and those with physical, behavioral, and emotional disabilities were traditionally considered "hard to place" in adoptive homes. These are the youngsters about whom much has been written in the literature on foster care, emphasizing how the lack of permanence and commitment allowed them to drift into adulthood without a permanent sense of belonging. Some spent a part or all of their childhood and adolescence in institutions. Others were moved repeatedly from one foster home to another. "Intended to be temporary, foster care often became a permanent arrangement. One national survey found that about one-fourth of all foster children spent over six years in care" [Shyne and Schroeder 1978:119]. "Many foster children, especially those with special needs, languished in care without the opportunity to return home or to be adopted" [Nelson 1985:1]. Some children may not have started with special needs but multiple placements and lack of adults' permanent commitment turned them into emotionally scarred young people.

Concern about foster care drift began to accelerate in the 1960s and 1970s in the United States and elsewhere. The permanency planning movement had much to do with the ultimate passage of Public Law 96–272, known as the federal Adoption Assistance Act. Under the law, agencies are held responsible for quickly and decisively returning children to their biological families or placing them permanently, preferably through adoption by families committed to them.

By challenging the assumptions that underlie adoption practice, the permanency planning movement brought about a revolution in the adoption scene. By asserting that no child is unadoptable, advocates have sought to free special-needs children from the hard-to-place label. They furthered efforts to extend adoption services to special-needs children by redefining the objectives of those services. In particular, the ideology of the permanency planning movement considers children awaiting placement rather than prospective parents as "the primary clients" of adoption services [Nelson 1985:3].

Of course, there are instances where children have spent their early years in particularly committed and caring foster homes. Children in such foster homes, given current changes in adoption philosophy and practice, are often adopted by their foster parents and do not join the ranks of special-needs children under discussion here.

Find Me a Family by Hedi Argent describes the new philosophy of finding homes for children with special needs. She describes Parents for Children, an experimental adoption agency in England founded in 1976 "to test out whether every child with special needs could be adopted. Adoption is for life. It is the only method of giving a child who has lost parents a secure and legal replacement" [Argent 1984:5]. Parents for Children not only pioneered adoption of older children but also of those with Down's Syndrome. The organization found families that were nontraditional in their needs and values. These families had the courage, commitment, and vision to do what had always been called not doable.

Some children with special needs have particular handicaps, such as blindness, cerebral palsy, or deafness; there are mentally retarded children and Down's Syndrome children. There are families who want to share their lives with these children, and derive much personal satisfaction from doing so. The challenge for the human services practitioner is to bring these various families and children together in a special support network.

Families have a wide and varied range of cultural values. Often professionals living in one value system find it difficult to understand people who live in a different one. At a time when young people seem to be moving away from the helping professions and other endeavors that require considerable personal effort with little or no financial remuneration, some practitioners may find it difficult to understand families who want to adopt children with special needs.

Special-needs adoption should function in collaboration with other service systems. It is best structured within an agency that has an array of services to avoid needless miscommunication, interagency bureaucratic slowdowns, and philosophic differences and biases.

The array of services may begin with an outreach preventive services department helping a biological family to think through possible adoption for their child as one solution to their life and parenting difficulties, and helping the child's special needs to grow. The child may need to be placed in an institution to work through the trauma of eviction from the biological family before the adoption process can begin. Residential staff must be in close communication with the outreach prevention staff, and very much involved with each phase of the termination or voluntary surrender of parental rights. In this way the child feels secure in knowing that the agency is there to care for her or him until a new permanent family is found.

Most children who need special preadoptive placement are no longer living with their biological families. Some are in foster homes; others are in group residences and child-care institutions. They have been in placement for varying lengths of time, and time is running out for them. The fact that these children are in need of parents implies that they have experienced serious losses; many have also been the victims of abuse and neglect, and have never felt truly secure and wanted during their most vulnerable formative years.

A potential adoptive family for an older child with a history of multiple placements must be told that this will be a troubled child. She or he will need a great deal of nurturance and professional help to become an optimally functioning human being. For many of these children, "love is not enough."

Carefully designed residential programs can be effective in preparing troubled older children for adoption. Residential units designed for this purpose can provide the support of a peer group to work through losses and help construct memory aids, such as scrapbooks, to help youngsters reexperience and understand their past and the many connections of importance to them. Social workers who help children during the adoption preparation process should see that they reconnect with and visit foster families, teachers, and, of course, relatives, if any can be found. This kind of experiential work is necessary for a young person to get a sense of wholeness as preparation for joining and bonding with a new family.

Allowing potential adoptive families to work as volunteers in a residential unit can be helpful in several ways. First, it helps family members assess whether they really can and want to continue the search for a special-needs child. It gives them a sense of what their own tolerance level might be in dealing with some of the demands, inappropriate behaviors, and developmental lags so characteristic of these children. Furthermore, the exposure allows children and families to search each other out. Natural interpersonal attractions crystallize without commitment on anyone's part. If a volunteer family and a child naturally relate to each other, staff can facilitate the initiation of a more formal adoption application.

The timing of adoptive placement is always an issue, and a great deal of conflict and disagreement usually surfaces when a child is "ready" to leave the protected environment of the institution. The residential staff have invested in the youngster and they seek to protect him or her. They are often looking for the perfect moment for separation which will never come. As children move closer to the time when they are to join their new families, they become frightened. With this fear comes ambivalence and inevitable behavioral regression, misinterpreted as lack of readiness to make the move. At times we expect the impossible of children, and refuse to validate what is normal. Of course these children will be frightened. They have previously been badly hurt, and they have a very understandable fear of the unknown.

What is usually not all right is how residential youngsters express their fear and ambivalence. Teaching the expression of feelings through appropriate behaviors needs to go on for a long time, and will become a primary task for the new adoptive family. Delaying placement because of a child's behavior is usually quite counterproductive. The adoptive family may see the institutional staff as causing the behavior. Families often live in the fantasy that when the child is no longer subjected to the negative influences of the residential environment the inappropriate behavior will disappear; of course, this rarely happens.

The only people who can assess when a child should leave residential care are the adoptive family members, but the staff should be open in expressing their concerns. We can assume that there will never be a right time, and that support services will have to be provided. Families who adopt older and handicapped children can benefit from belonging to a support group of parents with similar children. Other children in the family who become siblings to the newcomer often benefit from membership in sibling support groups. Staff and foster families with whom the child has lived can be very helpful.

We often speak of helping a child to say "goodbye" to previous caretakers, but this expectation is arbitrary and unrealistic. Children who have experienced multiple losses in the course of their short lives will need to live and rework these losses over a life span. Adoptive families should help them do so. Those relationships that do not need to be broken abruptly and permanently should be treasured and nurtured so that the young person can continue to reach out and reconnect for as long as the bond has meaning. These youngsters have usually been the victims of many arbitrary relationship cutoffs. There should be no need to repeat this hurtful cycle of events.

Children should be encouraged to call staff, foster parents, and friends to whom they feel close. As they begin to develop roots in their new family and new life, these contacts will naturally decrease. Postplacement and postlegal adoptive services, including respite services, support group participation, and individual family counseling, should be recognized as a right of families embarking on the adoption of older and handicapped children.

Minority Adoption

Many of the same issues that affect older-child adoption are relevant to minority adoption. But some issues are unique to minority adoption programs. Traditionally in this country, private voluntary agencies have not provided extensive service to the minority community. Minority community contact with social agencies usually has been with the public family assistance or child protective department. Many of these contacts have negative and even painful memories attached to them. Since it is this same public agency that also provides adoption services, potential African-American adopters in search of a child often shun contact with the public agency.

Furthermore, African-American and Hispanic families in the United States have traditionally cared for their children within their own kin systems. Both Hispanic and African-American families have lived in extended family community clusters, and childrearing was not necessarily done by the nuclear family. Households were held together by women who seemed to be very self-reliant in raising and nurturing the young. Only in situations where the larger family suffered a major breakdown was there an inability to raise another child.

However, major industrial forces pushing for geographic mobility have left many of these extended families unable to cope with new surroundings and confronted with too many adverse circumstances simultaneously. It is not surprising, therefore, given the levels of poverty, unemployment, and underemployment in the minority communities, that the number of minority children in the child welfare system has consistently been overrepresented. Yet the quality and quantity of services provided for them have not matched the need. "The most recent national data gathered by the U.S. Office of Civil Rights in 1980 indicate that 58 percent of the out-of-home child welfare population were white and 42 percent were minorities" [Hogan and Siu 1988:493], with black children comprising the most overrepresented group.

For the purposes of this discussion adoption issues are limited specifically to the African-American child, since this category remains a major area of concern in the field of adoption, although one in which much progress is being made.

African-American families have been very successful as foster families because their own family system is usually not closed. What are the reasons for the large number of these African-American children in foster care who eventually enter the pool of children waiting for permanent family ties?

Hall and King point out that according to the United States Census, already by 1970 there were among African-Americans 1.3 million female-headed family households as compared with 3.3 million two-parent households [1982:539]. The female-headed household and a deterioration in family cohesiveness have become the scapegoat for explaining why African-American children are drifting in foster care.

A great deal has been written about the slave origins of the African-American family. But only recently has there been a growing recognition of the remarkable family strengths that have evolved from this difficult and destructive past.

It was just over a decade ago that practitioners even considered that structure and functioning in black families might be more related to resiliency than to pathology. ... The traits commonly used by black families to meet individual needs and survive in society can be used advantageously by those who work with black families. ... The five strengths we have identified are kin-structured networks, elastic households, resilient children, egalitarian two-parent relationships, and steadfast optimism. [Hall and King 1982:540–541]

Thus we began to think ecologically in the sense of concentrating on "the sensitive balance between living things and their environments and the ways in which this mutuality may be enhanced and maintained" [Devore 1983:525]. Agency workers began to recognize how an inappropriate model of family assessment and care had gotten in the way of using existing family ties in the African-American community to provide that community the services to which they are entitled.

A knowledge of the black family value system can be helpful to the adoption worker who does not fully comprehend why more blacks do not adopt children through formal adoption agencies [nor why] ... the unmarried mother with little or no income will elect to keep her baby rather than select alternatives that would appear to be in the child's best interests. [Hall and King 1982:538]

We must, therefore, not lose sight of the key issues of poverty in the African-American community linked to single-parenting due to African-American male unemployment or underemployment. Even here there is bias in the assumptions commonly made, for the African-American poor are more likely to work than the white poor [Hill 1973:44].

We must understand the organization of the African-American community, including its heavy reliance on the church as a social integrator, helping system, and mutual aid group. The social welfare system has historic roots in the Elizabethan poor laws of Great Britain and has a moralistic and punitive stance toward parents who are perceived as not caring adequately for their children. It is not surprising that it has been insensitive to the needed protection of the African-American child from loss of kin and biological connections. Today this is more and more recognized in professional circles. We are beginning to see some work toward changing the philosophy of practice to assure a reduction in children who enter the foster care and adoption system in the first place. Schools of social work, professional conferences, and the literature have begun and must continue to address the issues of ethnic-sensitive practice on an ongoing basis.

Unhappily, we find ourselves confronted with polar alternatives. Historically, the white middle-class infant adoption agency did not provide for the African-American child because these agencies did not have African-American adoptive families as applicants. In any case, if African-American families had come forward, they would have been quickly disqualified for not meeting the agency's rigid and, for the African-American family, inappropriate, eligibility requirements.

As the number of Caucasian infants began to dwindle during the 1960s and 1970s, more Caucasian families began to press agencies to assist in finding African-American children for them. "In 1970 one-third of the 6,500 Black children in adoption were placed with white families" [Howard et al. 1977:184]. The transracial adoption movement began to grow, but has been surrounded by a great deal of controversy. As yet the research data and longitudinal studies are insufficient to determine the outcome of these placements.

The rationale behind transracial adoptions is that finding a permanent family committed to a child was more important than the race of that family. Concern, however, continued to linger about young people's resolution of identity issues as they reached adolescence. White families with African-American adopted children were encouraged to live in racially mixed neighborhoods and school districts so that the children would have exposure to other African-American families and children. Some families chose to join integrated churches or integrated organizations such as the local boys' club or neighborhood settlement house. Families that chose to adopt more than one African-American child in some instances made things easier for themselves and their adopted children.

Crucial issues remain, however: The Caucasian family cannot really protect their adopted African-American child from the overt or covert racism that still exists in the United States. An understandable outcome of racism is strengthening of racial identity and pulling together, leaving transracially adopted children to deal with problems of acceptance by the Caucasian community as well as rejection by their African-American peer group. For a young person already trying to cope with both adolescent development and adoption, the combination is very difficult. The issues can be negotiated, but they require unusually sensitive adoptive parents willing to experience a great deal of stress as their child struggles with these very complicated issues at a vulnerable age.

The American Association of Black Social Workers took a very strong position in April 1972 that "Black children should be placed only with Black families whether in foster care or adoption" [Madison and Shapiro 1973]. In response to this development and general changes in professional perception, many adoption agencies reexamined their practices. As a result some agencies reduced the numbers of transracial adoptions or gave them up altogether [Howard et al. 1977:184].

The successful "Black Homes for Black Children" movement, begun in Michigan, has demonstrated that, in order to provide African-American homes for African-American children, agencies must have African-American staff and use family recruitment practices that validate the assets of African-American culture and community.

Traditional criteria for family selection based on housing adequacy, size of household, and age of parents have to be abandoned. When an African-American child appears in need of placement, the youngster's extended biological kinship system must be contacted to understand and reaffirm the family's inability to absorb the child. The African-American family must be viewed as an extended kin support network in which the childrearing functions often are shared among several family members. Based upon a careful assessment, referral to preventive services should occur immediately.

If and when placement is necessary, and there is no hope of return to the birth family or kinship group, an African-American adoption program should be used. Unhappily, many African-American children in need of adoptive placement have been in the foster care system too long and have been seriously hurt by being in limbo. With sufficient ingenuity, hard work, and commitment, however, African-American staff have been able to find African-American families willing to share their lives with many of these youngsters. Families often must be recruited in geographic areas different from the ones in which the child is being cared for in foster placement, since many African-American families have successfully relocated away from the major urban centers from which the children come. In relocating, these potential adoptive parents have been able to find stable employment and improve their quality of life, which makes adoption possible and desirable for them.

As with many older-child adoptions, the African-American adoptive family often requires postadoption services. These are best provided by an outpatient clinic if one is available as part of an agency's array of services. The clinic should be staffed with a person not only experienced in older-child adoption but also in minority adoption.

A minority adoption program can be freestanding, but it can also function well as a subcomponent of any adoption or general social service agency. Professionally trained minority staff are difficult to find and even more difficult to keep because of their scarcity; the use of part-time staff can be helpful. Sharing of minority adoption staff with a clinic providing postadoption services can sometimes be arranged. Minority consultants can have major impact.

An agency that wants to undertake a minority or African-American adoption program must take many factors into account. A traditional agency may be viewed with suspicion by the minority community, which has a legitimate concern as to whether the commitment of the agency is genuine. There is no shortcut to building trust; it takes a long time to develop a legitimate track record. The agency's board of directors must be prepared to broaden services to all residents of a community and, through extensive board education, be helped to see that this kind of shift will require identifying board members representative of the minority community and perspective.

A successful minority adoption program entails a major educational component through African-American community channels such as the church and ministers' association, as well as discussions with key community leaders. A community advisory group to the professional staff can be invaluable in assisting recruitment, interpreting the program to the minority community, and identifying the key community leaders needed to help the program. As families go through the adoption process, a pool of well-qualified adoptive parents also becomes available for advisory board membership.

Intercountry Adoption

With the steep decline in the number of healthy Caucasian infants and toddlers for people seeking to adopt, many young children have been brought to this country for adoption from parts of the world overwhelmed by large numbers of children whose birth parents are unable to provide for them. As noted earlier, some countries have cultural prohibitions against adopting children from another blood line. Some countries lack the resources to provide good alternatives for orphaned or abandoned children. In 1980 approximately 5,000 babies were granted visas by the U.S. Immigration and Naturalization Service for the purpose of adoption. In 1987 this figure peaked at approximately 10,000, with a sharp decline to approximately 7,800 in 1989. A vast majority of these visas were issued to Asian babies; the next largest group came from Central and South America [Lewin 1990:B10]. For the purposes of this discussion, only the many placements of infants and children from South Korea, which comprised the largest single group, will be used as an example.

Since 1980 alone, more than 40,000 babies from South Korea have joined American families. The Korean War, postwar reconstruction, and industrialization brought rapid and almost overwhelming changes to South Korea. Population mobility, shifts in values and lifestyles, and the lack of funds for education and social services left mothers and children very vulnerable.

Young South Korean women left the protected environment of their family and countryside to move into the city in search of employment. They lacked birth control information and social survival skills. Out-of-wedlock pregnancy was not accepted in the culture, and a young woman who found herself pregnant could not return home to her family with her child. Without a father, the child could not be registered and could never attain full citizenship. Desperate young mothers frequently turned their babies over to a social agency or simply left the infants to be foundlings.

Several South Korean agencies developed placement programs to find homes for these children in the United States, Europe, and Australia, although from the beginning the agencies tried to liberalize attitudes about adoption in their own country. Very gradually in-country adoptive placements have begun to increase, and the long-standing cultural bias against the adoption of children from another blood line has diminished. With these developments and substantial improvements in disseminating birth control information, the number of Korean adoptions abroad has decreased sharply and will soon cease.

Some features of the Korean adoption programs are unique. Korean culture has a strong commitment to children, and foster homes do an unusually good job of nurturing the infant and toddler. The inability to care for all Korean children generated pain and concern for the social agencies and the South Korean government. The South Korean Ministry of Social Welfare has developed systematic procedures and requirements regarding the placement abroad with potential adoptive families, but there remains a great deal of concern and anxiety in South Korea about the out-of-country adoption of so many Korean children.

Early in the Korean adoption program, a few agencies placed children across the United States often in collaboration with other agencies. This process did not assure that the adoptive home study, postplacement supervision, and aftercare, if necessary, were provided by the placing agency. Some families and youngsters fell through the cracks when services were needed.

By the late 1970s, however, program development had become quite structured, and South Korean agencies caring for children in need of placement were asked by their government to develop contracts with selected foreign agencies. These agencies were to do family home studies, facilitate placement, and assure adequate postplacement supervision and postlegal adoption services. A close working relationship between the staff of the Korean child welfare agency and the American placing agency became an important component in the facilitation of placements. Through most of the 1980s the staffs of both agencies visited each other frequently to get to know and understand each other, and Korean social workers served on the staff of American placing agencies whenever feasible.

Children who come to adoption from South Korean family foster care have received much cuddling and body contact. This positive beginning stands the youngsters in good stead in the massive adjustments during the postplacement period. Large numbers of Korean children are also blessed with better than average academic potential, which allows for positive reinforcement for both the child and the family. The negative side of this equation is that the youngsters who are learning disabled—and a significant number are due to their often premature birth—bear a double burden since both the family and the teachers have high expectations. Despite the transracial nature of almost all of these adoptions, the limited research available suggests that Korean children adopted in the United States have adjusted well.

But issues remain in intercountry adoptions. According to Dong Soo Kim, in his article, "Issues in Transracial and Transcultural Adoption,"

The mental health of children is influenced and determined by all that goes on in their environment. Helping adoptive children make a healthy adjustment to the new environment is of great importance. In the placement of infants or very young children, such adjustment may be mainly a physiological adaptation with or without minor difficulties. However, the older foreign child's adjustment is a more prolonged process of accommodation and assimilation to the new home and community, in which the predominant cultural forms, ethnographic composition, and historical experiences differ from those of the child's background. . . . When adjustment problems are considered in a long-term perspective, they evolve into a general issue of how successfully the foreign child can achieve total socialization potential in American society. [Kim 1978:480]

Indeed, the adjustment of Korean or other children of non-Western background in the United States is a complex issue. We hear from many adoptive parents that they feel toward their non-Western child as they do toward their birth children. The experience of nurturing and caring for the child has bonded them so that physiological differences do not seem to play a significant role. In fact, it seems doubtful if racial physiological differences are factors impeding adoptive bonding and adjustment, unless major vulnerabilities already mitigate against mental health. Different ethnic characteristics are a reality in American society. During adolescence, only a relatively brief period in a human life, Asian children, like children everywhere, seek to accentuate their likeness to the dominant peer group, rather than searching out and accentuating their differences. Identity issues should be anticipated by service providers and are best worked through with thoughtful planning and problem prevention rather than crisis intervention.

Agencies that place Korean and other out-of-country children take on a sensitive responsibility in family education. The initial preparation of Americans applying to adopt should involve their families in sensitivity sessions to determine whether they are indeed prepared, willing, and excited about becoming a racially mixed family. Families cannot, and must not, expect their Korean or other out-of-country child to assimilate fully into the new ethnic and cultural environment. Instead, the family must be willing to learn about the child's cultural origins and ethnic history. Cultural traditions, foods, and dress for special occasions must early be woven into the child's now racially mixed family. Support groups that involve families with other children of the same cultural background are very helpful.

For example, when a Korean child and his or her family live near others with Korean children, play groups and informal get-togethers can be arranged. Families should select school districts that have other Korean children. Some communities have adult Korean populations and church groups. The assistance of these churches and other Korean social groups should be solicited. Korean or other foreign adoption programs, just like the African-American adoption programs, benefit from an active advisory group. These groups can be made up of adoptive parents and citizens of the children's ethnicity.

Agencies that bring children to the United States from abroad must provide services beyond the legally required six-month postplacement period. Some agencies have sponsored cultural summer or day camps. Parent education programs and workshops can be invaluable. Inevitably difficulties will occur and families should be encouraged to seek preventive help rather than allow tensions and anxieties to grow.

The possible need by the Korean children to search for their family of origin cannot be ignored. When feasible, return visits to Korea by the children as they grow older, together with their adoptive families, are very desirable. Some young people returning to Korea have made connections with their birth families. This can often be very difficult and confusing because the standard of living and culturally determined behavioral expectations are so different. When young people do have the need to search for their birth family, that search may be very helpful in giving some closure to their family fantasy. Fortunately, case records of adopted children are not sealed in South Korea, and South Korean child welfare agencies are free to share whatever information they have. These agencies are very willing to assist young people in their search.

Korean adopted children, like all adoptees, are the product of two sets of roots, their biological roots from their birth parents, and their second, equally important, roots given them by their psychological parents. The more aware and at peace all members of the adoption triad (adoptive parents, birth parents, and child) are with the integrity of the multiple rooting, the better the child's adjustment.

Professionals, government officials, and the judges responsible for legalizing the adoption are all left with the inevitable question as to whether uprooting children from their own culture is in their best interest. A thoughtful response to this serious question requires a careful assessment of what the children's lives would probably have been like had a foreign adoption not taken place. Under the best of circumstances, children should be raised by their own birth family in their country of origin. This is not always possible, in which case those responsible for decisions have to seek the next best alternative. Children should not be brought to this country from abroad primarily to benefit adults who want to raise children. Out-of-country adoption can only be professionally justified if the adoptions are in the best interest of the children who are being uprooted from their own land and culture.

The number of South Korean children in need of out-of-country adoption is rapidly declining. In 1987, 5,910 entry visas into the United States were issued to Korean children. By 1989, only two years later, this figure declined to 3,552 [Lewin 1990:B10]. The per capita income in Korea has been increasing, as have educational opportunities for women. There has been a substantial decrease in out-of-wedlock births, as well as attitudinal changes regarding in-country adoption, and the number of children coming into care of the South Korean placement agencies is dropping rapidly. This must be viewed as a very positive sign showing significant success on the part of the South Korean government and South Korean society in dealing with an issue that has caused a great deal of national pain, and at times very negative publicity. These Korean developments, however, leave many families in the United States and other Western countries unhappy about the loss of opportunity to parent Korean children.

Problems continue to arise in placing children from countries that are not as well organized as South Korea, and that seem not to have developed equally high standards of child protection for youngsters leaving their native land. Families in the United States are adopting children from these countries without the protection of professional family screening and follow-up supports for the child and family. They often seek help from the mental health system after serious damage has already occurred. The United States and the children's country of origin have a shared responsibility. Together they must build in safeguards to protect children on the hazardous road of intercountry adoptions. It may be interesting to note at this point that India, Thailand, and Fiji have enacted adoption laws similar to those promulgated in South Korea to facilitate responsible intercountry adoption for those children for which these countries are not able to adequately provide at this time [Kim n.d.:16].

POSTADOPTION SERVICES

Building families through adoption is different from building families biologically. By acknowledging this difference, we have eliminated the need for a destructive harboring of secrets. In most instances now, the family and the adopted child are quite open about sharing the information. But we have given insufficient help to adoptees in validating their dual sets of roots. Especially in adolescence, when young people struggle to establish their identity, this duality can raise concerns. Young people who have been adopted later in childhood and have distinct memories of, or have maintained their connections to, members of their birth family experience fewer complications from this duality.

Adoption is a major event not only in the life cycle of the adopted person, but in the life cycle of the adoptive parents and the birth parents. The reasons why people choose to adopt are complex and highly personal. Adoption is often a very legitimate way of coping with the loss of another child, or with being unable to bear children because of infertility, or with the sense of loss when children leave home. Birth mothers and fathers have their own reasons, equally personal. Planning adoption for their child rather than choosing to raise it themselves is a major life decision, about which anyone involved will continue to have some doubts. Life, however, never stands still, and major losses in life need to be worked through over and over again as the life cycle moves on.

For these reasons postadoption services are an essential component of any quality program. A great deal of work is still needed to assure that carefully designed services are available to all adoptees, adoptive parents, and birth parents. In addition to infant adoptions, there are now many older- and special-needs child adoptions that require specialized postadoption services. Many of the special-needs children are from minorities. Others come from foreign countries, often from non-Western cultures. They and their families have unique needs. Traditionally, the adoptees, adoptive parents, and birth parents have received counseling through established mental health services or through private practitioners in their communities if available.

The rationale for adoptive placement, as well as the process by which families and children come together, has changed over the last twenty years. Postadoption services are best staffed by people who understand and have had extensive experience in adoption and child placement, understand birth parents, and can philosophically validate the importance of the adoption triad and the part each member of that triad plays.

Crises in adoptive families are often no different than crises experienced by all families at nodal points in the life cycle. Adoption brings its own unique characteristics to the family situation, but needs to be understood within the broader context. An individual child may have special needs that contribute to the difficulties experienced by the family, and a careful assessment may be needed. Value judgments as to whether the adoptive placement should have occurred in the first place are of little help and can be detrimental. Instead of dealing with those issues that precipitated the request for help, energy is often diverted to searching for a scapegoat, usually the agency that facilitated the placement. Instead, a systemic approach to problems experienced by an adoptive family can be very useful.

The desire of birth parents to learn about their children's fate and the desire of adoptees to know more about and even meet their birth parents are now considered legitimate human needs. Postadoptive counseling for birth parents and adoptees who seek each other out is an essential program component. This process, however, is still surrounded by substantial controversy and disagreement. Progressive momentum has come from groups of adult adoptees, and research is beginning in the field on the differences between those adoptees who search for their birth parents and those who do not. Aumend and Barrett [1984] report that in their study of 131 adoptees, 71 wanted to search for their birth parents and 49 did not. There were differences between the two groups on almost every measure that was applied, yet the results

do not support the belief that adoptees, in general, have low self-concepts and identity conflicts, or that adoptees need information about their biological families and reunions to resolve their identity conflicts. . . . Although significant differences exist between the comparison groups, an important finding is that of all the adult adoptees, the majority scored above the sixtieth percentile of the TSCS and had positive scores on the Attitude Toward Parents Scales. Furthermore, they were happy growing up, with only 12% reporting being unhappy. These findings support . . . the belief that adoption is a legitimate way of building families. [Aumend and Barrett 1984:258–259]

New Zealand passed an Adult Adoption Information Act in 1985 that is far-reaching in its implications and very progressive in its thinking. It gives new rights to adults (age twenty and over) who were adopted as children, and to their parents, to get access to—or protect—information about each other. For example,

As an adopted adult or birth parent, you have the right to know more—or the right to maintain privacy. You have the right to choose. From March 1, 1986 you may have a veto put on the register, which will ensure that all information about you is kept confidential by the Registrar-General and the Department of Social Welfare. From September 1986 adopted adults over the age of twenty and birth parents are entitled to find out about each other, unless a veto has been put on the register. The law had been changed because it is recognized that people in the adoption process may feel more complete when they have knowledge of their origins and of each other. [Adult Adoption Information]

The concerns felt by adoptive parents about adoptees who seek to reunite with or learn about their birth parents are understandable. Some people fear that the right of adoptees to seek out their past could turn away some potential adoptive parents. Yet families who need to maintain secrets probably should not adopt. Older children, of course, are not able to be deprived of their knowledge about their past, because they come to the adoption with that knowledge. Today the number of infants in need of adoption is very few and the number of families who want them is large. Therefore, the movement toward opening information to the adoptees and birth parents if both parties desire this should in no way diminish the pool of potential adoptive parents.

Postadoption services should be a separate component in an array of services offered by an agency providing adoption services. Ideally this department should be separately staffed by professionals who have come from the ranks of the adoption department. Services should be preventive and allow for support groups, picnics, and other special social events, and respite and educational services, in addition to family counseling. One advantage to this model is that separating postadoption services from adoption services within the organization allows for the introduction of new staff. Because of their familiarity with a child and family and their sense of responsibility to the child or youth involved, adoption workers have particular difficulty managing a threat of disruption to an adoption. Yet, when not responsible for postadoption counseling, the placement staff of the adoption department can easily be available for consultation, along with those in foster care, residential, and other programs to whom the child and family may have been known.

When services are provided through a family counseling clinic licensed by a state mental health system, that clinic is usually able to collect third-party payments and state medical assistance payments for which special-needs adopted children are usually eligible. Some clinics also receive United Way and mental health financial support, which then allows the creation of a sliding scale according to income. Some practitioners believe that the government should fund postadoption services as a much less expensive alternative to government-funded institutionalized and foster children. The only way to fund a postadoption service at this time is by creatively combining a number of possible resources. This lack of predictable, comprehensive funding often leaves people most in need without service.

CONCLUSION

During the past twenty years there have been major changes in the philosophy of adoption. We have moved away from a service designed almost exclusively to meet the needs of couples seeking to adopt an infant because of their inability to have a child of their own. Today we seek to meet the needs of children whose birth families are unable to care for them, and who are therefore in need of permanent family connections. Adoption is regarded as a possible choice for a child, regardless of age, race, ethnic background, or special physical or psychological needs.

Eligibility requirements for adoptive families have also changed. Agencies no longer screen potential adoptive parents according to rigid requirements on age, race, religious affiliation, marital status, and fertility. They try instead to understand a family and its unique needs. The basic philosophic assumption is that the family members will know best what kind of child they can include in their family. Single parents and people with a variety of lifestyles have demonstrated their ability to parent children otherwise left to drift in foster care. Nevertheless, the decision for placement does remain with the agency, as the ultimate protector of a child's needs and rights.

A variety of specialized adoption programs have developed to address especially the needs for adoption of older children with special needs, minority children, and children from foreign countries. Given the complex needs of the children and families who will blend to form a new unit in adoption, appropriate preventive and ongoing services must be available. Specialized postadoption services, including counseling for those people, whether the adoptee or birth parents, in search of their biological kin, are now seen as essential.

The issue of interracial adoption for children requires much more study. The question is frequently asked by potential adoptive parents, "Why is it that agencies will place Latin American or East Asian children with Caucasian families and yet these same agencies will not place African-American children with Caucasian families?" The rationale that justifies these agency practices is driven by what is in the best interest of children. We now recognize that when appropriately recruited very desirable African-American families are ready to adopt. It is only in those instances when a family of the child's racial background is not available that an interracial adoption can be justified. There are those of us who wish that things were different. Unhappily, however, our society is still scarred by too much interracial bias and strife. Whenever possible, children should be protected from these identity struggles, which are then added to normal maturational tasks and the very special tasks attached to being adopted.

The research findings, although limited, point to adoption as a legitimate family-building option. It can meet the needs of people who seek to raise a child or children, often very different in background from their own. At the same time it can meet the needs of children in need of a permanent, nurturing family with whom they can bond.

NOTE

1. The Supreme Court decision in *Roe v. Wade*, 1973, legalized all but last-trimester abortion throughout the United States.

PART IV

Residential Group Care Services

In this section, the needs of youth not able to function in family-based services are examined. The community-based group residence is offered as one model of care with a variety of program alternatives for youth able to benefit from this option, while the campus-based residential program is designed for those youth who require more structure and protection. Again, these programs are suggested within a philosophic framework that finds only planning for the short term falls short of meeting the fundamental human need for permanent connections to others. It looks to ways to secure, create, or re-create these connections.

9

The Group Home or Community Residence: Dilemmas and Opportunities for Community Support

Group homes, or community residences as they are sometimes called, have traditionally been intended to provide a living environment for young people who cannot live with their families, are not with foster families, are not ready to live independently, and yet are able to live in an ordinary community. Given the complex needs of populations now being served, this model of care will be discussed with a focus on how it can best fit into an array of placement options.

INTRODUCTION

The children's group home, sometimes called a community residence, is at a crossroads. We in the profession of children's services need to establish what it can and cannot be expected to do in an array of placement services for young people and their families.

Historically, institutions for children went through a "children's home" phase. Some eventually became residential treatment centers for severely troubled populations. However, in some parts of the country "children's homes" continue to exist, are staffed by houseparents, and serve youngsters who have the necessary coping skills to live in the community. These youth attend public schools, participate in community activities, but live in these congregate settings, which sometimes are similar to a cluster of group homes.

A survey of the literature demonstrates that there are many effective community-based residential and group home programs in some communities [Adams and Baumbach 1980; Schneider et al. 1982; Walsh 1985]. Yet regardless of whether these models are referred to as institutions, clusters of group homes, or group homes, insufficient work has often been done on identifying the children's permanent connections or on finding alternatives that would provide connections for these youth when they leave the "house" or "home."

During the 1970s and early 1980s the group home or community residence model became a panacea as pressures increased nationally to deinstitutionalize children. The assumption was that a small residence in the community was less expensive to operate and a better environment for young people than the large, geographically isolated congregate facility. Group homes or community residences were developed to house a variety of populations with special needs.

The identification of the needs of specific youth populations must be coupled with philosophic integrity, carefully thought-through program design, adequate staffing, and physical plant. Young people who have experienced residential care and have progressed sufficiently to move on, but for a variety of reasons are not able to return to either their birth families or adoptive families, are often eligible candidates for a group home. Many of these youth are adolescents who have drifted through the foster care system; time is running out for them. It is probably no longer realistic to seek adoption for them, with the exception of those who truly want it. Many have been hurt in family foster care placements and are apprehensive about another failure.

For some youth the group home works well; for others it works well temporarily. Yet for still others this model works marginally or not at all. In fact, with a philosophic emphasis on deinstitutionalization, there is always the danger of a youth's ending up at a lower level of care than the best professional judgment suggests. But equally important, no youth should remain in an institutional setting if she or he can possibly succeed in a group home or foster family. At times it is necessary to risk sending a youth to a community-based placement in order to find out whether the demands of well-structured, appropriately supervised community living are really a viable alternative for that individual.

STRUCTURE

A small residence situated in the community is a more desirable environment for children and adolescents than a large congregate institution behind a gate and fence. Young people come because they are unable to live with their birth or adoptive families. Careful assessments have been made: There are some very specific reasons why other family living arrangements, such as return to original family, family foster care, or adoptive placement, are not viable options for the moment.

As we develop an array of services that can provide optimal differentiated services for children, youth, and their families, the group home or community residence program can establish its own identity and legitimacy. Pierce and Hanck [1981:476] speak of the group home approach as "based on increasing concern for the social adaptation of children who experience difficulty as they move from one level of care to another, as they re-enter the community after institutionalization, or for whom removal from the community is unnecessary." There are very special populations who for one reason or another will never be able to live wholly independently, and group home living has much to offer as a stepping stone to semi-independent adult living. However, for group residences to be effective as living environments, they should not exceed seven or eight youngsters at the very most or they quickly begin to resemble mini-institutions.

Case planning, as always, should have a broad perspective on what a particular program plan will accomplish in the long run. Programming for today is important; a child or adolescent needs care, protection, and education; but today soon becomes tomorrow and then the day after tomorrow. We are preparing these young people to function optimally in a society in which they need to know how to be group members. The group provides nurturance and commitment, but in turn these youth as they grow must learn to also offer nurturance and commitment to others. Everyone needs these skills in order to function in adult life. It is, therefore, not good enough to select group home living as an end in itself. The placement must be perceived as a highly specialized option to be used under very special conditions only. Group homes must not become a catchall when we don't know what else to do for a child.

Every effort must be made to help these young people define themselves in relation to their roots and origins. Young people may need to reject these roots temporarily, because in many instances these have caused them much pain and disappointment. However, as they grow and change, their perceptions as to the cause of the disappointments may also change. The option of reconnection with family, rather than its permanent rejection, needs to remain open.

Further long-range planning needs to be an ongoing part of the process. Youth placed in group homes without clear short- and long-term life goals and direction will soon begin to regress. We all need goals and directions; although the goals may shift and change, the need for goals must not be ignored.

How grouping in group residences can best be done can be viewed in a number of different ways. There are those who believe in grouping by age and gender. The assumption here is that adolescents do best in a peer group. This assumption may be true for those youngsters who are emotionally able to function at the adolescent peer-group level. In many instances, however, those young people who end up living in group homes during either their latency or adolescent years have had life experiences that have not allowed them to mature optimally. We therefore often find young people under care who are mistakenly placed in groups intended to accomplish tasks ordinarily appropriate to the chronological age of the child or youth but quite inappropriate for the emotional level of the specific young person.

Since staff are often reluctant to mix youngsters of different gender, ages, and types of difficulties, this may mean missed opportunities for normalizing the child by creative individualized programming. The placement, for example, of all physically large, acting-out adolescents in one house may generate fear both among the residents and sometimes the staff. This can escalate into unmanageable violence. Yet when there are bigger and smaller children in the house with entirely different needs and behavioral manifestations, youngsters begin to help and protect each other. Young people have to learn to live in environments with a variety of people at different developmental levels and with different needs. Each individual has something very special and very different to offer to the group. Therefore, the family model, made up of a whole range of ages and of both sexes, might work well in some settings.

The relationships that develop are much more like family than peer. Sometimes it is even possible to place a developmentally disabled child in such a house. The placement of more than one such child in the same house, however, is not advisable, because of the amount of physical assistance and supervision usually needed. Mixed grouping provides a unique opportunity to allow youngsters to be in touch with their ability to care for others. Often we design programs geared to our concrete and emotional giving to children but place insufficient expectations on their need to grow by experiencing their own unique contributions to others and the benefit of subsequent positive feedback.

Children and youth living in mixed groups that more closely resemble a normal family group usually do not exhibit the degree of acting-out behavior that peer groups of similar age and size show. For one, mixed groups stimulate less competition among youngsters, since very clear messages can be given by staff that everyone's needs are different and that these needs will be met on an individual basis.

STAFFING

Supervising a group home is a very taxing job and badly undervalued by society. Ideally, a house should be staffed by resident houseparents with the assistance of relief child-care workers. If the house is part of an agency operating an array of services, many of the concrete home management tasks, such as maintenance, food purchasing, and accounting, can be taken care of by the appropriate departments of the larger organization for cost-effectiveness and to relieve the houseparents of these responsibilities. Some funds, however, should be allocated for supplementary food purchasing, since most people running houses do want leeway to shop on their own.

Some group homes are now staffed by rotating shifts of child-care workers. This staffing pattern creates some disruption in the continuity of care and serves to dilute relationships, but that often works well for those young people who have experienced too many losses and are in need of respite from close and demanding relationships with adults. For other youngsters, the discontinuity of staffing and the absence of consistent adult parent models are not desirable.

The reality remains that in some parts of the country, especially in the more urban, industrialized regions, it is very difficult to find qualified couples with the necessary personal attributes and experience willing to assume the position and lifestyle required of group home parents. If a couple resigns, the residents of the house become extremely vulnerable until a new couple is recruited, hired, and trained. Noncouple child-care staff are more easily replaced because in most instances their loss affects one shift at most; the house, therefore, does not need to fall apart. The house manager model is another approach to staffing: An experienced supervisory child-care professional who does not live in the house is responsible for running the house, including programming and staffing. By removing the live-in requirement, the position often attracts a larger number of qualified applicants. The very real danger of burnout is also substantially decreased for people who can detach themselves from the very intensive job pressures by leading a personal life away from their agency responsibilities.

Some group home programs now find that the populations they serve are so troubled that the houses require awake night staff in addition to intensive daytime staffing. Night staff can, of course, assist with housework, laundry, and other chores. One should question, however, the use of group homes for populations of youngsters requiring twenty-four-hour awake supervision. Are these really group homes? Or are they in fact tiny, and sometimes not so tiny, mini-institutions that operate in the community? On occasion there may be some extenuating circumstances in which awake nighttime assistance might be necessary for a group home on a temporary basis. A temporary need, however, is very different from permanently staffing a group home with twenty-four-hour awake coverage.

The dilemma of how to staff a group home is related to the needs of the population, the availability of people able and willing to do the job, and funding. There are major programmatic arguments why a small group home appropriately staffed is a better alternative to the placement of young people in large institutions. However, some compelling administrative decisions have to be made to determine at what level of staffing it is no longer possible to maintain an isolated individual house in the community. Agency administrators and practitioners must be sensitive to cost–benefit issues in the selection of a specific group home model for youngsters.

The maintenance of children requiring a great deal of supervision in the community presents some real financial issues. Staffing patterns and youth–staff ratios, of course, determine the cost. Group homes that require very intensive staffing by shifts become extremely expensive. Intensive staffing usually also indicates that on-call back-up resources must be available. When the number of staff in relation to the number of youngsters becomes high, the program is no longer financially viable under current reimbursement rates. Group homes, therefore, if perceived as a viable program choice, cannot necessarily be selected on the basis of being less costly.

At some cost level, specific population needs as well as the prognosis for self-dependence no longer realistically allow for the provision of isolated community residences, if the intention is to offer a less expensive model of care. One can, of course, argue that it is indeed legitimate to operate expensive group homes for certain populations that require temporary or long-term care, as long as the cost does not exceed the cost of institutional placement. The careful selection of youths for specific programs becomes essential. Agencies must remain flexible in their constant evaluation of a house in relation to population needs. Group homes are small enough as units of care so that change should be ongoing and easy.

One alternative might sometimes be a congregate complex of two or three small houses situated in the same neighborhood close enough to each other for mutual staff support and back-up. Staffing patterns and the houses' geographic location are key determinants for the populations that can be served successfully in this way.

Group homes must have clinical coordination and input if the intention is to link together the past, present, and future for the young people under care. One hears the argument that many youngsters who live in group homes do not have families, that they therefore simply need care, which can best be provided by child-care workers and houseparents, and that one can save money by omitting staff clinicians. This argument is fallacious. Houseparents and child-care workers have a major task in providing for the day-to-day living of a group of young people with very special needs. House staff involved in the many struggles and crises of day-to-day care cannot be expected to assure that the life connections of each child and the emotional needs for bonding be addressed and worked with. Anything less than a comprehensive approach amounts to foster care "drift" and "warehousing." If these children and youth had no special needs, they would be living at home with their parents.

The very fact that they cannot live at home makes these youngsters vulnerable, in need of special care and attention. Most children in group homes have complicated, painful histories in addition to their separation from family. Clinicians responsible for working with these youth and those connected to them must be in constant communication with the house staff. Regular team meetings that produce clearly delineated plans are essential. The task of the clinician attached to the house is to keep the relationships among the child's past, present, and future alive and to continue working on realistic long-range goals.

The training for houseparents and child-care workers in group homes must include the skills needed for the day-to-day operation of the house. However, a great deal of experiential training in the meaning of the staff's own roots and connections should be built into the program. Only through the realization of what our own connections mean to us can we begin to understand what the loss of connections really means to those children and youth who find themselves in limbo and become the responsibility of the child-caring systems of their communities.

The agency has a further responsibility to staff the house with people whose values and lifestyles are as much as possible compatible with that of the neighborhood. It would not be appropriate to have staff for whom a high level of upkeep of the living environment is not of much significance in a very meticulous middle-class area where neighbors take immaculate care of their property. We all know outstanding child-care workers who have much to offer children, but who do not give the attention to house maintenance appropriate for a neighborhood in which house upkeep and meticulous housekeeping are relevant to the survival of the group home. These staff do better in an institutional environment in which the responsibility for the maintenance of the physical environment is left to the supervision of others.

PROGRAM

Programming in a community residence program should focus on the replication of a lifestyle as normal as that of any youngster growing up in the community. This programming should include the child's attending a community school if at all possible, and participation in community groups and activities such as Girls Clubs, Boy Scouts, community centers, and church groups. Youth need to be encouraged to form friendships and relationships within the house but also to develop relationships with people elsewhere.

Programming must emphasize the youths' assuming appropriate responsibility for maintenance of the living environment—participation in shopping, cooking, cleaning, laundry, and repair.

Youth need to learn to plan their own use of free time, to develop hobbies and activities that require other people but also those things they can do on their own. Youth growing up in the care of social agencies have often had their whole life so programmed that they are at a complete loss as to what to do with any unstructured time, except to get into trouble through inappropriate behavior.

Programming in group home living involves those very same tasks that other youngsters growing up in the community learn naturally. Self-dependence is acquired at different rates in different aspects of life as young people mature. Youth who have grown up in many different families and institutions have been the victims of so many disruptions and mixed messages that they are inevitably far behind in these simple skills of day-to-day living. A great deal of unlearning, relearning, and remediation is in order. Even though many school programs teach home management, child care, and living skills, the group home can provide a living/learning experience that even the best classroom laboratory program cannot do. With the extensive learning gaps of this population, practice in both the day-to-day living environment and the classroom is necessary, since there is usually so much catching up to be done.

Part-time employment for the older adolescent becomes an excellent opportunity to develop needed life skills not just in acquiring a job but also in holding on to it. The monetary rewards also provide opportunities for planning appropriate saving and spending. The desire to work and the value of work are established early in life when small children observe working parents and when their own efforts at play, equated with work, are rewarded. Many youth in group care have not had any opportunity to develop an appropriate work ethic early. A great deal of emphasis needs to be placed on this reparenting function. Clinicians working with families may also need to address this developmental issue, and may want to engage parents in working with their youngster in the group home on employment goals for the present and future. Parental support and encouragement remain major incentives for growth and accomplishment. Often, of course, we may have to help parents with their own personal attitudes about work and work satisfaction.

Any work that can be done in the house with a young person's family is usually very desirable. Some programs actively include families whenever this is possible. Parties, open houses, and picnics are vitally important. Youngsters who have parents, siblings, uncles, aunts, cousins, and foster parents to whom they have an attachment should be encouraged to allow these relatives and friends to visit. Families should be included in school functions such as plays and graduations. Families should also be kept informed and consulted on the issues of concern for their child. Circumstances vary, of course; but families often are unnecessarily excluded, and thereby rendered helpless. A natural response to being discounted is to distance oneself from the painful situation, and many families of children in group care often are forced to take that route, not by choice, but because they have come to feel that detachment is the only way to deal with their pain.

In addition to working on the youth's family ties, the house needs to function as a group, but only to the extent that a family functions as a group. Certainly there is room for planned house activities, but the planning of these activities must never be so tight and rigid that they stand in the way of appropriate community involvement or family involvement for youth. Too often reliance on the group activity of the house discourages any initiative to develop other relationships and seek out other activities. Staff must help these youth to learn how to use time optimally.

SPECIAL GROUP HOME POPULATIONS

Court-Referred Youth

Group homes or agency-owned boarding homes can make a valuable contribution as temporary respite environments for youth whose families have lost control over their children's behaviors. Even though foster family care is ideally suited for youth who come before family court judges, it is usually very difficult to have the right foster families available on a standby basis at all times. A program then has no choice but to refuse family foster care to a youth who might really benefit from it. In a group home or agency boarding home model, staff are employees of the agency, and the service system has much more flexibility in placement. The group home does not replace the family foster home ideal with its many unique assets, but it does serve as an alternative in youth placement in many communities.

Youth in need of temporary care sometimes require more long-term care when it becomes apparent that in spite of massive efforts on the part of outreach staff the family is so burdened that it cannot make the necessary changes to provide needed safety and direction to their child. Some of these youth can best be referred to foster family care, but for others the group home, with its less intense relationship demands, remains a better choice.

Group home placement has been quite successful with youngsters who come before the courts. Often the youths' inappropriate behaviors cease as the family examines its present commitment to them, and family and youth begin to think of the future. In some situations it is helpful to have a very concrete point system with built-in privileges and rewards that can be earned through appropriate behavior. Unfortunately, at times youth are placed in community residences when their behaviors are still quite inappropriate for community living simply because there is no better level of care or program available to them.

Refugee Youth

Group homes have proven to be particularly valuable for adolescents who come to the United States from other cultures and countries because of war or other catastrophes in their homeland. These young people find themselves displaced and uprooted, often after having experienced the major trauma of loss of family, home, country, and culture. Often these are youngsters who nevertheless have experienced caring and nurture in their early, formative years. Lutheran Family Services of North Carolina has operated group homes for Indochinese children and adolescents with remarkable success. Some of these young people moved on to foster families. Others left the group home after successful completion of high school and went on to college or vocational school.

One home was run by a Vietnamese couple who because of their own life experience were in an unusually good position to help their charges work on their losses while seeking to create a new life. The houseparents shared their family with the youth in care, and together they engaged in building a new life compatible with values that they brought with them. A great deal of work was done in helping these Vietnamese youth search for their families and reconnect with friends and relatives.

Developmentally Disabled Youth

Group residences are a very viable alternative for developmentally disabled populations. Many of these children have committed, caring families, who have nurtured their children and have done all they can for them. As the children grow older and physically bigger, however, the family often does not have the skills or physical capability to keep them safe. The separation from their handicapped children is difficult for these families, but they develop trust in the program and staff, particularly if they see progress. Some of these young people come into large residential centers where behavior modification and the teaching of basic life skills can occur. Those youngsters who become successful in caring for their own physical needs—bathing, toileting, dressing, and eating—and communicating their needs, wants, and feelings are able to move on to a well-supervised group home in the community. This opportunity should be made available to them and is best done by the agency that has had the youngster in residential care initially. Careful preparation for a slow transition is essential. Consistency of approach in both residential care and in the group home minimizes the risk of serious regression that can occur due to an abrupt move to an unfamiliar environment with unfamiliar people.

Houseparent staff, including relief child-care workers, are ideal for developmentally disabled youth but, as earlier mentioned, are difficult to find and keep in many parts of the United States. Given the need for constant supervision and the very slow progress of these clients, even the most committed staff become vulnerable to burnout. A nonresident house manager and child-care staff working in shifts are very useful in the long run, but recurring crises and disruptions caused by staff turnover are extremely detrimental and should be reduced as much as possible. Awake night staffing is usually necessary since so many developmentally disabled youngsters have very poor communication skills. Just the danger of fire warrants the constant presence of awake staff.

Family work with families of developmentally disabled youth is essential. Parents should remain involved with their child. Families are entitled to these connections and have a right to question policies and procedures. At times families may cause some discomfort for the staff. Parents often have expectations of staff that staff are unable to meet. However, parent involvement provides some checks and balances, and useful information. Frequently the youth do not speak and are unable to communicate their wants and needs. Parents of developmentally disabled youth are valuable advocates, and their demands are often legitimate, even if difficult to implement. Competent parents will not tolerate bureaucratic delay or agency responses that don't make sense. Programs change to become more responsive to people's needs under such pressure.

Families must be involved in setting goals for themselves and their youngster. Staff should not take over legitimate parent responsibilities and functions. If parents can be involved in medical appointments, clothes shopping, room decoration, and special events, it is well worth the extra time and attention that often must be given by a very busy group of child-care workers, particularly when new staff are being trained or when a unit is understaffed. The recruitment of staff who see themselves as family workers becomes crucial in a program for the developmentally disabled.

Developmentally disabled youth not ready for independent living nevertheless eventually become too old for an age-specific group care program. This, of course, remains a painful issue. When families bond to an agency for care of their disabled member, they are reluctant to see their child transferred into a different adult system. Agencies that do provide adolescent programs are often asked by families whether they would not consider developing adult programs also. No easy answer to this very human and understandable request exists other than to recognize that there will always be people who will require care for the rest of their lives and that arbitrary age cutoffs are not in anybody's best interest.

Certainly there is a place for systems that can continue to care for residents through their life span. The danger in this kind of system might well be, however, that it would need to be restricted to a specific population such as the developmentally disabled. This type of programming may take away some incentives for mainstreaming these people through including them in a variety of agencies providing services for different difficulties. But there is room for quality programs, both of the population-specific model, which can provide care throughout the life span, and the inclusion of developmentally disabled children and youth in systems that provide an array of services for a variety of difficulties, needs, and disabilities.

Parents of developmentally disabled youth should be included on boards of directors of agencies, since they have much to offer both in knowledge and perspective. Many parents also have additional skills related to their own occupations and accomplishments. Program parent advisory groups can be most helpful to supervisory staff responsible for program delivery.

Group Homes for Young Parents and Their Children

Group homes or residences for single parents of young children, particularly adolescent parents, continue to be an important need throughout the country. Often the separation of parent and child because of abuse and neglect can be prevented by expecting no more than is reasonable from very young parents without adequate social support. Of course, some model programs have been set up, often connected to programs serving pregnant teens and young mothers in need of maternity and postpartum care for themselves and their children. These options must be enlarged.

The private, voluntary not-for-profit sector has much to offer to community housing developments through the provision of services designed to enhance the quality of life for young residents with children and prevent child abuse, family breakup, and disconnection. A joint venture is possible between public housing and community residence staff in putting together some model programs involving supervised apartments for young people who are caring for their own children. Staff would help with life-skill building, counseling, and respite support. The goal would be to help young parents gradually move into nonsupervised apartments and use support provided by a family resource program, as discussed in chapter 5. The major difference between what is and what should be is that all these services are available in many communities, but are not necessarily located where the clients live who need them. Service contracts between the public and the voluntary sector could resolve some of these program design issues.

YOUTH GROW OLDER: AFTER GROUP HOME LIVING

Group home placement can often provide that in-between step necessary before a young person can move toward limited independence. Many community life and behavior skills can be taught in a group home. Ideally, the youth's last years of secondary school should be in the community. Clinically the group home experience should help the consolidation of future planning. The goal for those young people who have the potential to succeed can be that of moving on into a supervised independent-living apartment.

At best the youth's family was involved in the choice of plan and move toward independent living. If this did not happen, family connections should be reactivated. Sometimes this renewed connection can be accomplished even though previous efforts have failed. Often these young people are no longer seeking to live at home or share their lives with family members on a day-to-day basis; perhaps both family and youth are ready to reaffirm their bonds within the context of a new definition.

Whether a young person will be ready to move into independent living— sometimes only two or three years beyond the time of placement in a group home—must be assessed quickly. The work needed must be targeted and begun promptly. Are the youngsters capable of moving about the community freely and independently? Do they know how to use public transportation? Do they know how to manage money? Can they shop for their basic needs? Can they judge the quality of purchases? Do they know how to maintain their own living environment and that which is shared? Do they know how to save?

We must also evaluate their human relationships: Do they know how to select friends? How good is their judgment? How vulnerable are they in their associations with others? Many of our foster care youngsters have been so protected in their institutional environment that they lack the survival skills of youngsters who have spent most of their lives on the streets of tough communities. When moved into that environment, the group home child quickly becomes scapegoat and victim. These difficult issues cannot be ignored.

Are part-time jobs possible, preferably out in the neighborhood? With a job comes the responsibility for getting to work on time and following through on agreements. For some youngsters it is more realistic initially to work in the larger agency if the group home is part of an agency operating an array of services—the institutional kitchen, the maintenance crew, or the agency office are often excellent job placement possibilities. This more protected work environment may be one from which the young person may move later.

Live-in houseparents can be very helpful to youth coming into group homes to learn more about independent living, because residents are also being given an opportunity to observe a quasi-family model. Sometimes this observation of family member roles and relationships is possible at a distance, particularly for those youth who have been badly hurt and are fearful of any closeness.

Some group homes can put an apartment for independent living in the attic, on the ground floor, or in a separate wing of a large house. This apartment should have all the facilities young people will need to have when they move out into the community. An apartment shared by two young people is a preferred situation, since this will eliminate loneliness and isolation while providing an opportunity to share all housekeeping tasks and responsibilities. At the same time, while learning to live independently, they still have enough of the necessary protection and supervision.

The youth have to understand the purpose of an independent living experience. An agency should have several independent living units so that participants can form their own support group and learn how to reach out to their peers for help. Someday these young people will have to learn how to ask for and give help to their neighbors and friends. These are simple tasks that most young people learn naturally while growing in a family and in a community, but these young people have been deprived of this normal process. Child-care staff should continue their assistance at previous levels, but staff energy must be focused on specific tasks and issues that lead to self-dependence.

The opportunity to experience independent living while still in a protected group home environment, with much support and staff supervision, leads to the next step toward independence. Young people who leave the foster care system are particularly at risk during this most vulnerable of transitions. This is a population in their late teens and early twenties who have experienced many failures, who are often neurologically or intellectually handicapped, if only minimally, and whose life connections to kin and past are either nonexistent or very fragile. Yet they must graduate from the protection of the child-care system and find their niche in the world. At best they will have formed some connections with family or friends, and learned enough to work toward optimizing their strengths and assets. At worst, too many of these young people are not able to rise to the challenge of self-dependence, are isolated without supports, and end up in our penal system or among the homeless and street populations. The orchestration of the move toward independence for this population becomes a major challenge, particularly to the group home system, because this model of care is often the last stop for youth who have experienced an array of child welfare services.

This book cannot deal with program issues of young adult populations. However, at this point it is appropriate to note that the cycle can and will repeat itself in the next generation unless a great deal of thought and effort is built into appropriate management of the transition to adult living. A range of community services is essential, including supportive apartment housing. These youth should not be expected to make it on their own. While those populations that have benefited from family caring and protection all their lives continue to have these supports available as they make life decisions involving choice of lifestyle, relationships, and work, we jettison the most vulnerable youth.

There are voluntary agencies throughout this country that provide an array of services regardless of a client's age. These systems not only offer care to children, youth, and their families, but provide services for the aging, such as housing for senior citizens and nursing homes. There is here a promising opportunity to match the needs of isolated elderly people and of adolescents in need of connections. Each has something very special to offer the other. Creative program exploration and experimentation is now carried on in various places, although the literature on this is still very sparse. Group home programs are in a particularly good position to search for creative connections with senior citizen programs in their communities. Matching of adolescents and seniors must be done cautiously, however, as the elderly cannot take on the task of reparenting the most difficult children.

LOCATION: GROUP HOMES AND THEIR NEIGHBORS

A group home should be defined as a house in the community located among other houses on an ordinary city, town, or village street. The house needs to be maintained and equipped as any other house in the neighborhood. Houses are best selected in neighborhoods where multiple-family dwellings already exist. Many communities have neighborhoods where students rent apartments and people not related to each other already live together.

A major issue in the establishment of group homes is the response of the community and its willingness to allow the home into the neighborhood. The three most common fears are that the presence of a group home in a neighborhood will decrease the property values of the other homes in the area; that the children who live in group homes could have a negative influence on the other children in the neighborhood; and that youngsters in group homes may engage in community destruction and vandalism. These community fears and resistance cannot be ignored or minimized.

Administrators responsible for designing and operating group homes need to be very cautious where they choose to locate a group home. They have to work with the community in order to gain the acceptance needed for the program to work. I recall one group home that went into a community in spite of massive neighborhood resistance. The staff did a magnificent job working with the youngsters, but the amount of tension generated for them by angry neighbors ultimately polluted the quality of care they could provide. To be an unaccepted and unacceptable neighbor is a burden too difficult for group home youth and staff to carry.

Pierce and Hanck refer to Weber's article [1978] in which he "describes three strategies for entry into neighborhoods: the low profile entrance, the high profile entrance, and the combination approach" [Pierce and Hanck 1981:477]. There is no question that community members' involvement in planning for a group home in their midst is the most desirable way to go about this. But given the concern with real estate values in many communities, the perceived threat to residents is so great that except under the most unusual circumstances a high-profile approach is entirely unrealistic.

Fortunately, the courts have upheld the rights of many agencies to purchase property when these rights were challenged by neighborhood groups. Agencies have the legal right to purchase houses for children and do not need to be defensive and apologetic. The agency does have great responsibility, however, to be realistic in regard to which youngsters can succeed in community living without jeopardizing themselves or the home and the neighborhood in which they live. The way American communities are organized, it is in the children's best interest to live in a house that is maintained as well as any other in the neighborhood, and the neighborhood has a right to expect this of any owner whether the owner is a private citizen or an agency. Children's behavior in the community must be such that it not interfere with the rights of others. If a child does infringe on the rights of others, the staff must deal with this behavior. If behavior jeopardizes other children or neighborhood residents, the child does not belong in community living.

Once there is clarity about agency responsibility to the community and to the children, work with a few empathic neighbors can be very helpful. This approach is the same as family members getting to know neighbors in a community into which they have moved. Community connections are important and should be developed.

CONCLUSION

The group home or community residence programs across the country have suddenly found themselves in the unenviable position of being relegated to a catchall function for youngsters who cannot live at home. This model of care is perceived as being more cost-effective than institutional care, and more desirable since it is located in the community and does not have a campus institution's disadvantage of social isolation.

No doubt the group home/community residence model has much to offer to special populations of children and youth under particular circumstances. However, program design and populations selected for this type of living cannot be related just to cost-effectiveness and saving money. Group homes are expensive to run, because each one is for a small number of children or youth. When they exceed populations of seven or eight, they become mini-institutions. Furthermore, group homes are very difficult to staff; people willing to live in group residences are becoming harder to find. The child-care staffing model with rotating shifts clearly brings a different flavor and purpose. In some ways, child-care staffing of a group home is more expensive than running an institution, although at times programmatically more desirable. The intention of this chapter was to demonstrate that it is reasonable and realistic to fund some group homes for special populations at the same level of funding an institution may require.

Group homes are particularly useful for young people who have gone through the foster care system, have experienced multiple institutional and other placements, are not able to adjust to family life, or whose time in the service system is running out. Often they have learned in the institutional placement enough life skills for group home living. They may need to leave a foster home at a time when it is undesirable to look for or impossible to find another, and thus community residence placement can best meet their needs.

Programs preparing young people for independent or semi-independent adult living are essential as part of an array of services, since discharge cannot reasonably occur without these intermediary supports. Special apartment programs, perhaps in conjunction with public housing, can provide an opportunity for initially protected independent living. For single parents with young children, this type of housing, coupled with a variety of preventive support programs, can make the difference between successfully raising the next generation or continuing the revolving door through foster care and public dependence.

All group home programs require clinical input to insure that a youth's bonds and connections are clearly understood, utilized, maintained, and enhanced. Programs that function only to care for young people today without seeking to ensure optimum growth in the future are too limited in purpose and scope to be useful. Young people in need of residence away from their biological or adoptive families must be viewed as extremely vulnerable and in need of comprehensive programming and support.

10

Campus-Based Residence:
A New Purpose and Function

ORIGINS AND ISSUES

Campus-based residential care today finds itself in a strange position, one which badly needs clarification. Historically, campus-based residential care, previously known as institutional care, has been deeply rooted in the American orphanage, with the mission to care for dependent and neglected children. The further thrust of institutional care for youth, perhaps legitimately so, has been to remove children from environments in which they were victims of adult exploitation and abuse. The American orphanage was usually founded by philanthropic individuals and sectarian groups. These rescue and caring missions were likely to be joined to a punitive or moralistic attitude toward the adults who had not provided what was considered adequate care and nurturance for their children [Carlo 1985:15].

During the 1930s and 1940s, large congregate orphanages became cottage-based "children's homes." Many child-caring institutions in the United States today still take this form, where children whose parents are disconnected from them, or only marginally connected, do grow up. Other institutions became treatment centers for the severely emotionally disturbed or acting-out youngster. Of course, there were, and always will be, highly specialized institutions for children with handicaps such as blindness, deafness, or severe mental retardation.

In recent years, the care provided children in institutions has been under severe attack [*New York Times* 1987], sometimes excessive. In the best institutions, staff have often made a life commitment with major personal sacrifice. These institutions had strong values that allowed children to develop a sense of belonging. Some of our very valued citizens come from this background. Institutional children, however, even in the best of institutions, experience a unique set of problems.

Those children who have the ability to mingle in the community and attend public schools often experience rejection, and are referred to by other children as "the home kids." These youngsters lack a permanent support network that will continue throughout adult life. Meaningful relationships are, of course, built among some young people, as well as with a few committed individual staff members, but the lack of family ties remains.

The professional literature further documents that those institutions designed to deal with major emotional and behavioral problems in young people often have not produced the desired outcome [Fanshel and Shinn 1978; Kagan and Schlosberg 1989a]. One study in New York State, for example, shows that the outcome of out-of-home care, including institutional placement, is directly related to the amount of parents' involvement and the frequency of their visits. For many children, being able to return home successfully is related not only to the services received during placement, but also to continued contact with the parent(s) during that period [Ingalls et al. 1984]. These findings support those reported by Fanshel and Shinn [1978:110].

Residential care finds itself backed into a corner. Historically it was the prime model of care for children and youth in need of services. Many other models of care have evolved from needs first identified by the staff of such residential programs. People interested in working with children often opted for institutional work because the children were there. The staff in these settings had a sense of ownership *in loco parentis*.

But the ground rules have been changing rapidly, and the children's institution is being moved out of its "prima donna" position of caring for the "unwanted" child. Residential care is being rejected and isolated just as the young people it tries to serve are rejected and isolated. Today we have moved beyond the rescue mission of the orphanage; indeed the biological orphan hardly exists. Instead, "we are dealing with children who have been left in limbo because of increasingly complex social forces. Just as children cannot be left dangling in isolation, so the residential treatment center now needs to move into an appropriate position in the mainstream continuum of care and caring" [Finkelstein 1989:99–100]. We cannot, therefore, talk about the institution and its function without really considering where the youngsters come from and where they are meant to go.

All children need roots, belonging, and a sense of identity. Young people need to know from where they came, and equally important, they need to have a sense of where they are going. To help them, the service delivery system, too, must have an internal identity as part of a much larger model of care. [Finkelstein 1989:100]

Alternative models of care, whether institutional placement, foster family care, or adoption, must only be considered after every possible effort has been made to prevent the removal of the young person from kin. In the event removal does need to occur, it must be carried out only with a long-range permanent plan clearly in mind. This plan could mean eventual reunification with parents or other members of the original family system, whether biological, foster, or adoptive family.

Efforts at preserving the original family unit when children are in residential care have all too often been weak or nonexistent. When efforts to preserve the biological family have occurred, they have been, and often still are, provided by agencies and individuals with insufficient program adaptation to the needs of very frightened families. These parents may well have been themselves the victims of abuse, neglect, eviction, or institutionalization when they were growing up.

Some children and youth need to remain in institutional care, but the reasons for this decision must be very clear. From that well-thought-out decision, a plan must follow as to how these placements can assure permanent bonding and how these special bonds will be maintained and enhanced. Institutional campus placement should be thought of as a highly specialized component in an array of services for families and their children.

This change in philosophy of care means that some institutions have already closed and that others will close; the number of long-term beds theoretically should diminish. Yet the experience in New York State demonstrates that the same number of dollars spent on foster care beds are necessary to provide services to prevent children at risk of being removed from their families. The difference is that money has to be moved from the foster care budget to the preventive services budget.[1] Yet we are currently seeing an increase in the need again for institutional beds for severely damaged older children, which leaves one wondering whether the pendulum against institutional placement has swung too far.

Residential care decision-makers and practitioners must ask some crucial questions in order to clarify which needs residential care can best meet. Residential care should not be used by default simply because of the lack of appropriate alternatives. Business people know that when a product becomes obsolete they must develop a new product; educators know that when their curriculum becomes obsolete it must be reevaluated and redesigned to attract quality students. The evaluation of changing needs for residential care is no different than in other fields.

In some states the voluntary providers have been forced into program reevaluation, as public mandates no longer permit the arbitrary placement of children. In those states in which funding of children's institutions is still primarily from private sources, there is a luxury of more freedom in making decisions. Agencies there have the opportunity to evaluate their philosophy of care, their programs and services. Often it is a healthy mix of public agency pressure and provider awareness that brings about the most creative and innovative program shifts.

An organization that seeks to make major changes in residential program design and service delivery must begin with careful scrutiny of its agency mission. If the mission is articulated to provide for the rescue of abandoned and abused children, one model of residential care seems appropriate. If the mission addresses the care of children within a context of assuring the maintenance and strengthening of roots and permanent life connections, another model of residential care will emerge.

In some institutions, the pressure for change comes from line staff to the administration to the board of directors. As line staff experience more and more frustration with inadequate program outcomes for the populations they serve, they may press for alternatives. Professionals are aware of what is going on in their field. They attend conferences and read the extensive professional literature that discusses the dilemmas and limitations of traditional residential treatment and institutional care as well as innovative projects throughout the country emphasizing family permanence for children [Carlo 1985; Garland 1987; Keith-Lucas 1987; Lantz 1987]. Staff request permission to experiment with different approaches. The smaller world, with its rapid dissemination of information, quickly affects the field of residential care.

Sometimes the pressure for change comes from the agency administration. Administrators are confronted with serious resource allocation problems; above all, institutional care is very expensive. The cohort of available people willing to commit their lives to being cottage parents and child-care workers at low wages, often under inadequate living conditions, is rapidly shrinking in the United States. Staff turnover due to these conditions can be very detrimental to quality care. Continuously rising costs and lack of additional financial resources, coupled with new information in the literature, at conferences, and from larger umbrella agencies such as the Child Welfare League of America and the American Association of Homes for Children, may stimulate executives to engage their boards and staff in innovative problem solving. Before this can occur, the sharing of new approaches with board members, particularly those not knowledgeable about the history and methods of child care, is needed. In turn boards of directors themselves have knowledgeable members who may press the agency administration to seek change.

Regardless of where the process begins, the strategies for change should involve all relevant players: staff, administration, boards. The community, too, must be involved and, under the best of circumstances, those client families who will be affected by any changes in institutional philosophy and practice.

If in fact permanence in family living, especially with the family of origin, becomes the desired outcome of institutional care, several practices have to change. First, intake procedures should be such that alternatives to institutional care can be offered as a first option. This choice presupposes the availability of intensive outreach prevention-of-placement services. Families who can use the traditional community-based outpatient helping systems usually do not end up having children in placement. Outreach prevention-of-institutionalization programs are much less expensive to operate than residential care. In many instances, the cost may be approximately $3,000 per year for services for a family that includes several children, as contrasted with anywhere from $30,000 to $80,000 per year for services for only one child in residential care. Agencies should carefully consider using some of their resources now going into residential care toward establishing outreach family services to prevent institutionalization, or to shorten the stay in institutions. Outreach services assure the utilization of staff and resources on behalf of many more people than those in institutional care. Furthermore, outreach generates a healthy tension, which produces creative energy, rather than the destructive despair that often accompanies the eviction of child family members.

As long as institutional staff are only bent on rescuing children from abusive, neglectful parents, whatever is accomplished in institutional care is done at tremendous cost to individuals and to society. The results of the intervention are going to be very short-lived, ultimately destructive, and excruciatingly painful for all parties. If, after careful assessment, the need for temporary removal from the community does become clear, this must be done in partnership with the family. Discharge goals must be spelled out as early as the day of intake. No professional, no matter how competent or well-meaning, can define goals for the client; the professional can only assist a client in conceptualizing and articulating goals.

Once an agency has committed itself to shift from a child-centered to a family-centered approach and has established an appropriate philosophic base, many program design possibilities emerge. Five voluntary child-caring agencies in North Carolina have chosen this philosophic and practice change. Administrative support made the endeavor possible. Supervisory and line staff engaged in comprehensive didactic and attitudinal training that targeted the meaning of their own family ties for them. In order to absorb the meaning of family-centered work, the staff had to become comfortable with the imperfections of their own families of origin, and with their personal disappointments with them. This awareness then allowed for the good, warm, and caring feelings toward one's family to flow.

We cannot help youth connect with their families if we as practitioners do not value the assets and humanity of these families. Is there any reason for Alex or Debbie to ever learn to trust us if, in fact, we reject their family of origin? Through carefully designed experiential exercises, the institution's staff can be freed to come in touch with how much their own families mean to them. The staff then gain appreciation for what family and loss of family mean to another human being, in this case the children and young people under their care. Through extensive case presentations and discussion, each treatment plan must be conceived in terms of a youngster's past, present, and future in a context that validates all ties, both old and new [Coyle et al. 1986].

There will never be a time when a society as large and complicated as ours can function without children's institutions. The real issue is the kind of children's institutions that should exist, and what their attitudes, functions, methods, and tools should be [Maluccio 1989; Whittaker 1989]. How does the children's institution fit into an array of services that links young people to those who created them?

One criticism of institutional care in the United States is that it is too concerned with the "here and now." Institutional child care addresses the immediate nurturing, caring, and educational needs of the children. Staff emphasize the socialization and recreational needs of their charges. In many instances maladaptive behaviors of children mean their behavioral management takes an inordinate amount of caretaker energy. Some excellent, carefully thought-out behavior modification programs have been developed and are being implemented all over the country. In the main, however, some institutional care professionals have been weak, to the point of negligence, in trying to understand the meaning of maladaptive behaviors, such as running away, property destruction, and violence toward self and others, as an inappropriate communication of the pain because of lack of know-how in the constructive expression of feelings. Institutional staff often respond to behaviors, rather than directing their energy toward seeking out those for whom the communication is intended, i.e., the family the child has either lost or is afraid of losing.

Those of us in institutional care have been weak about planning ahead with the youngster on how he or she is to move through the life cycle, managing its many transitions and stresses. The dilemma is whether the institutional model can prepare youngsters to cope with ongoing losses and separations, career choices, marriage, childrearing, and old age. Unless the institutional experience is seen in this much larger context of a life continuum, we lose sight of a human being's future. "Each day in the life of a growing child needs to be the richest, best day we can possibly make it; that day will never come around again."[2] However, each very special day becomes a link in the life span.

In this rapidly changing environment those of us providing institutional services must have both the courage and foresight to redesign services. Effective institutional program design must assume that outreach preventive services have been used and that the institutional intake function is to assess whether everything possible has been done to offer alternative in-home services. In those communities where adequate in-home services are not available, institutional staff are eminently qualified to advocate and if at all possible implement these services in their own agencies or other appropriate community programs.

FIVE RESIDENTIAL OPTIONS

In those states that have implemented adequate permanency planning programs based on the federal Public Law 96–272 mandates and been able to provide an array of services, institutional programs are appropriate for five categories of family and child needs. The first provides children and families respite from each other; the second is for those youths whose primary symptoms threaten either their own safety or that of society, where an institutional placement is warranted based on the best available understanding of the child's behaviors; the third option discusses the role of residential care for youth who need to grieve the loss of their family so that they can move on to adoption; the fourth is for young people with clearly handicapping conditions, such as severe developmental difficulties, who cannot be cared for at home; and the fifth is the use of residential care for young people identified as mentally ill. We will discuss these five options in that order.

The Institution as Provider of Family Respite

Members of any family at times need distance from each other. Society is willing to spend thousands of dollars on institutional care for a child, but ordinary respite care for overburdened, overstressed families on a very temporary basis is almost impossible to obtain. Sometimes one or two weeks of summer camp for children allows families and children to be away from each other briefly. But the need for respite for overburdened families is hardly seasonal. Why can't we provide planned weekend respite care, or even for a week at a time, when the family's energy resources have been overtaxed, or preferably before they are overtaxed? As an alternative to nursing home care for the elderly, many programs throughout the country are beginning to organize respite for families who care for an elderly person. The needs of families caring for young people, particularly with special problems, are similar.

At times families may need respite from child-care responsibilities or from the care of a particularly demanding child in order to be able to think or feel their way through some critical issues in their own lives. Intensive clinical involvement may not be needed. It is not uncommon to send children off to visit grandma. But there are families who do not have this simple human option; if these families were not frightened, isolated, and lonely, they would not be in need of services. Institutions can make an important contribution by providing some of these natural supports to families that do not have their own.

A more complicated use of institutional respite services may develop in situations that come through the court system. Competent, caring judges often are at a loss when confronted with decisions on persons in need of supervision (PINS) or juvenile delinquents (JD). Often the difficulties lie in the family. Many of the families have been unable to benefit from traditional counseling programs and have had long histories of either making no changes or refusing involvement altogether. On the other hand, the young person's behaviors are such that the youth's own safety as well as that of others is clearly in jeopardy. Many parents look to the court for removal of their child. They have done everything they know how to do, but have been unable either to understand or manage the youth. A responsible judge, not knowing what else to do in these situations, will often refer the youth to an institution for a thirty-day assessment. Based on the institutional assessment, the court will then make a determination as to whether the situation warrants discharge to the youth's own home, to a less restrictive placement, such as a foster home or group home, or to restrictive institutional care.

This approach has some basic philosophic problems. If we assume that the youths in difficulty with the law (JD) or teetering on the verge of difficulty with the law (PINS) are sharing the pain of their families in the only language the young people know, they are then punished for this involuntary role by eviction from the family. The family, on the other hand, is given justification for their scapegoating of their most vulnerable family member. As perceived by the youngster, the institution joins the family in ganging up. A thirty-day institutional placement for assessment only tells us how the youth adapts to an artificial, very frightening environment in which the youth may continue to play the same role that required court involvement in the first place. And in the end the young person's behaviors may lead to an assessment that places the youth in institutional care, rather than release to noninstitutional care. The family that has been struggling with its own ambivalence toward the young person now hears from society, represented by the court and institutional staff, that it has indeed been right all along. Their "kid" is thoroughly "rotten" and only experts can help him or her shape up. The family will be happy to welcome the child back when he or she knows how to listen to adults.

However, an institutional thirty-day family assessment model similar to the CRY model described in chapters 6 and 7 in this volume could be developed instead. This placement approach is especially useful for youth whose behaviors are too unsafe for placement in foster family care, as is true with a youngster who has set fires. The intention of such an institutional program design would be to offer a thirty-day family assessment option to the court that would focus on the parents' ability to take charge of their son or daughter in order that the youth can safely be returned home. Placement would be defined as respite for the youngster and the family, with the clear message that all parties have worn each other out.

Thirty-day institutional placement that is for the purposes of getting away from each other to get a new perspective on how to manage things is very workable. Of course, placement of a child for family respite must never be conveyed by the adult or experienced by the child as its eviction. Often adults in families known to the child welfare system have themselves experienced multiple evictions in their growing-up years; there is therefore always some danger of misrepresentation of the purpose of temporary respite placement. Discussion of respite with parents can help put them in touch with feelings they experienced during their own childhoods when their parents could not take care of them. After these feelings are expressed, the difference in circumstances can be pointed out, and families can be coached to make their intentions clear to their own children. The young people must hear that others understand how much they must be frustrated and exhausted from not being heard or understood. Professionals can know and tell them that they are "O.K. kids," but that some of the family have had difficulty in hearing each other and understanding what the others are saying and feeling. The family in turn must hear that they have done everything the family knows how to do, that they are good and caring parents. The family needs to hear their son or daughter's assets and be given credit for them, the good they have given their child.

The professional intention is to engage the family in working with an outreach team. This contact is best done by an outreach prevention worker committed to engagement with the family, even after the youth's discharge home. The program objectives in this kind of placement are clear. Institutional energy should go toward helping the young person function effectively. Recreational programming directed toward feelings of success is valuable. Youth can do more than just hang around. Solid recreational programming for a child is needed in a structured, caring environment. The goal for family members is simply to ascertain whether they will work toward their child's return home and to identify one or two areas in which they can change things. We should not lose track of the needs of ordinary people whose situations are such that they are pushed into what are seen as "crazy behaviors" simply because the stresses outrun their coping capabilities.

The issue of schooling always comes up. According to law, youth must be in school or at least receiving home tutoring. Of course, young people in difficulty, or potentially in difficulty with the law, are notorious nonlearners. Yet these young people need not fall further behind from lack of classroom instruction during the assessment period. When young people have been separated from their families after a crisis, the school requirement makes good sense from a structural perspective. Youth in crisis, like their adult counterparts, do not have the energy to learn or reverse on their own the failure script that they have been so long acquiring. A structured classroom with much concrete, hands-on teaching connected with the respite placement is potentially valuable. A good collaborative effort by the institutional staff with the youngster's teachers in public school can create an appropriate individual program.

In respite placements we should look for a highly structured, collaborative team effort between the residential unit and the outreach preventive unit. As separate systems they provide checks and balances against any needless decisions to "rescue" the youth by residential care. The charge to the outreach prevention worker should be clear: Prevent ongoing placement, use respite appropriately, help the family cope and function in the community with whatever supports may be needed and are available. The preventive services worker must coordinate with residential staff for their professional input to help the family with child-management difficulties.

The residential social worker becomes the communication link between the outreach prevention worker and the residential staff. The social worker should understand the reason and goal for placement, work on contact between youth and family during placement, and supervise the individual program design for the young person while in residence. In court-mandated respite, the social worker's responsibility is to coordinate with the outreach prevention worker the input from child-care and educational staff so that a comprehensive, all-inclusive report can be submitted to the court. If long-term institutionalization does become necessary, the residential social worker can take over preparing the young person for this next step, while outreach preventive services can usually continue with the family to prevent their next youngster from being scapegoated into placement. When a longer-term placement is required because a family is not ready to cope or the youngster's behaviors are too dangerous, family work should sometimes be transferred to the residential social worker.

The dynamics of residential care are complicated. Sometimes what can be programmed depends on the staff on duty, their qualifications, how much experience the workers have had, and what the unit priorities must be in terms of the needs of the other youths in placement. The communication responsibilities should be left with the people who can devote time and energy to prevent misunderstandings, clarify communications, and integrate all the information into comprehensive programming.

The role of the child-care staff is the key to creating a program and environment in which young people can feel safe enough to benefit from the respite opportunity provided them and their families. Engaging young people in activities that can provide some sense of success and well-being is essential. Messages from the staff need to be given skillfully. The child-care workers must understand the purpose of placement to select the methods to accomplish that purpose during the critical "other twenty-three hours" [Trieschman et al. 1969]. Occasionally a particular child-care worker establishes a relationship with a young person that can be helpful even after discharge. They can also give the family more confidence and competence. All parties must recognize that they have worked hard and that the situation is not easy for the child, the family, or the child-care staff.

The challenge is to remain focused on the initial purpose of placement—to assess whether the family can become sufficiently motivated to accomplish the tasks that need to be done before the young person can return home. We need skillful, reinforcing messages signifying that whatever the difficulties, they are family difficulties that everyone will have to work out together. In the event that return home is not possible, a longer-term institutional, community residence, or family foster placement may be needed to target permanency issues. The family must be involved in this decision process.

Youth Who Act Out Family Pain

The second group of young people in need of institutional care are those who express family pain through severely disruptive behaviors, but for whom respite care is no longer an option. The people responsible for decisions fear for the safety of the youth and for that of others in the environment. These safety threats usually occur when the young person becomes the communicator for a family system at severe risk. The tensions and the coping mechanisms of the family are such that the young person is afraid of both physical and psychological eviction.

Those youngsters who end up in institutional care because of unsafe behaviors, in states that do provide adequate community-based alternatives for those who need help, are usually youngsters who do not have two biological parents living together. Most often, they are children of single parents, children living in reconstituted families, children adopted when older, or those legally surrendered but not yet adopted.[3] At times there are contributory neurological problems that have either been ignored or misdiagnosed. But unresolved permanency issues play a major role in the behavioral manifestations of these youth; often these issues are ignored or dismissed by the service providers.

Some of these young people are referred through the court system, where for legitimate reasons judges are often unhappy with the lack of alternatives available in the community for the placement of these young people. For many youth, a sojourn in a juvenile detention facility is no better than a holding action, with poor peer models and a built-in script for recidivism.

Family work is often nonexistent or at best marginal. Yet the key to understanding these situations and to reversing the negative, self-destructive scenario is both an intensive individual assessment of the youth and a comprehensive assessment of the family. Permanency issues must be openly addressed and explored. Families are often in multiple binds, giving messages that cancel each other out and/or mask unspoken secrets. Professional work must involve the young people, the family members with whom they are living, and the absent parent, as well as the extended family when there is one.

Institutional care is especially valuable in those cases where return to the original family is not possible because after careful, painful exploration it has become apparent that the family does not, and will not, have enough commitment to the young person for change to occur. The relationship demands on young people in institutional care are not as intense as in family living, and young people can be helped through a very difficult time while they and the family of origin are distancing emotionally. Extensive therapeutic programming directed toward nurturing, instant success, and hope for the child can be very helpful during this vulnerable, stressful period.

Supportive relationships with one or two staff members to whom the youth becomes attached can play a major role. There are many people in an institution, so the youngsters have some choice in selecting those with whom they feel particularly comfortable. Other youth in the unit are living through similar experiences but are at different stages in the process; some of them can be extremely supportive of each other.

The Institution as Facilitator for Adoption

Children and youth living through the psychological and legal surrender process while in institutional care, as well as those who enter placement already free for adoption, will continue to present major challenges to child-caring institutions. Creative institutional programs are often far more suitable for these youngsters than foster homes. An unusually experienced treatment family, such as those described in chapter 7, can also help a youth through this period. However, these families are difficult to find and have available when needed. The institution places many fewer pressures on young people, and there is an opportunity for them to benefit from the group experience. Some of the work that needs to be done, such as the reconstruction of the youngster's past, can take place very naturally within a group of children who are experiencing similar problems.

As discussed in chapter 8, potential adoptive parents should be allowed to serve the unit as volunteers; they provide a nonthreatening and successful means for older children to begin forming relationships with adults. In this more natural way a mutual selection process between children and potential parents can take place. The process allows for a "chemical" attraction between child and family to occur, eliminating some of the hazards when professionals match children with families. The living-unit milieu is an excellent environment in which adoptive families can decide whether adopting an older child with a difficult past is really for them.

On occasion difficulties arise with child-care and social work staff when an adoptive family feels ready to bring the child they will adopt home and the staff still see many unresolved issues. As institutional providers we do not own the children. The task is to facilitate the relationships between families and children. No developmental task will ever be completed in the institution, for developmental tasks really never get completed anyway; they keep shifting and changing. Emotional experiences are relived over and over again, as long as individuals have an intact memory. When memory no longer functions, we are, in fact, in trouble and need to unclog it so that the troubling memories can elicit appropriate feelings to create an equilibrium without excessive drain on energy.

All those who have experienced the loss of parents through surrender for adoption will need to deal with this sense of loss for the rest of their lives as will parents who have lost their child. If adoptive families can deal with these losses openly, the beginning of a bonding process with the youngster is on solid ground. The timing of when a child is ready for discharge to an adoptive family must, therefore, be a family decision arrived at mutually between family and child. No magic moment exists. The magic lies in the willingness to risk.

Ideally an agency that has a range of services, including outreach preventive services, outpatient clinics, residential programs, and an adoption program, is especially desirable. The process of relinquishing a child for adoption should begin with the work of an outreach preventive services worker who can remain as the primary communication link to the child's family of origin and to its other children. An institutional staff person works with the residential team on the adoptive child's day-to-day issues, which include grieving and the beginning of acceptance of an adoptive placement. The adoption program will carry out and monitor the placement. Intimate knowledge of the other service systems is important, and agreement on a philosophic practice base is absolutely vital. Intensive staff collaboration is necessary in order that children and families do not inadvertently get caught in the middle of emotional crossfire, communication mix-ups, and inter-program rivalry. None of the programs "own" the child. The objective is to assure secure, caring, permanent connections for the child. All of these efforts can more easily be accomplished within one agency. Families usually bond to an agency, and feel much more comfortable if they can use multiple services of one agency rather than having to work with a variety of providers.

Youth with Developmental Disabilities

The fourth kind of child or youth in need of residential care is a youngster with severe neurological or other physical problems where the burden of care cannot be borne by the family alone. This includes youngsters with autistic-like characteristics or who are severely retarded. Yet they too need committed families who will remain involved with them. Institutional staff often get to know families who have struggled long and courageously with children born with major communication disorders, recurrent seizures, or very low intellectual functioning. Many of these young people may have to grow up in institutional environments and then move on to long-term adult care.

When the children were little, the families managed, and they remained committed. They never wanted to evict their child. They hoped things would improve, that the children would somehow miraculously catch up. Fortunately, life and growth is such an ever-changing process that it is important to sustain hope on a day-to-day basis. Hope allows people to get through difficult days. We have no right to deprive families of hope.

But as the child gets bigger, the physical management of the child becomes much more difficult. A three-year-old who is not toilet-trained and given to temper tantrums is different from the six-, nine-, or twelve-year-old who manifests the same behaviors. Often the adults who can cope with the three-year-old, and with difficulty with the six-year-old, are desperate with the nine-year-old, and are looking for alternative living arrangements by the time the youngster is eleven or twelve. Safety issues, for example, may be involved with older, physically stronger youth who prowl around the house at night and place themselves and the entire family in jeopardy of fire by playing with a gas stove. In some ordinary family homes a twenty-four-hour awake system is needed, yet is simply not possible.

The study done for the New York State Council on Children and Families states that

While there are families with multiple severe problems who will place their developmentally disabled family member in spite of provision of services and supports, the results of the study suggest that families likely to place can be characterized by a constellation of risk factors. The disabled person tends to be older, to be more severely disabled, and to exhibit more behavior problems than persons who are not placed. The families tend to be larger, to have more emotional problems and/or marital conflict, and perceive that having a developmentally disabled person to care for has been disruptive of family life. Furthermore, the families who make out-of-home placements tend to have been those who lack informal sources of assistance with caregiving and who also have received comparatively few client services. [Sherman and Meyers 1985:38]

The study identifies specific services that families themselves perceive as beneficial. These are day programs with transportation, respite care, homemaker assistance, counseling, and parent training.

Something may be learned from these findings for institutions designing appropriate programs for these populations. The more vulnerable the people in the family, and the lower their level of stress tolerance and commitment to each other, the more vulnerable is the handicapped person in this environment. In the case of severe disability in a family member, we must only cautiously apply our desire to avoid placement at all costs. Given lowered tolerance of stress by the adults in charge, placement of the child under such conditions may be far less detrimental to all concerned than remaining in the family.

Many service supports for the handicapped child's family can and should be provided. Too often, however, these family supports lack continuity. Paid homemakers are human: They come and go; their cars break down; their relatives get sick. Complete dependence by a family on an outside homemaker is often not realistic.

Respite care for families with disabled children is very important for institutions to consider as a component in program design. Respite care can be particularly useful in a continuum of care. Day services with transportation are often badly needed. In addition, if those staff who provide institutional respite care can also provide brief at-home respite for the families and youth they work with, the program is even more helpful.

Even those families that are not isolated and do have family and friendship support can quickly become isolated when they have to deal with the growing problems of a severely disabled family member. Problems are easier for friends and family to understand when they are more universal and there is more knowledge about them. A cancer patient or otherwise terminally ill child or adult in the family evokes unambivalent empathy. By contrast, unintentional but implied criticism of the parents of a developmentally disabled child may surface. For example, not long ago mothers were blamed for insufficient emotional warmth toward their autistic child when an infant. In fact, parent perception of criticism may be connected to the inevitable and painful guilt that some experience when they have a disabled child, no matter what anyone says. A developmentally disabled child makes people uncomfortable, and when people are uncomfortable, they are quick to offer advice.

The family's response to others was feelingly articulated by a parent of a developmentally disabled child:

Often, people who have no idea what a family suffers feel compelled to give advice—you should love your child more; you smother him with love; discipline him more; discipline him less; and the old platitude "God never gives you more than you can handle" only soothes the one who says it. . . . The abnormal becomes the norm and family life takes on an out-of-focus, topsy-turvy existence contrary to the expectations and conditioning of most families. The family tends to turn inward, since outsiders usually can't understand or relate to problems a family of a handicapped child deals with daily. [Colangione 1980]

Even though in many instances with sufficient support for the family, the child's out-of-home placement can be avoided, there will always be equally caring families who will do better with their disabled family member in placement. If placement is the program of choice or necessity, family-centered institutional programs should be available. The family who places a developmentally disabled child is often in as much or more pain than the child. Since they need each other, any arbitrary disconnection is extremely destructive for both child and family. The bond between the disabled child and its family is particularly tight. The child has never reached age-appropriate separateness and is bonded for survival at a much younger level. Programs should see family members as partners in this endeavor and must be sensitive to all the family's needs while caring for the child. As already indicated, recognition of these joint needs requires much self-awareness by staff.

In contrast to the chronically disorganized family, many parents who seek out-of-home placement for developmentally disabled children are competent people, who have achieved much educationally, economically, and professionally in their own lives. The birth and condition of this special child have left them very scarred and vulnerable. None of the usual ways of working through problems which have always worked for them in the past have proved useful—hard work, dedication, patience, education, money. The damage to their lives is irreversible, and their task is to learn new lifelong ways of adapting and coping.

These vulnerable people, especially when articulate and powerful, can become very threatening to professionals. Still, this outwardly threatening presentation must in no way frighten us, although at times it can be very difficult and trying. Of course, the placement institution will be less than perfect, but so was the home environment or the placement would not have occurred. At intake, when placement is considered by the family, all the institutional liabilities should be pointed out, and the family must be put into the decision-making position as to whether they do, indeed, want to use the services of the institutional center—where their child's possessions will get broken by other youngsters, where child-care workers will try hard but often do less than a perfect job with the laundry, where that blue sock always seems to end up in the white wash and nobody knows how or why.

The family is engaged in getting to know the staff, to identify their vulnerabilities, and to learn how the staff affects them. Likewise, institutional staff members must recognize their own vulnerabilities and be open about their feelings: There is nothing to hide or be ashamed of.

Families have much to teach institutional staff. They have shared a life with their son or daughter. They understand every communication and response. What may seem totally bizarre to someone who does not know the child can have important meaning that should not be missed. For that reason alone, frequent visiting is very important to the young person and to the family, and should be encouraged.

Many parents, siblings, and grandparents are willing and able to contribute to the life of the residential unit in which their child lives. We have worked with families who wanted to paint, decorate, and even install a new floor in their child's room. Institutional regulations, therefore, should be flexible. Parents should be actively involved in the selection of the youngster's clothes. The children should wear the clothes their parents have bought them or helped staff select. Special functions and activities in the living unit should be designed to involve families in both the planning and execution of events. Those institutions that take children from parents at a distance should be equipped with living quarters where they can stay overnight during visits.

In many instances the goal for young people with neurological conditions will be to move into a community residence with long-term adult care. Family members should be encouraged to contribute to the design for needed programs and facilities. They know what is necessary and have the potential to be powerful advocates for their young people.

Work with developmentally disabled youth takes a great deal of patience and skill. Child-care workers must be very carefully selected for this job. They are working with youngsters who can be very difficult to manage physically while unable to communicate verbally what is hurting them. These child-care workers should be people who can engage with parents in a real child-caring partnership. Family-centered care must give equal respect and importance to every family member regardless of which member is actually in residence away from home. The social worker will need to work hard to assure that life connections remain intact and healthy so that families, including siblings and extended family, will be available to their youngsters as they grow into adulthood.

The Child Designated as Mentally Ill

Those children and youth who exhibit symptomatology to warrant a clinical diagnosis of mental illness can be served in specially designed and staffed institutional residential programs. Often stabilization through use of psychotropic medication at a psychiatric hospital or in the psychiatric unit of a general community hospital is needed prior to admission. However, long-term institutionalization of children in state psychiatric facilities is seen neither as clinically desirable nor as cost-effective.

The adequate service for this type of youngster in a child-caring institution is dependent on appropriate, easily available hospital back-up services when necessary. In addition to a sufficient number of child-care workers and social workers, these programs require adequate psychiatric and nursing personnel. Psychologists, recreational therapists, and other specialists are needed to adequately serve this population.

In 1979 the Residential Treatment Facility system was developed in the state of New York. Currently 397 youngsters are being served in sixteen child-caring institutions providing this level of care, contracted for by the New York State Office of Mental Health and funded with Medicaid dollars. It is the intent to bring the number of beds up to 600 as soon as financially feasible. This particular program initiative is demonstrating that severely emotionally disturbed youth who previously would have spent their growing-up years in large state mental hospitals can do well in a community-based child-caring institution, provided that adequate staffing, programming, and hospital back-up services are available.

The New York State Residential Treatment Facility (RTF) program is "based on the belief that many severely emotionally disturbed youth could benefit from a secure, environmental milieu-oriented approach to treatment as an alternative to traditional hospital care" [New York State Residential Treatment Facilities 1990:1].

However, the philosophic issues addressed earlier in this volume remain crucial in this initiative since youth who come into care through the mental health system have often been completely disconnected from their families, yet many are also in the custody of a county commissioner of social services who is mandated to assure permanency planning. It is often hard to separate what came first, the fact that these children are mentally ill and therefore ended up as dependent and neglected, or whether indeed their neglect and unattended dependence made them mentally ill. Regardless of which came first, to make them as well as possible, therapeutic intervention cannot be effective unless the issues of permanence are addressed. The service agencies responsible for these young people must develop a comprehensive mandated approach that will assure permanency planning as a part of the treatment design for these youngsters. Dr. Wander deCarvalho Braga [1989] deals with the complex challenge to bring the best of systemic thinking and individual developmental theory together. Unless the youths' individual developmental needs can be dealt with within the broader context of where they came from and with whom they are ultimately connected, no psychiatric intervention can really alleviate their pain and dysfunction.

Institutional program design requires a special educational component that may begin on the living unit to avoid difficult transitions early in treatment. Assets must be targeted to assure successful program experiences. Often one-to-one staffing must be available because many of these youths can tolerate group activity for only very brief periods. Yet slow targeted work can bring about amazing progress and improvement in daily living and functioning.

We must not lose sight of the normal developmental tasks of childhood and adolescence, tasks that include socialization, education, and recreation. Residential programs must meet all these needs. Furthermore, from the day of intake a long-range plan must be established to meet not only therapeutic needs but long-term development of kin connections. In order to reactivate connections, the agency will have to work with both parents, who usually are not living together, and with both of the youngster's extended families. Any effort less than this will not assure a reasonable discharge plan.

The institutional program for the youth should focus on assets and preparation for community mainstreaming as much as possible. It is exhilarating to watch these very troubled youth participate at a school dance or prom. The behavioral disabilities seem to disappear and their energy is absorbed by the rhythm of the music. If the program does not work for its youth, the program must be reevaluated and redesigned. Youth don't fail; only programs fail.

CREATIVE USES OF THE RESIDENTIAL SETTING

A number of very interesting models using residential programming and facilities have been designed. Astrachan and Harris [1983] describe an imaginative "weekend only" use of one particular type of residential care in an agency offering other programs also. Some youngsters in this particular setting come to stay only on weekdays and return home on weekends. The living unit, therefore, is left with some empty weekend beds. This particular agency has worked out a way to use consistently available space and staff talent to design a whole series of options for weekend use that are individually tailored to meet family and child needs. In fact, any program with an intensive family-centered approach will have some youngsters in care weekdays only; the weekends are used by the family and child to practice at home the new ways of interacting learned during family sessions and in the residential milieu.

The empty weekend beds offer an opportunity to program for youngsters referred to full-time residential care for whom there is no immediate opening. Family work can begin right away and the child comes in only for weekends. In some instances full-time care may even prove to be unnecessary. Where full-time care is clearly necessary, weekend programming provides immediate family respite and allows for an easier transition into residence for both family and child.

Weekend care also can be very helpful as part of an aftercare plan for youngsters who are moving out of the residence. This type of flexible arrangement can be very useful for special-needs children who have joined adoptive families but who are difficult to manage. Giving these adoptive families respite every weekend, every other weekend, or as needed is a very good preventive measure against the disruption of placement. Foster families who care for unusually difficult or demanding children can find this type of respite helpful also.

Child protective services know families in which the child is more at risk on weekends, with its very special strains and pressures, than during weekdays when time is more structured. For these families, weekend placement of the vulnerable child may be an alternative while an outreach prevention-of-institutionalization worker provides intensive services to the family. The intention is to keep the family together and to prevent full-time placement and educational discontinuity for children in community schools.

While providing badly needed respite for stressed families, weekend residential care offers nurturance and constructive programming to the children. The key message to child and family is that they belong together, that the family has not surrendered the in-charge and caring role.

Weekend family marathons and residential family camping have potential in using residential expertise and facilities. These experiences should be made available as treatment options in conjunction with family work. The family systems marathon uses the residential milieu to bring in approximately three families to spend the weekend together in carefully designed, structured activities directed toward relaxation, fun, improved communication, and growth. This is particularly useful for the underorganized family, often referred to as the "resistive" or "multiproblem" family. These are families that have an inordinate amount of difficulty in negotiating their environment. The parents lack nurturing and well-structured parenting models from their own past; constant stress further diminishes whatever coping skills they possess.

This program option can be available to families of youngsters in residential care and to families with youngsters in other agency programs [Finkelstein 1976]. Residential family camping uses the same principles as the family systems marathon, but takes the whole family to a campsite. Our experience shows that, although there is much initial apprehension about joining this type of experience, the outcomes for all concerned have invariably been beneficial. The benefit of these experiences lies in the preparation and in the family's participation. Planning for these weekends should actively involve the participating families. The more responsibility that can be delegated to family members for both planning and implementation, the more valuable the experience becomes for them. Residential staff are well-qualified to facilitate these projects.

Vassil [1978] describes one agency's creative involvement of families in camping. This program involves families of economically and socially disintegrated communities for an eighteen-day residential camp experience. Families are put in charge of planning, and function as camp counselors to groups of children, which do not include their own. Staff function as consultants and facilitators. Teenagers have work responsibilities in the kitchen and on the waterfront. They also have their own living quarters away from their families. "It was pointed out to families in the initial precamp and contracting stage that, in addition to fun, relaxation, and play, as constituent members of a community, everyone had to learn from, work with, and depend on each other for the camp to function" [Vassil 1978:607].

All of these programs address issues of the whole family, and emphasize health, not pathology. The methods employed—group work and education—of course are intensely therapeutic. The programs zero in on the deprived life situations of the participants, and offer extensive nurturing, role-modeling, and education for living. All of these programs are fiscally sound, and could, in fact, save millions of dollars now spent on duplicating fragmented, ineffective services for these populations.

PREPARATION FOR INDEPENDENT LIVING AND AGING OUT

Even with the new emphasis on keeping children in their own families or placing them in adoptive homes, inevitably there will be youngsters who find themselves in institutional environments as adolescents, because of deficiencies in planning, unavailable resources, or failure of all other intervention. The goal for these young people is "independent living." This assumption faces a contradiction, however, because as programs become more sophisticated and preventive in nature, those youth capable of independent living are no longer still in an institution in their later teens. Group homes and family foster homes prepare young people for independent living much more adequately because they simulate a more normal community life than an institution can ever do. Therefore, young people who find themselves in an institutional setting with the goal of soon living independently are probably those for whom a more appropriate place in the community is lacking, or because they will require a more protected semi-independent living environment.

The professional's objective is to teach them living skills over and over again. The institutional environment should be designed so that self-care tasks can be done with and by the young people, rather than for them. They should learn how to do cooking, housekeeping, laundry, and other minimal maintenance tasks. Many institutions have institutional kitchens located too far from the living unit and not designed to teach these skills. Cooking in the living unit allows the young people to help at their individual levels of ability. From this kind of realistic institutional unit living, some young people can gradually move into a group home or into carefully supervised apartments.

Adolescent "aging out" at arbitrary, artificially given ages has created havoc in the child-caring system. Many youngsters graduate from the institution into a brief interim stay in an unrealistic independent situation, and then move right on into jail. They do not know how else to find some structure and safety in a world in which they are unable to survive on their own. Parents of college-bound children know how much support families provide for these young people as they make the critical transition from a sheltered home environment to independent living. Yet we expect unrealistically or even cruelly that somehow those young people who have had a terrible struggle growing up can suddenly, miraculously make the transition into self-dependence without those same supports that are accepted as a right and necessity for the well-integrated, well-functioning adolescent from an intact family.

It is heartening to see some recognition of these issues by Congress through the enactment of the Foster Care Independent-Living Initiative (Section 477, Title IV–E of the Social Security Act) in April 1986. This legislation is designed to provide funding for needed services to youth ages sixteen to eighteen to help them make an easier transition from foster care to independent living. It usually takes extensive legislative effort to keep these programs funded, but individual states also are demonstrating major recognition of these very serious issues. Senator Daniel Patrick Moynihan, in his foreword to *Independent-Living Services for At-Risk Adolescents*, edited by Edmund Mech, commits his support to the funding of the Independent-Living Initiative with these very poignant words:

We might learn from the clarity and truth of a poem titled "We Are," written by Salena H., a young woman in New York City's foster care system when she composed it several years ago:
    We are the gifted, but we do not know . . .
    We all have a dream, but we do not know how to fulfill this dream,
    We have goals, but need guidance to reach them.
    WE, US, YOU and I have the FUTURE in our hands,
    "We are the FUTURE!!" and sad but true we do not know.
[Mech 1988:iii–iv]

Energy and work must go into finding meaningful connections for young people who will never return to their families. These young people and their families should know each other and be available to each other for whatever each can offer. Throughout residential placement, the building of these connections is absolutely a first priority, or else all other gains will disappear. If there is absolutely no one out there—and in most instances this is not the case—volunteer families, staff members to whom the young person has been connected, former foster families, former teachers, all need to be engaged in searching for someone willing to assume the role of a noncustodial parent for a young person leaving the child-caring system. The child-caring agency should, of course, be willing to stand by as help is needed.

CONCLUSION

Campus-based institutional residential care needs to be one alternative in a carefully designed array of services. The strength of that array lies in the ability of the model to provide service options through which people in need of intervention can move as change occurs. Institutional residential care needs to be a very specific program of choice to be used in a very specific way; it should not be seen as the "last resort."

Residential care can no longer provide for a child only in the here and now situation by putting all its emphasis and energy on today. Merely managing children's immediate behaviors is insufficient. Unless there is a coordinated professional effort, the child remains "in limbo," programmed only for being moved into the next phase of life without having made the connections necessary to continue through the life cycle. When we offer residential institutional care as an alternative to family living, we often forget to build the foundation needed to make those connections that help people to become functioning adults. The challenge to residential care is to understand its mission, which is to help young people get in touch with their past, integrate the past into the present, and provide focus for a future through innovative, creative programming.

NOTES

1. From 1981 to 1984, there was a decline of $75.8 million in New York State foster care maintenance costs, while preventive services costs increased from $9.3 million in 1980 to $62.4 million in 1984 [New York State Division of the Budget 1985].

2. Ray Schimmer, assistant executive director of residence and education, Parsons Child and Family Center, Albany, New York.

3. Nineteen percent of children in institutions licensed by New York State Department of Social Services have two biological parents living together, while 48 percent of children in developmental centers for the retarded have two biological parents living together [Ingalls et al. 1984:65].

PART V

Organizational Implications

The final part of this volume examines organizational implications; development, function, recruitment, organization, and training of agency board of directors are discussed. The relationship between the board and the executive and how this relationship affects the health of the organization are explored. Styles of executive leadership are examined. Most important, we must identify the need for a cadre of child-care professionals, educationally equipped to handle problems presented by current populations. Staff recruitment and training are the key to quality services. We will review professional development options for the major disciplines with emphasis on the needed education and certification for the badly undervalued discipline of child care. Finally, we identify methods and organizational implications of interagency mergers as creative solutions to fiscal constraint and service enhancement.

11

The Process of Change: Organizational Implications

As human needs and our perceptions of human needs change, so must the service delivery system change. Children's services in this country, rooted in the orphanage with its tradition of rescuing children from immoral, uncaring families, have come a long way toward accepting prevention of family dissolution as their primary goal. Yet many agencies providing institutional care with great commitment to children at times pay mere lip service to working with the child's family. There is an inherent, obvious, and sometimes semi-conscious destructive criticism of the family. As long as these critical attitudes persist, even the best-intentioned attempts to engage family members with their child are programmed for failure. There are, of course, some magnificently successful programs serving those same families who have otherwise been labeled as "unworkable," "multiproblem," and, worst of all, "resistive to change." This chapter will address the issues of organizational change so that family change can indeed occur.

We begin by recognizing that raising children in a protected, isolated environment, such as an institution, without primary regard to permanent family roots and connections fosters a revolving door of disabled people coming through the welfare system. A redesign of publicly mandated programs must follow, as well as reallocation of funding. The validation of roots and a need for permanent belonging must be an inextricable part of child welfare and mental health treatment programs.

Many institutions throughout the country have begun to work intensively in their own institutional milieu with families of the children in care. Through the reallocation of resources and the redesign of programs, it has become more evident that some children can and should be discharged from institutions; others should never have been admitted. Changes in philosophic thinking in an agency bring with them commitment to change feelings and attitudes among service providers, as well as among the lay and professional communities responsible for creative implementation of these changes. People who have committed themselves to caring for children not their own understandably become concerned when confronted with the challenge of seeking preventive models as alternatives to institutionalization. The process is usually slow and painful, but also exciting and rewarding.

As agencies seek to broaden their range of services, excitement begins to permeate the system. The threat felt from loss of the familiar generated by the broadening of practice opportunities is replaced by hope and creativity.

CREATIVE CHANGE

The impetus to effect necessary changes in program design and service delivery in a democratic society is ongoing. The change process can be perceived as circular. Pressures come from the community, including people in need of services. Through elections citizens register their desires with those who hold public office through their choice of elected officials. At the same time, through a variety of communication and social action tools, pressure builds up for legislative mandates for new perspectives and new methods. These in turn have an impact on services, clients, and the community.

Simultaneously, the community and client populations express their needs to the line staff of human services agencies as people come to seek help and are assisted in engaging a variety of community sources of support and control, such as schools, courts, physicians, attorneys, friends, and relatives. Line staff in turn communicate with supervisory and administrative staff, share their perceptions of service needs and service gaps, and define the resources needed to provide what they perceive as necessary and desirable. Agency executives in turn communicate these needs to their boards of directors so that change can become part of policy. Furthermore, executive staff are in direct communication with funding sources in constant search for public and private resources to deliver needed services. The executive is responsible not only for the professional direction of the agency, but for board orientation and education. Boards in turn recruit and hire the executive of an agency. The board is responsible for raising the agency's funds, for putting appropriate pressure on legislative bodies to assure funding for programs, and for monitoring their accreditation, licensing reviews, and contracts. Larger professional advocacy bodies such as the Child Welfare League of America, Family Service America, American Association of Children's Residential Centers, United Way, and community planning councils are additional linkages through which executive staff in collaboration with agency boards can effect change.

BOARD OF DIRECTORS

Each particular voluntary board of directors of a not-for-profit human services agency has its own form and board composition. Some organizations have large boards but only a small working nucleus. Other organizations involve all members in active committee work. Combining committees for special issues is useful. The board of directors of a voluntary agency, with its overall responsibility for policy setting, has to be much more than a rubber stamp. The board is a major resource on which professional staff can draw for expertise and guidance. The board is also an important link to the community and to funding sources. Board members are formally and informally called upon constantly to interpret the purpose, goals, and methods of the agency to large numbers of citizens in a variety of capacities. The public relations capability of a board of directors should never be undervalued.

The composition of the board should be directly related to the mission of the organization, so that it can best represent the community and contribute to the needs of the organization. Some people believe that a board should consist only of those people who either are able to contribute money or have access to funds. Others are interested in a board that consists primarily of representatives of the consumers of agency services, or of people familiar with the professional activities of the organization.

A balanced board seems preferable. The fiscal integrity of the organization is paramount: Competent fiscal monitoring and efforts to find funding for agency operation, plant, and new program development are essential board functions. People knowledgeable in finance, law, personnel, and fundraising are sorely needed. People who are familiar with the professional activities of the organization are also very helpful. Some service consumers should be members, and so should others who represent the community at large. This balance of various skills, attitudes, and types of knowledge on the board can provide the most appropriate direction. The more knowledgeable and involved the board is, the stronger the organization will be. The questions raised by board members not only hold executive staff accountable but open up new avenues for thought and problem solving.

Board building and recruitment is important. There must be enough seniority and continuity among the members to provide competent leadership for the organization, as well as the kind of dedication that can only be developed over time. Many voluntary boards in the United States exist on which families have had members over several generations. This commitment can be valuable indeed, so long as it does not allow board membership to become exclusive, and prevent assimilation of new members, perspectives, and ideas.

Board orientation and training should be the responsibility of the executive staff. An interview with the executive director of the organization before an invitation to membership on the board is one excellent way to explore mutual interests and compatibility. Potential candidates should have an opportunity to consider whether a particular board is really compatible with their interests and whether the demands made by the organization may exceed what they are able or willing to offer. Orientation to the organizational purpose and the responsibilities of board membership should begin at this time.

Ongoing board training should be provided in a variety of ways; often a combination of methods is best. A great deal of board training inevitably takes place on committees with staff and other committee members providing input on a given area of responsibility—program monitoring and development, finances, personnel policies. A clearly designed and articulated inservice training program that requires participation by all board members is essential. This should include description and discussion of the organization's mission, philosophy, and structure, as well as its program and services. If specific topics are presented by a unit director or responsible supervisor, this enlarges board exposure to the administrative staff and vice versa. A comprehensive training program offered annually to all new board members with an invitation to other board members is one model. Although it is extremely valuable, however, some boards may find this too time-consuming. Another possible option is to spend the first twenty minutes of every board meeting with a particular program presentation to familiarize board members with the diverse activities of the organization. Only a knowledgeable board will have the involvement, commitment, and opportunity to lend its own expertise to the improvement of the quality of service.

The success of the organization is closely linked to the delicate balance between the board and executive staff. Mutual respect, openness, and clarity in the definition and allocation of responsibilities are essential. Difficulties at the top of the agency quickly impede the effective functioning of the organization.

EXECUTIVE STAFF

Selecting the executive staff of an organization is critical. The executive director provides leadership for organizational direction and quality of services. Organizations are made up of many people: Some agencies can go a long time without dynamic leadership because of the quality of their other staff. Such organizations, however, lack a way to organize change in response to rapidly changing client, community, political, and fiscal needs and pressures.

The executive director should be responsible for recruiting and hiring associate executive- and director-level staff. The executive director's skill in selecting and keeping competent people on the leadership team is crucial.

The board of directors must support the executive director, while holding this individual to concrete measures of organizational integrity, financial accountability, and program quality. The executive director should give full support to the administrative staff, while holding them accountable for their performance. Creative professionals require direction, leeway for creativity, and validation of their accomplishments. They need the ability and permission to pass these qualities along to the people they supervise.

Many leadership styles work well. The important ingredient is that the executive director understand his or her own style and seek an administrative team with compatible and complementary styles; otherwise the entire operation is in danger. Style incompatibilities sometimes camouflage lack of respect for the philosophy, values, goals, and methods of the executive. However, style incompatibility should not be confused with differences of opinion, disagreements, or healthy conflict—all necessary ingredients for growth in individuals and organizations.

Organizational leadership is transmitted through structured processes and recognition of staff achievements. Therefore continuous staff dialogue and training are needed. Administrative training is important so that all agency administrators share common values and beliefs, methods and goals. Administrative training serves to build the administrative team. Depending upon the size and organizational structure of the agency, the executive director should meet regularly with executive staff and the administrative staff directly responsible for the coordination and direction of professional programs and support services. Much of the philosophy of care and methods of implementation in agencies that do provide multiple programs are negotiated and defined at meetings such as these.

STAFF TRAINING

Inservice training begins with the orientation for all new staff to the organization's history, mission, philosophy of care, administrative structure, and personnel policies. Orientation further needs to deal with a whole range of practical operational issues so that the nitty-gritty of survival in an organization does not take needless energy. But a comprehensive inservice training curriculum above and beyond ongoing individual and group supervision is also essential.

Direct service staff should have training to further skills in their own particular disciplines. The training sequence for social workers, psychologists, creative art therapists, teachers, child-care workers, and foster parents expands on applying the basic philosophy of care and should include professionals from all agency components, while recognizing that any practice philosophy can provide only an underlying framework. However, the practice method must be adapted to meet the unique and special needs of a given client population.

To assure good interprogram communication and continuity of care, the agency should deliver basic philosophic training to mixed groups of professionals from all agency programs and disciplines. As people learn together, they get to know one another, and share and communicate in a common professional language. As questions are raised and new insights gained, individuals begin to understand staff in other programs. These connections are invaluable as staff struggle to give direction to families and children in need of services that require expertise and skills from more than one agency component.

Beyond these essentials specific training must be structured to address individual discipline issues. Support staff in any agency delivering services to families and their children are very important. The agency must train staff in how to deal with families and youth on the telephone, in the waiting room, in the living units, on the playground, in the dining rooms and kitchens. An approach committed to helping people deal optimally with their physical and social environment warrants intensive orientation and training attention.

Psychologists, social workers, and other clinical staff must begin by familiarizing themselves with the organization's philosophy of care and with the specific client group with which an organization works. There are, of course, a whole range of technical issues, such as clinical recording and compliance with monitoring, licensing, and accrediting bodies. From there the basic curriculum must address issues such as client engagement and assessment, understanding behavior from the normal to the specific dysfunctions presented by client groups, such as abuse of children, domestic violence, alcohol abuse, posttraumatic stress, and so forth. Behavior must further be viewed within a cultural and historical context. The curriculum must then address client goal setting, treatment planning, and understanding of the treatment process over time.

Once these fundamental areas have been covered, intensive family systems work in an organization committed to assuring permanent connections for its clients is essential. The Bowenian model of family therapy lends itself to adaptation in agencies working with youth at risk of losing family connections. In addition to the Bowenian approach, a variety of strategic approaches can also be very useful, and a seminar based on an integration of Brief

Problem-Focused Therapy and Solution oriented approaches can yield impressive results [Bryan, Kagan, and Walsh 1990:6–13].

The Bowenian model of family therapy can provide a good philosophic foundation for a training model in agencies dealing with families and their children with special needs. Philosophically Murray Bowen uses a school of thought that validates family scripts and connections over several generations. Its assessment and intervention methods are clear and easily transmittable. The model provides an orientation that focuses on health. It allows room for a variety of styles to function within one philosophic context. A great deal of emphasis is placed upon work on the therapist's own family; there is no better vehicle to learn how to help others than by understanding oneself.

The major reservation often articulated about the use of the Bowenian model of family therapy is that it is thought to work best with motivated families who seek therapy. The Bowenian model has been developed largely in private practice. On occasion, practitioners struggling with difficult children referred by courts and child protective units feel put off when Bowenian trainers use examples and tapes of articulate middle- or upper-middle-class families: The practitioners may see these as irrelevant for their own client families. And they are keenly aware how difficult the therapeutic engagement is while assuring minimal safety for the child. Furthermore, these workers do not have the luxury of giving up on a difficult, often assaultive, client.

Training thus is best provided by people with the skills and experience to adapt the content and presentation to the needs of the practitioners. Supervised practice opportunities with skilled practitioners experienced in the use of the Bowenian model with hard-to-reach families become important. The basic human issues remain the same for all people regardless of socioeconomic category or symptom presentation.

If institutional, community residence, and family foster care are part of the organization's array of services, a curriculum for child-care workers and foster parents should be part of the agency training program. Child-care staff and foster parents function in real-life situations. Their messages to the young people in their care are ongoing and around-the-clock [Trieschman et al. 1969]. How these key life-space therapists deliver their messages and translate them into tangible program activities are vital. Unless training is built around validating a youth's family ties and other enduring connections, training in all other areas can quickly become nonproductive. Advanced child-care practitioners and supervisory staff may want to participate in family-systems training delivered to clinicians in order to enhance their child-care supervisory and practice skills.

However, inservice training for child-care workers remains a major challenge and is closely connected to the lack of professionalization of this critical

230 *Organizational Implications*

field. At this time most people entering this discipline come from a variety of backgrounds and need to acquire skills on the job. Minimal training must include child development, routines and structure of daily living, management of behaviors, effective communication and listening, constructive use of activities, and conscious use of self. This list can go on and on and only highlights the desperate need to professionalize this group of key service providers to vulnerable children. As discussed later in this chapter, professionalization will put in place some basic educational requirements allowing agency inservice training to do what it can do well without needing to do the whole job.

Teachers and educational specialists need their own training program. Given the difficulty of youth in care they must be very sensitive to and knowledgeable about the young person's psychological issues. Knowing how to be a competent, effective member of a psycho-educational team is key to being able to create a learning environment needed by youth requiring their services. Beyond that, the psycho-neurological deficiencies and numerous accompanying learning disabilities are increasing the challenge and inevitable knowledge gaps for even the best special educator. Every possible training resource must be made available to these key professionals.

Special topic areas of concern to all disciplines working directly with children and their families include loss, separation, and disconnection. A genuine appreciation of the cultural and ethnic background of not only children and families but of other team members and colleagues is essential. The sexually abused and abusing parent and child, the AIDS epidemic, drug and alcohol issues, and the many multiply-handicapped children with substantial developmental deficiencies and medical needs point toward the design of training modules requiring input and expertise from pediatricians and pediatric neurologists. The pooling of knowledge resources among human services, child-care, special education, and public health professionals is more critical than ever before.

STAFF RECRUITMENT AND SELECTION

The recruitment and selection of staff is a complex issue in a family and children's services organization seeking to provide a close-knit array of services. Not only does the organization need to offer an attractive work environment in an occupational field difficult to staff, but the organization has to be highly selective in recruitment and hiring practices in order to assure quality of care. Fiscal constraints further complicate the process.

An agency is only as good as the staff it can hire and keep. Recruitment and staffing should follow a plan balanced by the recognition that not all staff will remain with the organization for an extended period, but that a very competent core staff and the people who will eventually join the ranks of the core staff are essential for all agency disciplines. Even staff who will later leave should be selected on the basis of their intention to commit themselves for a minimal two-year period. Staff turnover with less than two-year tenure is undesirable. An organization that is a revolving door with constant staff turnover is an extremely expensive, dysfunctional operation. The recruitment and training of new staff is very costly financially, and even more so in its impact on client services. In trying to create connections for people with lost or fragile ties, an agency with excessive turnover does not have the continuity and connections for healthy operation.

Realistically some staff turnover is inevitable. Indeed, an agency from which staff are selected for more advanced positions in other agencies is making an important contribution to the field. Often the promotional pyramid in an organization is such that people find themselves blocked from moving up because the number of advanced positions is limited in any organization. It is counterproductive to try to keep staff within the organization when the organization is no longer able to meet their professional or personal needs. Staff mobility, of course, is always much more of an issue when more jobs are available than there are qualified candidates for them. At the same time, when there are no opportunities for mobility, an agency may find itself with locked-in dissatisfied staff, experiencing unhealthy, undesirable frustration, but with no place to go.

Program staff, regardless of discipline or how they were trained, must be flexible in their thinking and willing to adapt their practice to an agency philosophy. Interviewing for staff positions should, therefore, focus on their flexibility of thought and their willingness to change and learn.

Many practitioners come to the field of children's service because of a desire to work only with children. Often these are people who are experiencing much difficulty in their own relationships with other adults. But direct work with children is only a small part of the service tasks that need to be accomplished. The ability to work empathetically and collaboratively with other team members, staff from other programs, and the child's past, present, and future family cannot be overlooked. Those practitioners who seek to work with children exclusively can only function well in some very special positions, as in children's recreation. But even in those limited roles, it is far more useful to have a recreation specialist who has the desire and ability to involve families in recreational programming with the children whenever possible if reinforcement of family connections is the organization's philosophic intent.

For example, a community residence has planned an outing for a long time. Suddenly Dan's father appears on the scene and wants to visit Dan on the day his group will be away. Dan has not seen his father for a long time, and his father has not been reliable about follow-through. It would be easy and natural for the staff to say, "Sorry. The group has made other plans. Your visit is unscheduled and it's inconvenient." Yet, understanding the meaning of the father's attempt to reach out to his son and the importance of this connection to Dan, the staff should consider other responses. What arrangements can be made for Dan to remain behind? Is it possible for Dan and his father to join the outing? Could they join the group later? These are only a few alternatives that a child-care or social work applicant should be willing to consider.

Individuals who are at ease in exploring their own family connections and the meaning of these connections do best. Given the difficult life experiences of most people who need professional help, those practitioners who can come to terms with their own and with their family's imperfections have much to offer their clients.

In the selection of child-care practitioners and family foster parents, it is useful to structure the interview around the question, "If you were to have children of your own, how would you raise them—the way you have been raised? Or how would you do it differently?" The question, of course, can also be phrased, "If you have children, in what ways are you raising them the way you were raised and what are you doing differently?" This question gives rather quick access to applicants' feelings about their upbringing by their own parents and the extent to which they feel free to conceptualize alternatives. The absolute, rigid conformity to or complete rejection of how one has been raised may point toward possible difficulties in the child-care role. Some balanced awareness, insight, and empathy toward one's own family is important to be able to accept a child's family who may appear rejecting or even abusive. The interviewer must, of course, be skillful and cautious in order to protect the applicant from revealing irrelevant personal information. The intent of the interview is to assess only the applicant's attitudinal flexibility.

DIFFICULTIES IN STAFF RECRUITMENT

The philosophic integrity, leadership, and training in an organization, although essential, remain only part of the whole. Client care can only be as good as the dedication and quality of people who work directly with the agency's clientele. Agencies across the nation recruiting staff are confronted with a dilemma that will not go away soon.

Values in American society have become weaker over the years in commitment to people over things. So much emphasis has been placed on increasing one's standard of living, on the acquisition of material comforts as the primary measure of success, and on an extreme individualism placing the needs of the "I" above the needs of the "we," that value placed on people has diminished. These disturbing trends and how they affect commitment to marriage and raising of children have been reviewed in this volume. These same issues also arise when we seek qualified staff to serve children and youth who have suffered because of lack of sufficient commitment from the adults who brought them into this complicated world.

The more successful the parents of young people, the more inclined their offspring are to seek professions that will afford them the same if not a higher standard of living as early as possible, not recognizing that it may have taken these parents most of a working lifetime to be where they are and that it may hardly be realistic for their children to achieve these goals so soon after completing their education or training. The reality remains, however, that only a few of our better college graduates seek the challenges of nursing, social work, education, or child care as their professional goal.

Professor Laurel Eisenhauer of the Boston College School of Nursing is quoted [Duffy 1986:11] as saying: "Nursing has been a victim of the women's liberation and feminist movements. The young woman of today has so many career opportunities to look into, and nursing remains, in concept, a traditional role." Judith Shindul states

All the service professions—nursing, teaching, social work—are suffering from the materialism and egocentricity of this generation. How do you change the attitudes of an entire generation? When I was a student, we were more concerned with social issues. We were more concerned with what we could give to society than what we stood to gain. [Duffy 1986:11]

Professional careers in law, business, investment banking, and computer technologies rank highly among college students' career choices. Young people who have excellent interpersonal skills often choose the travel industry or the insurance business. Those individuals who are willing to commit themselves to long hours and hard work also seek a level of financial remuneration that human services are simply not able to offer. To further this bleak scenario, those people who do enter the helping professions often find that they cannot take some of the creative opportunities offered in the voluntary not-for-profit sector because the salaries and fringe benefits offered by the public sector are much more advantageous. Social workers in particular do not seem to select child and family services, because of the low salaries and the amount of paperwork and monitoring that has been inflicted in many states on practitioners in agencies under public funding contracts. The legitimate concern is that low salaries in not-for-profit agencies are no longer compensated by the advantages for more creative, innovative work opportunities due to excessive, often inappropriate, accountability demands and paperwork.

Some talented social workers who have much to offer agencies now seek their basic training in a voluntary agency, but then move out into private practice as soon as they can. There are social workers who combine agency work with after-hours private work. Some social workers go into private practice before they have had enough supervised training to be able to provide high-quality services. Others, of course, provide excellent service to many middle-class clients at a price they can afford. But those most in need lack their services.

The social work profession, its origins rooted in community service, is unable to meet the demand for workers in most parts of the country. As a reasonably new, organized, and credentialed profession, social work has begun to make itself felt in our society and to prove itself necessary. One of two things may follow. Salaries for social workers will have to increase substantially to come into line with other fields that require the same amount of professional education, or else the number of available jobs in the financially more lucrative fields must decline to make social work more attractive by comparison.

Education specialists are difficult to recruit and keep in those systems committed to serving unusually difficult populations, because these staff have the option of moving into mainstream public school positions often perceived as less stressful and more remunerative. Particularly those trained in a voluntary not-for-profit organization develop highly specialized skills and find it easy to move into either public school special education or regular classrooms at higher salaries, with many fewer working days, and many more benefits.

Consultants in special disciplines such as psychiatry, neurology, and psychology are becoming more and more difficult to recruit also, although part-time arrangements are sometimes possible. Many practitioners in private practice welcome the opportunity to share their knowledge and skills with an agency staff and in turn benefit from the interaction with other professionals. Although the fees paid by an agency are sometimes lower, there is no overhead or risk of appointment cancellation, unlike in private practice. Given this context, many salary arrangements can be considered quite competitive.

PROFESSIONALIZATION OF CHILD CARE

Agencies committed to developing an array of services have a unique opportunity to contribute to the development of child care. Child care, of course, presents its own dilemma. We in the United States consider ourselves one of the most advanced countries of the world. Our energy has gone into the development of such expensive games as Star Wars. Our standard of living and per capita income are still among the highest in the world.[1] However, we do not have a bona fide profession that includes educational requirements and licensing for those people who take care of our children. The youngsters placed at risk include our most vulnerable children, such as those in child-caring facilities or the little ones in day care who need nurturance while their parents are at work.

Child care is not a new profession. Most industrialized European countries have had professional child-care workers for years, and have clearly designed training and educational requirements for them. An "educateur" in France or Switzerland or an "Erzieher" in Germany or Austria does not need to explain apologetically what he or she does for a living, a constant experience of American child-care professionals, who are perceived at most as glorified babysitters. Efforts toward professionalization are ongoing but spotty, and a great deal remains to be done. We have not even been able to agree upon a designation for the profession. One hears "child-care worker," "sociotherapist," "counselor," "therapy aide," and a variety of other terms. I prefer the term "child-care professional" because it delineates its function, and places a professional identity at its core. It distinguishes the professional from the lay person caring for children in a variety of capacities, including family babysitting.

Once in a while a really good professional training program emerges on the associate, bachelor's, or master's degree level. There are a sprinkling of excellent programs in child care throughout this country and Canada, such as those offered by the University of Pittsburgh, the University of Victoria in British Columbia, and Dutchess Community College in New York State; but these are few and far between. Many legitimate programs are part of another discipline for fear they would not enroll a sufficient number of students if they maintained pure child-care professional integrity. This may be realistic; young people are understandably reluctant to confine themselves to a field that for years has had difficulty in legitimatizing its status and its remuneration, in a social climate that gives the care of children a low priority.

The creation of *Child Care Quarterly* in 1972 was a major contribution to the developing professional field of child care. In 1987 the name was changed to *Child and Youth Care Quarterly* to reflect the importance of adolescent program content. The quality of the journal has been high from the beginning, and it has taken a place in the professional literature that addresses the needs of children and families. This journal addresses current child-care information as well as providing professional articles and reports on the status of the profession. In 1985, Roy Ferguson and James P. Anglin from the University of Victoria School of Child Care in Canada—where progress toward the professionalization of child care took hold much earlier and with more vigor than in the United States—examined articles in *Child Care Quarterly* since its inception, tracing the struggle toward professionalization. They pointed out that

Some early entries in the journal refer to child care as an "emerging profession." . . . However, over time, we witness a gradual movement from discussion of child care as "a developing profession" to concern with "the development of the child care profession." . . . The second shift noted in the literature is the decreasing preoccupation with the search for a precise definition of child care. Such a development parallels the adolescent's struggle leading from the painful cry "Who am I?" to the hard-won acceptance that "I am who I am." The early volumes of *Child Care Quarterly* reflect an anxious searching for a unified and unifying definition (Foster 1972; Becker 1973) whereas the recent report on a major Project on Child Care Education and Training (Vander Ven, Mattingly, and Morris 1982) reflects increased acceptance of diversity and complexity within the field. [Ferguson and Anglin 1985:86]

The imaginative umbrella drawing devised by Denholm, Pence, and Ferguson [1983, as quoted in Ferguson and Anglin 1985:95] illustrates clearly what needs to happen in the profession of child care as it moves beyond its historic locus in the orphanage and child-caring institutions. With the many changes in American lifestyles, including single-parent households and two-career families, the demands for professional child care will continue to increase. Figure 11.1 shows the many practice fields in need of child-care expertise. The umbrella handle depicts the various levels of training necessary.

Those professionals who come to their positions after having completed professional training and qualification for appropriate certification and licensing, such as psychiatrists, psychologists, social workers, nurses, and special education teachers, have already invested in and made a major commitment to their professions. Child-care staff and family foster parents, of course, often use an initial employment situation in the field to explore their interest and suitability. Such child-care staff then often seek advanced degrees in one of the more professionalized helping occupations.

There can be collaborative agency ventures with regional educational institutions, coupled with the allocation of financial training grants to staff willing to pursue certificate or degree programs. Assisting staff toward their educational goals cuts down turnover and allows people to remain with the organization for a longer time. Educational incentives also attract people who might otherwise not want to be committed to this demanding occupation. An agency in turn has much to offer educational institutions for curriculum

Figure 11.1
The Umbrella Model of Child Care

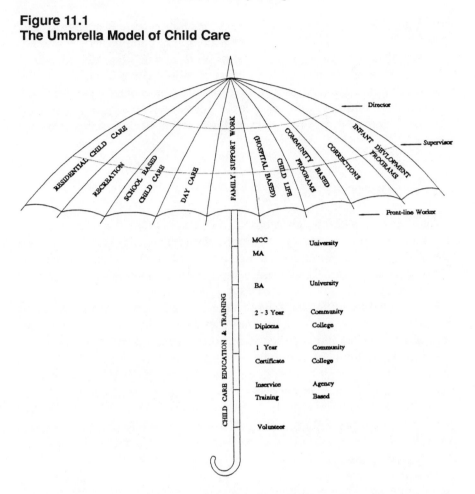

Source: Roy V. Ferguson and James P. Anglin, "The Child Care Profession: A Vision for the Future." *Child Care Quarterly* 14, 2 (Summer 1985): 95. Used by permission of Human Sciences Press, Inc., 233 Spring Street, New York, NY 10013–1578.

development, as well as field placement sites for their students. Staff pursuing a degree can also participate in intensive agency inservice training that is philosophically oriented toward the validation and reinforcement of family connections. They are then well-equipped to move from one agency program to another and contribute in a variety of functions that require unique hands-on life and program skills of the child-care profession.

Educational institutions, agency boards, and agency administrations should work hard to seek licensing for child care. State bodies that license service providers should in turn insist on the employment of licensed staff. Children and youth who grow up in a complex, complicated, so-called "developed" country deserve this kind of protection. With professionalization, education requirements, and licensing should come a more realistic allocation of salary. One can hope that some of our talented young people will then seek child and family services as a career with the same enthusiasm with which computer expertise, law, and investment banking are now being pursued.

USE OF VOLUNTEERS

Young people and families needing connections at times overwhelm the professional helping system often burdened by a financially feasible caseload size. Yet support can come from a creative use of volunteers to supplement professional activities. Clients can benefit from volunteers as an informal network of support and for practice of interpersonal skills.

Agencies have traditionally used volunteers in a variety of capacities, such as tutors, big sisters and brothers, and child-care living unit and classroom aides. Enriching the life experience and options of isolated people so that they can begin to raise their own families effectively may require new initiatives for community involvement and caring [Daly 1989]. Staff should seek out natural helpers in the client's own living environment, or if none seem available, go farther afield. As people in need begin to interact informally with nonprofessionals willing to listen, offer advice, and assist with concrete tasks, these skills can then be used to redefine old relationships and form new relationships.

An attitude among professionals that allows for inclusion of volunteers on the helping team may be initially difficult to implement. But allocation of resources for volunteer recruitment, training, and supervision is professionally sound and cost-effective. The voluntary not-for-profit sector is a model of care that benefits substantially from its volunteer boards of directors and other volunteers.

In adopting volunteer participation in a social work setting on a greater scale than is currently the case, and in defining its parameters more clearly, social workers and social service agencies will be able to add another dimension to their services. [Mitchell 1986:298]

Engagement of volunteers in network and support building for others in their community often serves to recruit foster families, child-care professionals, and other human service people who are currently difficult to hire.

Yet these rich resources often go untapped. Finding and involving them require an organizational commitment at all levels to assume the risks involved in enlarging the pool of people who can provide services to families and young people in need of functional connections. This involvement must not be seen as a duplication or replacement of professional staff. Finding resources for a comprehensive volunteer program is constant and time-consuming. Its rationale is a commitment to improving the quality of care and of life for the people to whom the organization is committed.

FUNDING

As discussed earlier, the staffing for human services is becoming increasingly difficult for many reasons, and it remains a key issue. Especially agencies entirely dependent on voluntary funding have difficulty developing the program quality they want. United Way allocations do not allow for much growth, and organizations are in keen competition for these limited dollars. Many voluntary agencies have chosen to contract with local departments of mental health, social services, and education. A few agencies have large endowment portfolios. This gives them some freedom, and is, of course, ideal. Given organizations' funding dilemmas, building up endowments is becoming crucial to allow for traditional experimentation and innovation by the not-for-profit sector. Today a multiply-funded system seems the healthiest, because this allows some autonomy in allocating funds. Any voluntary agency entirely dependent upon one source of funding finds itself at a severe disadvantage in the delivery of quality services.

Each type of funding has its advantages and disadvantages. Building a private endowment is expensive and requires ongoing fundraising. Deferred-giving programs are very effective, but mean long-drawn-out funding schedules—building for the future is essential; yet today's needs also must be met. Some creative organizations have linked their activities to a for-profit enterprise and are beneficiaries of their profits. This model has great potential for the future.

It seems desirable to delegate service development to the voluntary not-for-profit sector, where more innovation and creativity has traditionally taken place. However, often there are difficulties because there are not equivalent resources allocated to purchased service contracts as when government itself provides these services. Government contracts are very important in not-for-profit funding. Some services have been mandated by law, and ultimately it is the government's responsibility to provide them. Government operation of human services is very expensive, and the systems are too vast to provide quality services. Government salaries and benefit packages are usually substantially higher than in the private sector, and the administrative overhead costs are much higher also. In subcontracting, however, there is much concern with accountability, and huge quantities of paperwork are demanded by government to monitor information that is often of little, if any, use; with government funding comes overregulation. Human services professionals are particularly vulnerable to burnout from paperwork overload perceived as neither useful nor satisfying, and cutting into valuable client time. There will, however, always be a need for government-run services, particularly for populations requiring very restrictive facilities.

Developing programs through special federal, state, and foundation grants has always been possible. But the application process is tedious and time-consuming. Government requests for proposals are often distributed with minimal time to respond. Many potential applicants are discouraged from even trying. Those grants that are received are usually for a limited time period, and agencies are then left with the dilemma of whether to drop the program or to try somehow to continue it without adequate funding. The inclination is to continue a successful program, but the program usually requires overburdening a system already working too hard with too few resources. Whether small short-term grants for program innovation are really useful or cost-effective, considering the start-up time and resources taken from other programs, is an issue in need of more assessment.

MERGING SERVICES

As new program options gain credibility and momentum, each organization engaged in the change process discovers that it is faced with inevitable service gaps. Some of these service gaps may be within the agency's own system; others may exist in the community. As present resources become more limited and the intervention needs of troubled youth and their families appear to require more service options, some agencies may choose to merge as previously discussed in chapter 4. This stimulates an intensive dialogue between two or more agencies. Organizational goals are clarified, and merger advantages and disadvantages evaluated.

Professional staff have to review their respective philosophies of care. Mergers are best accomplished when the professional leadership in the organizations supports the merger. Dialogue between executives can create the necessary environment for encouraging boards of directors to consider the possibility of consolidating services and organizations.

The rationale for mergers should be enhancement of service quality. At times mergers occur in response to fiscal crisis, although this is usually not the optimum time to effect philosophic or programmatic changes. When professional staff are resistant to or excessively fearful of a merger initiated by the boards of agencies, the process is much more complex, though still possible. Merger talks can initiate destructive power struggles, which, if at all possible, should be avoided or at least kept to a minimum.

Child guidance clinics, family counseling agencies, and children's agencies that provide a range of institutional and family foster care and adoption services should seek to pool their resources. These mergers naturally validate the need for an array of services and recognition that in-home care for children with their own families of origin is always the preferred choice. When agencies with different philosophies are combined, the merger assists in the redesign of a comprehensive service system with clearly articulated objectives.

The purpose of the merger is to provide continuity of support. When mergers are contemplated, all board members of the original organizations should have an opportunity to serve on the newly created board. Sometimes their enlarged size can make combined boards unwieldy, but this problem is easily dealt with through normal attrition or reduction in the number of new board members elected during the early years after a merger. The new board can decide what its optimum number should be and gradually work toward that goal.

If individual program components can remain intact initially and be allowed to continue to function as they have, the outcome is enhanced. The administrations can join together in administrative groups and assume responsibility for operating the new agency. The differences can be dealt with gradually. One way of dealing with inevitable differences is to keep salaries, working hours, and benefits as they were for those staff in the original agencies. But each new appointment contract is geared to the new structure. The continuation of existing separate personnel practices can then be increasingly limited over time, and a uniform package mandated after a specified date.

Philosophic differences and communication among staff are best worked out as staff begin to share interprogram cases. As staff openings occur, agencies can begin to encourage staff to move from one program to another. Consultation on individual cases between skilled practitioners from one program and another is also helpful. Mergers take time to work through, but the results are heartening.

Changes are never smooth and easy, whether they occur through merger or by the development of a series of new program offshoots from the parent agency. The key to understanding the purpose of the merger remains recognition of young people's need for validation of their roots and for supportive connections to aid their move to adult living.

Family services and children's services can no longer be seen as two unrelated components: They are one and the same, regardless of how a family is constituted. Psychiatric child guidance services must be family services, as should institutional and preventive services. Adoption is just another method of family building.

One can hope that in the future more definitive national standards in support of the American family will emerge and that child and family mental health will become a high-ranking national priority as measured by fiscal allocation. With enough hard work on the part of committed people, this can happen.

CONCLUSION

Reinforcing family ties and building new connections for young people whose lives have rendered them particularly vulnerable are formidable tasks. The voluntary not-for-profit agency in the United States has much innovative leadership to offer in this area.

But too often the human services providers have opted for the separation of children from their kin when this was neither necessary nor desirable. We propose an agency model designed to provide an array of services through a variety of linked programs. This model can be built by allowing new program offshoots to develop from a parent program, usually in a child-caring institution, or by allowing two or more agencies to merge. Program redesign and reorganization occurs through the stimulus of government mandates, of service recipients, and of professional administrators and staff. Competent agency management work with their board of directors to inform them of new needs and trends in the field.

Board membership, orientation, and training are important parts of executive management responsibilities so board members can use this knowledge and skill to meet the needs of the organization. The board of directors should hold the executive officer accountable for programmatic innovation, excellence, and fiscal integrity.

Staff recruitment for the voluntary not-for-profit human services sector remains a major issue. Available social workers, nurses, teachers, psychiatrists, and psychologists are scarce. Child care, scarce also, has to undergo further professionalization. Recognition of the many needs that can be met so well by this discipline can be reinforced if educational opportunities in the field are expanded and legitimate licensing is instituted to assure child-care practice by well-trained, qualified personnel. The development of a variety of volunteer programs utilizing natural helpers in the communities in which isolated client families live can be another means for creative program development and innovation.

The decline in number of young people seeking human services as a profession has been alarming, though most recently schools of social work report an increase in the applicant pool. The expansion of volunteer opportunities is one effective recruitment vehicle for the human services professions, although not a replacement for professionals.

Training models committed to an agency philosophy of practice that looks to build and reinforce permanent family connections must be developed. These models need to be carefully structured and implemented, or else services will be counterproductive or even cancel each other out.

Funding remains an ongoing concern, which requires much thought and action. For the voluntary not-for-profit sector in human services to continue to be creative and innovative, purchase-of-service contracts with government agencies have to be coupled with fundraising, deferred-giving programs, and affiliation with for-profit organizations. A healthy diversity can protect the voluntary agency from the "second-class-employee" status of having to submit to excessive paperwork requirements and overregulation by government while enduring lower salaries, fewer benefits and inadequate administrative overhead.

NOTE

1. U.S. Gross National Product (GNP) (1986): $4.2T; U.S. per capita income (PCI) (1985): $13,451 [Hoffman 1989: 731].

   Sweden's GNP (1985): $100B; Sweden's PCI (1985): $11,989 [Hoffman 1989: 719].

   Finland's GNP (1985): $54B; Finland's PCI (1985): $11,007 [Hoffman 1989: 673].

Epilogue:
Future Directions

Within a broader global context these are historically significant but very unsettling times. We have moved from a cold war with the Soviet Union to an unprecedented, volatile struggle toward freedom and democratization in the USSR, Eastern Europe, and South Africa. East and West Germany have become one country. North Korea and South Korea are struggling to develop dialogue. Yet even today, after "Desert Storm," we are engaged in major crisis in the Middle East and have American troops in a part of the world we know far too little about and have no sense of consequences or cost. Although we may wish otherwise, the future of our children and their families is tightly linked not only with our national climate but with how we fit into this rapidly emergent interconnected world.

THE NATIONAL ECONOMIC CRISIS

Nationally we are confronted by a deficit crisis that requires immediate attention and action. "[A]fter months of debate among economists about whether the economy was in a recession, events have given the answer . . . that the business cycle has taken a lurch for the worse, whether you call it recession, or, like the Federal Reserve chairman, Alan Greenspan, a 'meaningful downturn,' or like the sardonic Cornell University economist, Alfred Kahn, you call it a 'banana' " [Silk 1990:E5]. The immediate downturn may be merely a symptom of long-term U.S. economic problems of deindustrialization, unproductive investment, lack of research and development, a deskilled work force, misallocated government resources, a collapsing infrastructure, and other unresolved economic and political issues.

Some of our most industrially advanced states, such as Massachusetts, New York, and California, are struggling against the threat of insolvency. We are living in a climate resistant to increased taxes and in a society unwilling to pay for human needs.

Our economic ability to compete globally has dramatically decreased compared to Western Europe and the Pacific Rim. Although our shops are full of consumer goods and our standard of living is still one of the highest in the world, "the latest Census Bureau numbers, for 1989, confirm that, for all the fanfare of the Reagan Boom, median family income is in real terms barely above the level of 1973. Even more strikingly, the Bureau of Labor Statistics (BLS) records that average real earnings have fallen to the level of 1961" [American Living Standards 1990:19]. The social consequences of enormous U.S. federal budget and international trade deficits, and the high level of government, corporate, and personal indebtedness, have left a rising number of American families in deep trouble—unemployed, homeless, hopeless, and broken. At the same time, these same conditions have meant fewer resources for dealing with family crisis.

THE WORK FORCE

Work force needs in the year 2000 will demand the development of optimum skills by every man and woman. Beyond that, the means of production are changing. With the change in means of production must come a changed educational philosophy, structure, and curriculum. But the first step is a work ethic established early in life through the bond between parents and children. Yet the importance of early bonding between parent and child must be recognized as a basic social value with the necessary family and social supports to allow this process to occur, as has been done so successfully by the Japanese [White 1987]. But, as is so dramatically being demonstrated in Russia, a work ethic is not transmitted from parent to child unless there is hope that hard, targeted work will improve one's own quality of life or at least that of one's children.

FAMILIES AND THEIR NEEDS

In the context of U.S. economic developments, there are significant trends that will affect the provision of family and children's services in the United States at least through the year 2000. In 1988, out of 63.2 million U.S. children under 18, 15.3 million or 24 percent were living with only one parent, compared with 12 percent in 1970 and 9 percent in 1960 [Saluter 1989:14]. It is estimated that 60 percent of the children born today will spend at least some portion of their childhood with only one parent [Saluter 1989:14]. Single-parent households are being created by young women who are not married but keeping their children, and by separation, divorce, or widowhood of the married, or by adoption of children by single individuals. Of all children, 15.5 percent live in a blended or stepfamily household [Saluter 1989:16]. These life situations create a whole realm of stress, with attendant service needs for the children to grow into optimally functioning adults. It is well known that single-parent households are disproportionately represented among the poor of this country. In 1987, 16.2 percent of the population lived in poverty, but 64.1 percent of this group were single mothers and their children. Within this category 38.7 percent were white, and 59.5 percent were African-American [Saluter 1989:25].

It appears that demographic trends show that we may have reached a plateau in the creation of new families, and can anticipate relative numerical stability during the next decade. A general aging in the population will be coupled with greater longevity, leaving middle-aged parents to assist their aged parents. Yet these middle-aged parents can also be expected, because of economic conditions, to be taking in many of their young adult children. There is further demographic evidence that the absolute and relative population of ethnic minorities will increase.

EDUCATION

The educational system is confronted with a major and difficult challenge to change not only curriculum but philosophy and method. It is clear that American education has to be adapted to the cultural and lifestyle needs of the increasingly diverse populations being served.

Education resource allocation must be set with priorities that recognize the realities of the year 2000 already mentioned.

1. More than half of the children being served by family services will live in single-parent households.
2. There will be more and more children from a growing variety of ethnic minorities.
3. Most mothers will be part of the work force.
4. Assistance to students and teachers will be available from an increasing number of competent, healthy senior citizens.

Some school districts are already moving in needed directions. Both observation and the literature point to innovative modes of education, which demonstrate that day care can be and often is located in a school building. More and more frequently after-school programs are attached to the school curriculum. Some schools offer physical space to day care, leaving its financial support to parents and the Department of Social Services for those who cannot pay.

Appropriate adult role models must be available to youth. Adolescent role models can be very helpful in work with younger children and youth with special problems, such as those with physical or learning disabilities. Programs must be culturally sensitive to strengthen culture rather than superimpose an alien system. Curricula must be designed for success of all populations rather than targeting the college route as the only desirable one, leaving half the young people disheartened and disinterested. Creative vocational education and technical hands-on experiences must begin early in the educational curriculum. These approaches must become equally prestigious and desirable when compared to academic achievement to assure a competitive adult work force.

SERVICE DESIGN

Services for children and families must be easily and readily available. The best services can be offered in a public-private partnership. For this partnership to be wholesome and viable, government has to become user-friendly for those wishing to contract with government to provide human services.

Contracts must be simple, and funding must flow with minimum bureaucratic encumbrances. Accountability to government must demonstrate the practical outcome of services rather than compliance with a myriad of conflicting, often irrelevant requirements. Preferably contractors should have to deal with only one oversight agency responsible for services to children and families. Only such simple contracting and accountability structures will allow for the delivery of optimum human services to children and their families within limited resource constraints.

Given the present lifestyles of family caregivers, "one-stop service shopping," available close to the children's school, can make access easier. Community centers, libraries, and physical fitness facilities are also best positioned in these areas to pool expensive resources. In designing family and children's services, the skills and talents of the retired should be used on both a volunteer and paid basis.

For those young people and families with more than usual need for support and help to prevent pathology, there must be a mechanism designed for funding to follow the needs of the family and child, rather than their being forced to fit artificially into a rigid system of service structures. Otherwise, they often cannot access needed services or are offered a level of care no longer needed, but are unable to move to a lower level of care because funding is not available.

A FAMILY-SUPPORTIVE WORKPLACE

We are seeing some progress of family support in the workplace. With the changing demographics of the United States, it is imperative for employers to adjust work schedules flexibly so that workers are not constantly being confronted with choosing between home and work responsibilities. Those employers who at best can provide child care, as well as human resources counseling and referral programs, will have a better work force. Some progressive employers are beginning to develop work-family coordinator positions. One of the key functions of these professionals is to sensitize management to family-work-related issues. The agenda of family-work-related concerns in the 1990s may well be of comparable significance to the equal-opportunity agenda in the 1960s [Deutsch 1990:F27].

A PHILOSOPHY OF CARE AND SOCIAL POLICY

America's children and therefore America's future will remain at high risk until rhetoric and action begin to coalesce. Given our culturally diverse origins, we must develop and implement a philosophy of care acceptable to the many peoples of diverse cultures in our country as well as to our political representatives, who are often in conflict. "We need a new family policy that transcends the polarized debate between liberals, who emphasize economic pressures while neglecting family structure and behavior, and conservatives, who preach family values while neglecting economics" [Kamarck and Galston 1990:A19].

Once we acknowledge that every human being was put here by the reproductive capability of a man and a woman together, who in turn are needed to support this young human being until the fully matured individual can care for her- or himself without serious jeopardy to well-being, a family and children's policy truly in support of the American family can flow. Ideally we must continue to strengthen the two-parent and the multigenerational family. On the other hand we also know that unless the workload and stress placed on the two-parent family are reduced, the family disruption rate will continue at least at the level now familiar to us. In any case, children and those adults responsible for nurturing them must experience more than rhetorical support from government. This volume has addressed many program options that work. However, none of them can work without adequate

legislative and fiscal support. Kamarck and Galston [1990:A19] cite six ways
to a new national family policy:

1. Restore the federal tax exemption for children to the value it had in 1948;
2. Create a nonpoverty working wage;
3. Reform divorce laws in order to put children, and not marital property, first;
4. Promote parental responsibility by holding them legally responsible for their children's behavior and education;
5. Make the workplace "family-friendly" by reconciling childrearing and work outside the home;
6. Develop alternatives to foster care by emphasizing home-based strategies to help parents deal with acute stress.

If these very basic policy proposals were agreed to, we would be well on our way to a national commitment to the principle that children and their caretakers are of primary importance to the well-being of our society. A meaningful, comprehensive family policy can then move us into the next century, utilizing our multiple talents and cultural diversity to bring about the best possible living and working environment for generations to come.

Bibliography

Ackerman, N. W., ed. 1970. *Family Therapy in Transition*. Boston: Little, Brown and Co.

Adams, Morris, and Baumbach, Diane J. 1980. "Professional Parenting: A Factor in Group Home Programming." *Child Care Quarterly* 9, no. 3 (Fall): 185–96.

Adult Adoption Information Act of 1985, Birth Link, Adult Adoption Information. n.d. Wellington, New Zealand: Postal Center, Department of Social Welfare (information pamphlet).

Allerhand, M. E.; Weber, R.; and Haug, M. 1966. *Adaptation and Adaptability: The Bellefaire Follow-up Study*. New York: Child Welfare League of America.

"American Living Standards, Running to Stand Still." 1990. *The Economist* (November 10): 19–22.

Argent, Hedi. 1984. *Find Me a Family: The Story of Parents and Children*. London: Souvenir Press.

Arieli, Mordecai, and Feuerstein, Reuven. 1987a. "A Four-Fold Program: A Rejoinder to Lewis, Maluccio, Polsky, and Whittaker." *Child and Youth Care Quarterly* 16, no. 3 (Fall): 193–95.

———. 1987b. "The Two-Fold Care Organization: On the Combining of Group and Foster Care." *Child and Youth Care Quarterly* 16, no. 3 (Fall): 168–84.

Astrachan, Myrtle, and Harris, Don M. 1983. "Weekend Only: An Alternate Model in Residential Treatment Centers." *Child Welfare* 62, no. 3 (May/June): 253–61.

Aumend, Sue A., and Barrett, Marjie C. 1984. "Self Concept and Attitudes Toward Adoption: A Comparison of Searching and Nonsearching Adult Adoptees." *Child Welfare* 63, no. 3 (May/June): 251–59.

Barden, J. C. 1991. "When Foster Care Ends, Home Is Often the Street." *New York Times* (January 6): 1, 15.

Basic Course for Residential Child Care Workers. 1977. Chapel Hill, NC: Group Child Care Consultant Services.

Billingsley, Andrew, and Giovanni, Jeanne M. 1972. *Children of the Storm*. New York: Harcourt Brace Jovanovich.

Bowlby, John. 1965. *Child Care and the Growth of Love*. New York: Penguin Books.

———. 1966. *Maternal Care and Mental Health*. New York: Schocken Books.

Boyd, L., and Remy, L. 1978. "Is Foster Parent Training Worthwhile?" *Social Services Review* (June): 276–96.

Brace, Charles Loring. 1872. *Dangerous Classes of New York*. New York: Wynkoop, Hollenbeck and Thames.

Braga, Wander deCarvalho. 1989. "Developmental and Systemic Approaches: The Clash of Paradigms." In *Permanence and Family Support: Changing Practice in Group Child Care*, edited by Gary O. Carman and Richard W. Small, 61–82. Washington, DC: Child Welfare League of America.

Brozan, Nadine. 1988. "Leaders and Experts Join the Child Care Drive." *New York Times* (October 2): 22.

Bryan, David; Kagan, Richard; and Walsh, Tom. 1990. "In-House Training Programs 1990–1991." Sidney Albert Institute, Professional Development Programs, Parsons Child and Family Center, Albany, NY.

Carlo, Paul. 1985. "The Children's Residential Treatment Center as a Living Laboratory for Family Members: A Review of the Literature and Its Implications for Practice." *Child Care Quarterly* 14, no. 3 (Fall): 156–70.

Carman, Gary O., and Small, Richard W., eds. 1989. *Permanence and Family Support: Changing Practice in Group Child Care*. 61–82. Washington, DC: Child Welfare League of America.

Child Welfare League of America (CWLA). 1989. *Standards for Services to Strengthen and Preserve Families with Children*. Washington, DC: CWLA.

Colangione, Isabel. 1980. In a panel entitled "Parents as Partners in Special Education," at Parsons Child and Family Center's Fall Institute.

Cole, Elizabeth S. 1984. *Implementing Permanency Planning*. Paper presented at Permanent Families Project National Launching Conference, National Council of Juvenile and Family Court Judges, June 11, Washington, DC.

Council on Accreditation of Services for Families and Children, Inc. 1987. *Provisions for Accreditation*. New York.

Coyle, N.; Haimes, R.; Johnson, M.; Langhorne, N.; Risk, P.; and Stamper, D. 1986. "Keeping Families in the Center: A Manual of Family-Centered Services in Out-of-Home Placement of Children."

Crotty, Gerald C., Chair of the New York State Council on Children and Families. 1988. *The State of the Child in New York State*. Albany, NY: NYS Council on Children and Families.

CWLA. *See* Child Welfare League of America.

Dail, Paula W. 1990. "The Psychosocial Context of Homeless Mothers with Young Children: Program and Policy Implications." *Child Welfare* 69, no. 4 (July/August): 291–308.

Daly, Margaret. 1989. "Helping Homeless Families." *Better Homes and Gardens* (March): 21–25.

Denholm, C.; Pence, A.; and Ferguson, R., eds. 1983. "The Scope of Professional Child Care in British Columbia," Part I, 2d ed., University of Victoria, as quoted in Ferguson and Anglin, 1985: 95.

Derdeyn, Andre P., M.D. 1977. "A Case for Permanent Foster Placement of Dependent, Neglected and Abused Children." *American Journal of Orthopsychiatry* 47, no. 4 (October): 604–14.

Deutsch, Claudia H. 1990. "Corporate Advocates for the Family." *New York Times* (November 11): F27.

Devore, Wynetta. 1983. "Ethnic Reality: The Life Model and Work with Black Families." *Social Casework* 64, no. 9 (November): 525–31.

Duffy, Carolyn. 1986. "Where Have You Gone, Florence Nightingale?" *Boston College Magazine* 45, no. 2 (Spring): 10–13.

Dullea, Henrik N., Chair of the Task Force on Children and Youth. 1988. "Local Planning for Children, Youth and Families: An Analysis and Recommendations."

———. 1989. *There ARE Better Ways to Serve Children*. Albany, NY: New York State Task Force on Children and Youth.

Edna McConnell Clark Foundation. 1986. *1986 Annual Report*, (October 1, 1985–September 30, 1986): 9.

Fanshel, David; Finch, Stephen J.; and Grundy, John F. 1990. *Foster Children in Life Course Perspectives: The Casey Family Program Experience*. New York: Columbia University Press.

Fanshel, David, and Shinn, Eugene. 1978. *Children in Foster Care: A Longitudinal Investigation*. New York: Columbia University Press.

Ferguson, Roy V., and Anglin, James P. 1985. "The Child Care Profession: A Vision for the Future." *Child Care Quarterly* 14, no. 2 (Summer): 85–102.

Festinger, Trudy. 1983. *No One Ever Asked Us: A Post Script to Foster Care*. New York: Columbia University Press.

Finkelstein, Joseph. 1986. "The Third Industrial Revolution—Questions and Implications for Economic Historians." Paper presented at the 9th International Economic History Congress, August, Berne, Switzerland.

Finkelstein, Nadia Ehrlich. 1976. "Family Systems Marathon."

———. 1980. "Children in Limbo." *Social Work* 25, no. 2 (March): 100–5.

———. 1981. "Family-Centered Group Care—The Children's Institution, from a Living Center to a Center for Change." In *The Challenge of Partnership: Working with Parents of Children in Foster Care*, edited by Anthony N. Maluccio and Paula A. Sinanoglu. New York: Child Welfare League of America.

———. 1988. "The Role of Residential Care: Facilitating a Permanent Sense of Belonging for Children in Jeopardy of Rejection and Isolation." In *Permanence and Family Support: Changing Practice in Group Child Care*, edited by Gary O. Carman and Richard W. Small. Washington, DC: Child Welfare League of America.

Flango, Victor Eugene. 1990. "Agency and Private Adoptions, by State." *Child Welfare* 69, no. 3 (May/June): 263–75.

Fogarty, Thomas F. 1984a. "Evolution of a Systems Thinker." In *Compendium I, The Best of The Family 1973–1978*, edited by E. G. Pendagast, 17–34. New Rochelle, NY: Center for Family Learning.

———. 1984b. "Thoughts on Divorce." In *Compendium I, The Best of The Family 1973–1978*, edited by E. Pendagast, 142–49. New Rochelle, NY: Center for Family Learning.

Framo, James L. 1970. "Symptoms from a Family Transactional Viewpoint." In *Family Therapy in Transition*, edited by N. W. Ackerman et al. Boston: Little, Brown and Co.

Gardner, Richard A. 1983. *Psychotherapy with Children of Divorce*. New York and London: Jason Aronson.

Garland, Diana S. Richmond. 1987. "Residential Child Care Workers as Primary Agents of Family Intervention." *Child and Youth Care Quarterly* 16, no. 1 (Spring): 21–34.

Gersh, Eileen S., and Gersh, Isidore. 1981. *Biology of Women*. Baltimore: University Park Press.

Gewirtman, Rena, and Fodor, Iris. 1987. "The Homeless Child at School: From Welfare Hotel to Classroom." *Child Welfare* 66, no. 3 (May/June): 237–45.

Giordano, J., and Giordano, G. P. 1977. *The Ethno-Cultural Factor in Mental Health: A Literature Review and Bibliography*. New York: Institute on Pluralism and Group Identity, as cited in McGoldrick 1982: 4.

Goldstein, Joseph; Freud, Anna; and Solnit, Albert J. 1973. *Beyond the Best Interests of the Child*. New York: The Free Press.

Grossman, S.; Shea, J. A.; Adams, G. R. 1980. "Effects of Parental Divorce during Early Childhood on Ego Development and Identity Formation of College Students." *Journal of Divorce* 3: 263–72.

Guerin, Philip J. 1984a. "Family Therapy: Style, Art and Theory." In *Compendium I, The Best of The Family 1973–1978*, edited by E. G. Pendagast, 3–8. New Rochelle, NY: Center for Family Learning.

———. 1984b. "System, System, Who's Got the System?" In *Compendium I, The Best of The Family 1973–1978*, edited by E. G. Pendagast, 9–16. New Rochelle, NY: Center for Family Learning.

Hall, Ethel H., and King, Gloria C. 1982. "Working with the Strengths of Black Families." *Child Welfare* 61, no. 8 (November/December): 536–44.

Handlin, Oscar. 1990. *The Uprooted*, 2d ed. Boston: Little, Brown and Co.

Hartman, Ann. 1990. "Children in a Careless Society." *Social Work* 35, no. 6 (November): 483–84.

Hess, Peg. 1982. "Parent-Child Attachment Concept: Crucial for Permanency Planning." *Social Casework* 63, no. 1 (January): 46–53.

Hill, Robert. 1973. *Strengths of Black Families*. New York: National Urban League.

Hoffman, Mark S., ed. 1989. *The World Almanac*. New York: Scripps-Howard.

Hogan, Patricia Turner, and Siu, Sau-Fong. 1988. "Minority Children and the Child Welfare System: An Historical Perspective." *Social Work* 33, no. 6 (November/December): 493–97.

Howard, Alice; Royse, David D.; and Skerl, John A. 1977. "Transracial Adoption: The Black Community Perspective." *Social Work* 22 (May): 184–89.

Hubbard, Ruth; Henifin, Mary Sue; and Fried, Barbara, eds. 1979. *Women Look at Biology Looking at Women*. Boston: G. K. Hall and Co.; Cambridge, MA: Schenkman Publishing Co.

Ingalls, Robert P.; Hatch, Rebecca P.; and Meservey, Frederick B. 1984. *The Out-of-Home Project, Characteristics of Children in Out-of-Home Care*. Albany, NY: New York State Council on Children and Families.

Jones, Mary Ann, and Moses, Beth. 1984. *West Virginia's Former Foster Children: Their Experiences in Care and Their Lives as Young Adults*. New York: Child Welfare League of America.

Kadushin, Alfred. 1970. *Adopting Older Children*. New York: Columbia University Press.

Kagan, Richard M., and Reid, William J. 1986. "Critical Factors in the Adoption of Emotionally Disturbed Youths." *Child Welfare* 65, no. 1 (January/February): 63–73.

Kagan, R.; Reid, W. J.; Roberts, S. E.; Silverman-Pollow, J. 1987. "Engaging Families of Court-Mandated Youths in an Alternative to Institutional Placement." *Child Welfare* 66, no. 4 (July/August): 365–76.

Kagan, Richard, and Schlosberg, Shirley. 1989a. *Families in Perpetual Crisis*. New York: W. W. Norton.

———. 1989b. "When Love Is Not Enough: Creating a Context for Change." In *Permanence and Family Support: Changing Practice in Group Child Care*, edited by Gary O. Carman and Richard W. Small, 171–85. Washington, DC: Child Welfare League of America.

Kamarck, Elaine Ciulla, and Galston, William A. 1990. "America's Children, Still at Risk." *New York Times* (November 19): A19.

Kamerman, Sheila B., and Kahn, Alfred J. 1988. *Mothers Alone, Strategies for a Time of Change.* Dover, MA: Auburn House Publishing Company.

———. 1989. *Social Services for Children, Youth and Families in the United States.* New York: The Annie Casey Foundation.

Kaplan, Lisa. 1986. *Working with Multiproblem Families.* Lexington, MA: Lexington Books, D. C. Heath and Company.

Keefe, Frank T., 1988. Introductory Letter. *Progress Report to the House and Senate Ways and Means Committee*, February 1.

Keith-Lucas, Alan. 1987. "What Else Can Residential Care Do? And Do Well?" *Residential Treatment for Children and Youth* 4, no. 4 (Summer): 25–37.

Kim, Dong Soo. 1978. "Issues in Transracial and Transcultural Adoption." *Social Casework* 59 (October): 477–86.

Kim, Do-Young. n.d. "The Policy on the Intercountry Adoption, the Adoption Laws, and the Future of Adoption in Korea." Seoul, South Korea.

Kingston, Maxine Hong. 1976. *The Woman Warrior: Memoirs of a Girlhood among Ghosts.* New York: Random House, Vintage Books.

Kozol, Jonathan. 1988. *Rachel and Her Children: Homeless Families in America.* New York: Crown Publishers.

Lantz, James E. 1987. "Family Intervention during Residential Treatment." *Residential Treatment for Children and Youth* 4, no. 4 (Summer): 39–52.

Lee, Judith A. B., and Nisivoccia, Danielle. 1989. *Walk a Mile in My Shoes.* Washington, DC: Child Welfare League of America.

Legislative Commission on Expenditure Review. 1988. *Program Audit of OMH Residential Facilities.* Albany, NY: The Legislature, State of New York.

Lewin, Tamar. 1990. "South Korea Slows Export of Babies for Adoption." *New York Times* (February 12): B10.

Lewis, W. W. 1987. "Adding Ecology to Two-Fold Care: A Response to Arieli and Feuerstein." *Child and Youth Care Quarterly* 16, no. 3 (Fall): 185.

Libov, Charlotte. 1987. "A Day-Care Center for Ailing Children." *New York Times* (November 22) Section 23: 14.

Lindsey, Robert. 1987. "Adoption Market: Big Demand, Tight Supply." *New York Times* (April 5).

Low, Brian J. 1984. "A Therapeutic Use of the Diagrammatic Family Tree." *Child Welfare* 63, no. 1 (January/February): 37–43.

Macchiarola, Frank J., and Gartner, Alan, eds. 1989. *Caring for America's Children.* Montpelier, VT: Capital City Press.

McGoldrick, Monica. 1982. "Ethnicity and Family Therapy: An Overview." In *Ethnicity and Family Therapy*, edited by Monica McGoldrick, John K. Pearce, and Joseph Giordano, 4, 13, 21. New York: The Guilford Press.

McGowen, Brenda G., and Meezan, William. 1983. *Child Welfare: Current Dilemmas, Future Directions.* Itasco, IL: F. E. Peacock Publishers, Inc.

McKelvy, Doris. 1981. "Agency Change: A Response to the Needs of Black Families and Children." *Child Welfare* 60, no. 3 (March): 183–90.

McRoy, Ruth G.; Grotevant, Harold D.; Zurcher, Louis A.; and White, Kerry L. 1985. "Adopted Adolescents in Residential Treatment," University of Texas at Austin.

Madison, Bernice Q., and Shapiro, Michael. 1973. "Black Adoption Issues and Policies." *Social Service Review* 47 (December): 531–59.

Maguire, John. 1985. "History of Parsons Child and Family Center." Albany, NY.

Maluccio, Anthony N. 1987. "Toward Ecologically Oriented, Family-Centered Practice in Child Care: A Response to Arieli and Feuerstein." *Child and Youth Care Quarterly* 16, no. 3 (Fall): 187–88.

———. 1989. "The Role of Group Child Care in Permanency Planning." In *Permanence and Family Support: Changing Practice in Group Child Care*, edited by Gary O. Carman and Richard W. Small, 13–28. Washington, DC: Child Welfare League of America.

Mech, Edmund V., ed. 1988. *Independent-Living Services for At-Risk Adolescents.* Washington, DC: Child Welfare League of America.

Minuchin, Salvador, and Montalvo, Braulio. 1967. "Techniques for Working with Disorganized Low Socioeconomic Families." *American Journal of Orthopsychiatry,* 37, no. 5 (October): 880–87.

Mitchell, Manzell. 1986. "Utilizing Volunteers to Enhance Informal Social Networks." *Social Casework* 67, no. 5 (May): 290–98.

Moore, Barbara; Grandpre, Marcella; and Scoll, Barbara. 1988. "Foster Home Recruitment: A Market Research Approach to Attracting and Licensing Applicants." *Child Welfare* 67, no. 2 (March/April): 147–60.

Nayman, Louis, and Witkin, Stanley L. 1978. "Parent/Child Foster Placement: An Alternate Approach in Child Abuse and Neglect." *Child Welfare* 56, no. 4 (April): 249–58.

Nelson, Katherine A. 1985. *On the Frontier of Adoption: A Study of Special-Needs Adoptive Families.* New York: Research Center, Child Welfare League of America.

New York State. 1990. *Executive Budget 1990–1991*, Briefing Book, Section IV, Human Services. Albany, NY.

New York State Citizens Task Force on Aging-Out. 1988. "Goal Statement," October, Albany, NY.

New York State Citizens Task Force on Aging-Out. 1989. "Legislative Report," January, Albany, NY.

New York State Division of the Budget. 1985. *Child Welfare Reform Act: An Evaluation Report to the Governor and Legislature on Impact and Implementation*, October, Albany, NY.

New York State Residential Treatment Facilities for Children and Youth. While They're Still Kids. 1990. Residential Treatment Facilities Coalition.

New York Times. 1987. "A System Overloaded: The Foster Care Crisis." (March 15):1, 32.

Pendagast, E., ed. 1984. *Compendium I and II, The Best of The Family 1973–1978.* New Rochelle, NY: The Center for Family Learning.

Pendagast, Eileen G., and Sherman, Charles O. "A Guide to the Genogram." 1984. In *Compendium I, The Best of The Family 1973–1978*, edited by E. G. Pendagast, 101–12. New Rochelle, NY: The Center for Family Learning.

Phillips, Kevin. 1990. *The Politics of Rich and Poor: Wealth and the American Electorate in the Reagan Aftermath.* New York: Random House, as cited in Hartman 1990: 483.

Pierce, Lois H., and Hanck, Victor B. 1981. "A Model for Establishing a Community-Based Foster Group Home." *Child Welfare* 60, no. 7 (July/August): 475–82.

Pinkerton, Elsie M. 1984. *Care of the Elderly.* Elmsford, NY: Pergamon Press.

Pittman, Frank S., III. 1985. "Children of the Rich." *Family Process* 24, no. 4 (December): 461–72.

Polsky, Howard W. 1977. *Cottage Six—The Social System of Delinquent Boys in Residential Treatment.* Huntington, NY: Robert E. Krieger Publishing Co.

————. 1987. "On Diluting Powerful Communities: A Response to Arieli and Feuerstein." *Child and Youth Care Quarterly* 16, no. 3 (Fall): 189.

Polsky, Howard W., and Chester, Daniel S. 1968. *The Dynamics of Residential Treatment.* Chapel Hill, NC: University of North Carolina Press.

Ransom, Jane W.; Schlesinger, Stephen; and Derdeyn, Andre P. 1979. "A Stepfamily in Formation." *American Journal of Orthopsychiatry* 49, no. 1 (January): 36–43.

Regional Research Institute for Human Services. 1976. *Barriers to Planning for Children in Foster Care*, vol. 1: Evaluation of "Freeing Children for Permanent Placement" Project. Portland, OR: Portland State University.

Reid, William J.; Kagan, Richard M.; Kaminsky, Alison; and Helmer, Katherine. 1987. "Adoptions of Older Institutionalized Youth." *Social Casework* (March): 140–49.

Saluter, Arlene, ed. 1989. *Changes in American Family Life.* Current Population Reports, Special Studies Series P–23, no. 163. Washington, DC: U.S. Department of Commerce, Bureau of the Census.

Schneider, Kurt; Kinlow, Melvin R.; Galloway, A. N.; and Ferro, Don L. 1982. "An Analysis of the Effects of Implementing the Teaching-Family Model in Two Community-Based Group Homes." *Child Care Quarterly* 11, no. 4 (Winter): 298–311.

Schowalter, John E.; Patterson, Paul R.; Tallmer, Margot; Kutscher, Austin H.; Gullo, Stephen V.; and Peretz, David, eds. 1983. *The Child and Death.* New York: Columbia University Press.

Seaberg, James R. 1986. " 'Reasonable Efforts': Toward Implementation in Permanency Planning." *Child Welfare* 65, no. 5 (September/October): 469–79.

Selig, Andrew L. 1976. "The Myth of the Multi-Problem Family." *American Journal of Orthopsychiatry* 46, no. 3 (July): 520–31.

Sherman, Barry, and Meyers, Rebecca. 1985. *Critical Factors Affecting Families' Decisions to Place Developmentally Disabled Family Members.* Albany, NY: New York State Council on Children and Families.

Shyne, A., and Schroeder, A. 1978. *National Study of Social Service to Children and Their Families.* Washington, DC: U.S. Government Printing Office.

Silk, Leonard. 1990. "It Isn't Just a Downturn, It's the Bill for the 1980's." *New York Times* (December 30): E5.

Smith, Eve P., and Gutheil, Robert H. 1988. "Successful Foster Parent Recruiting: A Voluntary Agency's Effort." *Child Welfare* 67, no. 2 (March/April): 138–45.

Spencer, Marietta E. 1980. *Understanding Adoption as a Family-Building Option.* Boulder, CO: Social Science Education Consortium Inc.

Spoor, Barbara J. 1986. "Issues in the Transition of Young Adults with Disabilities from the Education to Adult Services Systems." NYS Office of Advocate for the Disabled, Albany, NY.

Tinsley Institute. n.d. "Transition Planning: A Parents' Guidebook and Resource Manual," prepared for NYS Citizens Task Force on Aging-Out, Berlin, NY.

Titterington, Lee. 1990. "Foster Care Training: A Comprehensive Approach." *Child Welfare* 69, no. 2 (March/April): 157–65.

Trieschman, Albert E.; Whittaker, James K.; and Brendtro, Larry K. 1969. *The Other 23 Hours.* Chicago: Aldine Publishing Company.

U.S. Bureau of the Census. 1990. *Statistical Abstract of the United States: 1990.* Washington, DC: U.S. Government Printing Office.

Vassil, Thomas V. 1978. "Residential Family Camping: Altering Family Patterns." *Social Casework* 59 (December): 605–13.

Waldinger, Gloria. 1982. "Subsidized Adoption: How Paid Parents View It." *Social Work* 27, no. 6 (November): 516–21.

Wallace, Steven, and Estes, Carroll L. 1989. "Health Policy for the Elderly." *Society* 26 (September/October): 66–75.

Walsh, James Mackin. 1985. "A Model Community-Based Residential Treatment Program." *Child Care Quarterly* 14, no. 1 (Spring): 48–55.

Walters, Laurel Shaper (of *The Christian Science Monitor*). 1990. "Massachusetts Trade School Students Put Training to Use, Build Child Center." *The Sunday Gazette.* Schenectady, NY (December 9): C–8.

Washington, Valora. 1987. "Community Involvement in Recruiting Adoptive Homes for Black Children." *Child Welfare* 66, no. 1(January/February): 57–68.

Weber, Donald E. 1978. "Neighborhood Entry in Group Home Development." *Child Welfare* 57 (December): 627–42.

White, Merry. 1987. *The Japanese Educational Challenge, A Commitment to Children.* New York: The Free Press.

Whitman, Barbara Y.; Accardo, Pasquale; Boyert, Mary; Kendagor, Rita. 1990. "Homelessness and Cognitive Performance in Children: A Possible Link." *Social Work* 35, no. 6 (November): 516–19.

Whittaker, James K. 1987. "Combining Group Care and Foster Care: Solution or Problem: A Response to Arieli and Feuerstein." *Child and Youth Care Quarterly* 16, no. 3 (Fall): 191–92.

————. 1989. "Family Support and Group Child Care: Rethinking Resources." In *Permanence and Family Support: Changing Practice in Group Child Care,* edited by Gary O. Carman and Richard W. Small, 29–55. Washington, DC: Child Welfare League of America.

Williams, Robin M., Jr. 1970. *American Society: A Sociological Interpretation.* New York: Alfred A. Knopf.

Index

Community residences. *See* Group homes

Community services: activity/work programs, 101–2; child/day care, 88–89; day treatment programs, 98–101; family resource centers, 91–92; housing, 87–88; mental health clinics, 92–97; schools, 89–90; special education, 97–98; special family services, 90–91; vocational programs, 102–4

Council on Accreditation of Services to Families and Children, 118

Coyle, N., xii, 202

Crotty, Gerald C., 22

CRY for Help Program, 122–24

Cuomo, Mario, 13

CWLA. *See* Child Welfare League of America

CWRA. *See* Child Welfare Reform Act

Dail, Paula W., 88

Daly, Margaret, 238

Day care, entitlement to organized, 88–89

Day treatment programs, 98–101

Denholm, C., 236

Derdeyn, Andre P., 143

Deutsch, Claudia H., 249

Developmentally disabled youth: adoption of, 160; in campus-based residences, 210–14; in group homes, 188–90

Devore, Wynetta, 164

Divorce: emotional, 33, 35; impact on families, 35–36; reasons for, 33–35

Down's Syndrome, 160

Drug abuse, 40

Duffy, Carolyn, 233

Dullea, Henrik N., 13

Dutchess Community College, 235

Economic crisis, impact of national, 245–46

Edna McConnell Clark Foundation, 119–120

Education: activity/work programs, 101–2; day treatment programs and, 98–101; family services and, 18–19; foster care and attitudes of schools, 134; future for, 247–48; respite placement

and, 206; responsibility of, to the community, 89–90; special, 97–98

Eisenhauer, Laurel, 233

Elderly. *See* Senior citizens

Emergency/assessment foster care, 135–38

Employment for youth in group homes, 186

Estes, Carroll L., 39

Ethnicity, family and, 25–29

Executive staff, role of, 226–27

FALC. *See* Family Activity Learning Center

Family/ies: alternative forms of relationships in, 31–33; blended, 36–38; dissolution and role of mental health clinics, 93; ethnicity and, 25–29; factors that have an impact on, 24; function of, 23–24; gender roles and, 29–31; geographic and socioeconomic mobility and, 27–28; homeless, 40; independence from the, 27; reasons for the breakup of the, 33–36; respite and campus-based residences, 203–7; single-parent, 31, 33, 38–39; social dilemmas facing, 40–41; taking care of the elderly and impact on, 39–40

Family Activity Learning Center (FALC), 121–22

Family resource, support and education (FRSE) services, 91–92

Family service agencies: array of services in, 80–82; coalition of, 82–83; types of, 75

Family Service America, 224

Family services: designs for, 248–49; education and, 18–19; mergers and integration of programs, 75, 83; program design alternatives, 79–83; segmentation of, 74–75; special, 90–91; values and, 19–20. *See also under type of, e.g.,* Community services

Family therapy/therapist, use of term, 76

Fanshel, David, 132, 198

Federation of Jewish Philanthropies of Greater New York, 75

Ferguson, Roy, 235–36

Festinger, Trudy, 132

ABOUT THE AUTHOR

NADIA EHRLICH FINKELSTEIN is the Associate Executive Director of Parsons Child and Family Center in Albany, New York. A member of the Academy of Certified Social Workers, she has contributed to several books on family-centered social work and children's agencies and published articles in professional journals.